The
Social Studies Teacher's BOOK OF LISTS
Second Edition

Updated with over 200 New Lists, Including
Web Sites, Standards, Teaching Ideas, and Activities

Ronald L. Partin, Ph.D.

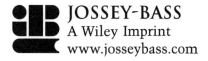
JOSSEY-BASS
A Wiley Imprint
www.josseybass.com

Published by Jossey-Bass
A Wiley Imprint
989 Market Street, San Francisco, CA 94103-1741 www.josseybass.com

The illustrations in this book are from Art Today, Dover Clip Art, Dynamic Graphics, and Art Explosion.

Library of Congress Cataloging-in-Publication Data
Partin, Ronald L.
  The social studies teacher's book of lists / Ronald L. Partin—2nd
ed.
    p. cm.
  "Updated with over 200 new lists, including Web sites, standards,
teaching ideas, and activities."
  Includes bibliographical references.
    ISBN 0-7879-6590-1 (pbk. : alk. paper)
    1. Social sciences—Study and teaching (Elementary—United
States—Handbooks, manuals, etc. 2. Social sciences—Study and teaching
(Secondary)—United States—Handbooks, manuals, etc. 3. Teaching—Aids
and devices—Handbooks, manuals, etc. 4. Activity programs in
education—United States—Handbooks, manuals, etc. I. Title.
    LB1584.P29 2003
    300'.71'073—dc21
                                        2002154412

Printed in the United States of America
SECOND EDITION
PB Printing 10 9 8 7 6 5 4 3 2 1

About This Book

LEARNING SOCIAL STUDIES can be fun while at the same time intellectually stimulating and practical. Yet it takes time and effort to research and compile the facts, activities, and ideas that bring social studies to life. The lack of sufficient planning time and the scarcity of ready-to-use materials challenge all social studies teachers. To help you, this updated and expanded edition features 200 new lists.

The Social Studies Teacher's Book of Lists, Second Edition, gives you a broad range of interesting and challenging information to use in teaching United States history, world history, American government, sociology, consumer economics, psychology, and geography. It is packed with illuminating facts, startling statistics, practical checklists, and relevant research findings, which will enhance your social studies courses. The array of lists can be helpful in planning lessons for grades 4–12.

For easy access and use, the 554 lists in this resource are printed in a reproducible form, numbered consecutively, and organized into the following seven sections:

    I. LISTS FOR UNITED STATES HISTORY (Lists 1–132)

    II. LISTS FOR WORLD HISTORY (Lists 133–210)

    III. LISTS FOR AMERICAN GOVERNMENT (Lists 211–261)

    IV. LISTS FOR CONSUMER ECONOMICS (Lists 262–319)

    V. LISTS FOR SOCIOLOGY (Lists 320–409)

    VI. LISTS FOR PSYCHOLOGY (Lists 410–495)

    VII. LISTS FOR GEOGRAPHY (Lists 496–554)

The National Council for the Social Studies has established ten interdisciplinary thematic standards that encompass the subject areas of social studies. The lists provided in this book can augment instruction in at least one and often several of these ten thematic standards. This updated edition includes a thematic table of contents, organized by the NSCC's ten thematic areas. In addition, a special introductory section presents a variety of stimulating activities for introducing the lists into your lessons to spark students' interest and enthusiasm. Each activity is accompanied by detailed directions and specific suggestions for its effective use.

The possibilities for using the lists are limited only by the imagination. Many can be reproduced and used to encourage thoughtful discussion and problem-solving (e.g., How many things can students list that were around in 1960 but are hard to find today?). Have students work in small cooperative groups to predict the contents of a list before you present it (e.g., What are the ten largest companies in the U.S.? Which are the hottest job prospects for the coming decade?). Challenge individuals or teams to complete their own lists (e.g., What are the greatest engineering achievements of the twentieth century?).

Lists can be used not only to illustrate important points in your lesson, but also to provide practice in interpreting data and as springboards for discussion. Lists of frequently used terms (e.g., "Forms of Government" and "Therapeutic Techniques") can be used as student handouts for instant review. Some lists make stimulating posters or can be distributed as "sponge" activities for students to ponder as they wait for class to begin or when they finish an in-class assignment. Incorporate the lists into simulation and query games, such as the classroom versions of "Jeopardy" and "Who Wants to Be a Millionaire" as described in "Activities to Use With the Lists." Learning centers can also incorporate lists for interpretation and problem solving. Most importantly, design your own creative uses of these lists to add spice and variety to your lessons. Use them to expand, enrich, enliven, and excite your social studies classes.

Ronald L. Partin

About the Author

RONALD L. PARTIN has spent 33 years as an educator, beginning as a high school social studies teacher. He was one of the first to be certified to teach psychology and sociology in Ohio. He earned his doctorate in educational psychology and counseling at the University of Toledo. Ron continued working with teachers as a professor in the College of Education at Bowling Green State University, where he taught courses in educational consultation, group dynamics, counseling, and learning psychology.

Ron is in frequent demand as a speaker, trainer, and consultant. As a facilitator of fun-filled, interactive workshops, he has been invited to present programs by over 400 schools, businesses, and professional organizations.

He is the author of five books and numerous journal articles in the areas of time management, goal setting, creative problem solving, stress management, and effective teaching skills. His most popular book, *The Classroom Teacher's Survival Guide* (Paramus, NJ: The Center for Applied Research in Education, 1999), was recently released in Spanish—despite the fact that his vocabulary is limited to "dos tacos."

Ron and his wife, Jan, are enjoying their second adulthoods in the beautiful mountains of western North Carolina. He collects hobbies: genealogy, woodworking, hiking, stained glass-making, golf, and square dancing.

Dedicated with much love to my grandchildren,
Brooke Nicole Partin, Braedon Long, and Jake Partin.

Contents

SECTION I: Lists for United States History

Diversity in the U.S.

Business, Industry, and Transportation

Entertainment and Culture

SECTION II: **Lists for World History**

SECTION III: **Lists for American Government**

SECTION IV: Lists for Consumer Economics

SECTION V: **Lists for Sociology**

SECTION VI: **Lists for Psychology**

SECTION VII: **Lists for Geography**

Activities to Use with the Lists

THE LISTS IN THIS BOOK may be used in a spectrum of creative learning activities to enrich and enliven the social studies. Generally, it is not suggested that they be memorized or used as test material. While many teachers would expect their students to know the content of some lists such as the states and capitals (List 502) or the items of the Bill of Rights (List 213), it is hoped that the lists will be used primarily to stimulate students' thinking, to spark enthusiasm for the social studies, to invite discussion, and to challenge students' assumptions and attitudes.

The following provides a variety of specific suggestions for using *The Social Studies Teacher's Book of Lists* with your students. With imagination you can create other uses. Your students may even suggest possible learning activities incorporating lists. Experiment, adapt, and refine. Classes differ; the same activity may not work the same with two seemingly identical classes. Also employ a variety of approaches. The element of surprise can be a most valuable motivator.

CLASSROOM CHALLENGE

This activity is adapted from the television game show "Family Feud." It can be played with two or more teams of 4–6 persons each.

Preparation:

In bold letters at least 2 inches high, print each list on newsprint or cardboard. Cover each individual item with a strip of paper that is attached lightly so that the strip can be removed easily. Leave the title of the list uncovered. Make a master copy of each list so that individual items can be uncovered as they are correctly identified.

Directions:

Select 2–4 teams of 5–6 students. Try to assure that the teams are about equal in academic ability. Hang the list on the front wall so that all will be able to read it. The teams stand or are seated on either side so that they do not block the view of the list by the nonparticipants. The individual items of the list are each covered with their slips of paper. Appoint a scorekeeper and an assistant to reveal the individual items on the list as they are correctly identified. You may either serve as the master of ceremonies or choose a student to fill that role after the game is understood.

Toss a coin to see which team will begin. The master of ceremonies describes the type of items included on this list. One at a time and without consultation, each participant of the beginning team suggests one item he/she believes will appear on the list. If the participant's response is correct, the strip of paper covering the item is removed before the next person on the team responds. For each incorrect response, the scorekeeper marks a large X on the chalkboard. If the team records three incorrect responses, they lose their turn and the next team may attempt to finish the list.

A team scores 5 points when each person on the team responds and no more than two incorrect responses occurred. For example, on a 6-student team 5 points will be awarded if four or more items are correctly identified from the list. In the event that a team has three incorrect responses, the next team may attempt to complete the list. The second team receives credit for the items already correctly guessed by the first team. For example, if the first team (of 6 members) had correctly identified two items from the list before recording three incorrect responses, the second team only has to correctly identify two more items from the list to win the 5 points.

The winner may be the first team to win 25 points, or you may choose to set a time limit. Whoever is ahead at the end of the time limit wins.

Suggested List (with List Numbers):

Earliest Colleges (14)
The Confederate States (31)
Flags Flown over Texas (42)
Seven Wonders of the Ancient World (133)
The Axis Powers of World War II (168)
Former Republics of the U.S.S.R. (178)
The Cabinet Positions (212)
Early Black Civil Rights Leaders (247)
Religious Symbols (339)
Things Not Around in 1960 (348)
Major World Religions (357)
The Endocrine Glands (449)
Parts of the Brain (450)
Provinces and Territories of Canada (509)
The 20 Most Populous Countries (510)
The Great Lakes (521)
Soybean Products (530)
Major Wheat Producing Countries (532)

COOPERATIVE LEARNING REPORTS

You can develop the attitudes and skills of cooperation by assigning small groups to work together on projects selected from the lists.

Preparation:

Select the list on which students will base their projects, for example, "Famous American Indians." Write each item on the list on a different piece of paper and place the slips in a box or bag.

Directions:

Break the class into cooperative learning groups of 2–4 students. (For more information on effectively developing cooperative learning groups, see D. W. Johnson and R. T. Johnson, *Learning Together and Alone* [Englewood Cliffs, NJ: Prentice Hall, 1987], or R. E. Slavin, *Cooperative Learning* [New York: Longman, 1983].) Each group draws a slip of paper selecting their topic for the project.

Describe the type of final product desired—written report, oral report, videotape, display, skit, etc. Encourage the groups to be creative in their approaches. Announce the final due date and if possible allot some class time for the groups to meet together to plan their projects.

Suggested Lists (with List Numbers):

Household Implements of the Pioneers (24)
Major Civil War Battles and Campaigns (40)
Inventions of Thomas Edison (56)
The Muckrakers (60)
Women's Rights Pioneers (61)
Fads and Fancies of the 1920's (69)
The Alphabet of the New Deal (70)
Fads and Fancies of the 1930's (72)
Fads and Fancies of the 1950's (82)
Notable African Americans (102)
U.S. Women's Firsts (106)
American Inventors and Their Inventions (112)
Major Egyptian Deities (138)
Greek Dieties (141)
Roman Deities (145)
Major World Philosophers (200)
The Bill of Rights (213)
Investment Opportunities (282)
American Architectural Styles (305)
U.S. Social Reformers (322)
Contemporary Social Problems (346)
Major World Religions (357)
Eminent Pioneer Psychologists (412)
Counseling Approaches (415)
Common Defense Mechanisms (429)
Self-Help Groups (436)
Provinces and Territories of Canada (509)
Major Crops of the United States (517)
Nations of Africa (539)
World's Most Populous Metropolises (541)
Common Contaminants (544)

SCAVENGER HUNT

Arouse curiosity and encourage students to enter the room early by hiding items from one of the lists. This can be a fun way to introduce a new topic.

Preparation:

On separate 4″ × 6″ index cards, print individual items from one of the lists. Laminate the cards so they can be reused in future classes.

Directions:

Before students begin arriving for class, tape the cards around the room. Place them so they can be easily found, but in somewhat unusual spots (e.g., near the baseboard, on the waste-basket, beneath the pencil sharpener). Students should write down the items of the list as they discover them. It may stimulate enthusiasm to award a small prize or privilege to the person recording the most items from the list before class begins.

Suggested Lists (with List Numbers):

Witticisms and Quotations of Ben Franklin (8)
Achievements of Thomas Jefferson (18)
Civil War Military Leaders (35)
Inventions of Thomas Edison (56)
Popular Songs of 1900 (57)
Woodrow Wilson's Fourteen Points (65)
Fads and Fancies of the 1920's (69)
American Automobiles of the 1930's (73)
Slang of the 1950's (81)
U.S. Women's Firsts (106)
American Inventors and Their Inventions (112)
Timeline of Toys (117)
Ancient Units of Measurement (134)
"Love" in Other Languages (194)
Irish Proverbs (198)
Portraits on U.S. Currency (218)
The Federal Reserve Banks (223)
Early Black Civil Rights Leaders (247)
Labor Unions (300)
Tips for Wise Online Shopping (317)
Folk Medicines (325)
The Golden Rule in Many Religions (338)
Words Borrowed from African Languages (342)
Australian Slang (344)
Things Not Around in 1960 (348)
Forms of American Music (350)
Advice from Aesop (355)

Major World Religions (357)
Phobias (414)
Research-Based Suggestions for a Happier Life (428)
Common Defense Mechanisms (429)
The Most Common Fears (438)
Multiple-Intelligences: 8 Ways of Being Smart (452)
Time Management Strategies (470)
Hearing Impaired Persons of Note (486)
Current Names of Old Places (496)
Nicknames of the States (504)
The 20 Most Populous Countries (510)
Weather Signs from American Folklore (513)
Largest Islands (524)
Geographic Nicknames (528)
Major Crude Oil Producing Countries (533)
World's Most Populous Metropolises (541)

PAIRING PUZZLES

This is a fun way to break the class into pairs.

Preparation:

Select a list that offers pairs of items such as vocabulary, nicknames, or achievements. Print the pairs on a sheet of paper as a matching quiz (for example, writing the names of inventors on the left and their invention on the right half). Cut each card in half such that the key word (inventor) and its match (invention) are on separate halves. Use a zigzag cut so that no two halves will be exactly the same. Shuffle the half-page sheets to mix up the order. There should be a sufficient number of cards for each pair of students.

Directions:

Distribute the cut card so that each student ends up with one half. Students must mingle to locate the student with the piece that matches their half. In pairs, students may now complete activities such as the Matching Game or Cooperative Learning Reports. If you have an odd number of students, include one "Wild Card." That student becomes a third member of a selected group. You may let the student choose which pair to join, or you may select it.

Suggested Lists (with List Numbers):

Slang of the 1920's (68)
Slang of the 1930's (71)
Slang of the 1950's (81)
Slang of the 1960's (86)
U.S. Women's Firsts (106)
Nicknames of Famous Americans (126)

Major Egyptian Deities (138)
"Hello" in Other Languages (192)
"Love" in Other Languages (194)
Nicknames of Various World Leaders (202)
Fathers of . . . (204)
The Cabinet Positions (212)
Portraits on U.S. Currency (218)
Nicknames of the Presidents (239)
Household Measures (272)
Esperanto Vocabulary (327)
Australian Slang (344)
Southern Foods (347)
Phobias (414)
Counseling Approaches (415)
Current Names of Old Places (496)
Nicknames of the States (504)
Countries and Capitals of South America (535)
Nations of Africa (539)

PRESS CONFERENCES

Get students personally involved in social studies content and encourage listening skills with simulated press interviews.

Preparation:

Select an appropriate list related to a topic the class will be studying. Lists of names work best for this activity. Type each item from the list on separate sheets and mix in a box or hat.

Directions:

Allow each student to draw a card from the box or hat. Students are assigned to research that person. Allow at least a week for the research. Encourage students to enmesh themselves into the lives of the persons they are studying, to learn as much as they can about that character and the world in which he/she lived. On the due date(s) individuals are interviewed by the "press corps," which might be a selected group of 4–5 students. The format is much like that of a presidential news conference. Rotate interviewers as each new person is interviewed. As an option, students may be encouraged to dress as their "character." Interviews might be spread out over several weeks. This activity may be used as an extra-credit option.

Suggested Lists (with List Numbers):

Patriot Leaders of the American Revolution (10)
Major Native American Leaders (1500–1900) (32)
Civil War Military Leaders (35)
Infamous Outlaws of the West (46)

The Muckrakers (60)
Women's Rights Pioneers (61)
U.S. Women's Firsts (106)
Labor Leaders (108)
American Inventors and Their Inventions (112)
Nicknames of Famous Americans (126)
Nicknames of Various World Leaders (202)
Fathers of . . . (204)
Recent Nobel Peace Prize Laureates (206)
The Cabinet Positions (212)
U.S. Supreme Court Chief Justices (219)
Early Black Civil Rights Leaders (247)
U.S. Social Reformers (322)

BRAINSTORMING

Encourage cooperation and develop listening skills through small-group brainstorming. This is also an effective technique for introducing a new topic.

Preparation:

Minimal preparation is required beyond selection of the appropriate list.

Directions:

Divide the class into small groups of 4–5 persons. Identify a leader for each group. A fun way to select leaders is to ask for each group to determine who got up earliest that morning or who has the most brothers and sisters. The leader's role is to keep everyone on task and to record the group's answers. For variety, large-group brainstorming can be done with the entire class. Select two students to write the list on the board as items are suggested.

If the students are not familiar with brainstorming, explain that the focus is upon quantity, to name as many items as they can that belong to the selected list. Allow a maximum of 5 minutes for the brainstorming session. Have each group in turn share two items from their list until all are mentioned. Reveal the total list on a transparency or handout, or just read the ones that have not been mentioned by the students.

Suggested Lists (with List Numbers):

Earliest Colleges (14)
Largest U.S. Cities in 1790 (15)
Northern Advantages During the Civil War (33)
Southern Advantages During the Civil War (34)
Civil War Military Leaders (35)
Nineteenth-Century American Authors (52)
Occupations of the Nineteenth Century (53)

American Automobiles of the 1930's (73)

Sources for Genealogical Research (128)

Signs of the Zodiac (151)

Major Languages of Europe (191)

Greatest Engineering Achievements of the Twentieth Century (176)

Richest Countries (184)

The Bill of Rights (213)

Current Supreme Court Members (220)

Top 10 Lobbyists' Expenditures in Washington, D.C. (251)

Hottest Job Prospects in the Next Decade (275)

Effects of Mandatory Overtime (278)

Most Dangerous Jobs in America (279)

Top Consumer Complaints (293)

Ways to Improve Gas Mileage (297)

Labor Unions (300)

Biggest Companies in the U.S. (309)

Careers in Sociology (320)

Problems Facing Teenagers (323)

Predictors of Successful Marriages (371)

Research on Effective Schools (375)

Recipe for Avoiding Poverty (396)

Fizzled Fashion Fads (405)

Research-Based Suggestions for a Happier Life (428)

Barriers to Effective Communication (446)

Leadership Qualities (447)

Major Stressors for Adolescents (458)

Physical Symptoms of Stress (459)

Stress Reduction Techniques (465)

Time Management Strategies (470)

Causes of Procrastination (475)

The 20 Most Populous Countries (510)

Potential Effects of Pollution (546)

BINGO

You'll be surprised how much students remember when lists are incorporated into versions of Bingo. This can be an effective technique for emphasizing the breadth of a list, such as contributions by women, or the variety of religions in the world. It is a fun way to introduce a new topic.

Preparation:

The easiest way to make the game cards is to duplicate the blank Bingo card given here. Give each student a copy or write the selected list on the chalkboard. The lists used should have at least 24 items. Have the students fill the 24 open boxes on their Bingo cards with separate items from the list. They should mix up the order of the items as they write so that no two cards will be exactly the same. You will also need about 20 markers for each student.

Cut up a copy of the list so that each item of the list is on a separate slip of paper. Be sure each item on the list is included. Place all slips in a box or bag and shake. You may choose to laminate and save the game cards for use with future classes.

Directions:

When each student has a game card with items of the list written in the open boxes, the game is ready to begin. It is played much like the traditional game of Bingo. As a slip is drawn from the box, it is read aloud. Each student who has that item on his/her card places a marker on that box. The winner is the first person to get five items in a row vertically, horizontally, or diagonally. Everyone begins with the center box covered as a free one. A winner calls out "Bingo." It is probably a good idea to verify that the person does indeed have five in a row.

To build enthusiasm for the game, award a small prize to the winners. It can be a classroom privilege, small token, poster, button, free sports tickets, or other freebie.

Suggested Lists (with List Numbers):

Civil War Military Leaders (35)
Major Civil War Battles and Campaigns (40)
Occupations of the Nineteenth Century (53)
Automobile Brands of 1906 (62)
Slang of the 1930's (71)
Popular Radio Shows of the 1940's (77)
Innovations of the 1980's (98)
U.S. Women's Firsts (106)
Women Inventors (107)
Entrepreneurs Who Shaped American History (111)
American Inventors and Their Inventions (112)
The Greek Alphabet (142)
Roman Deities (145)
Presidents of the United States (229)
Things Not Around in 1960 (348)
Phobias (414)
Counseling Approaches (415)
Stress Prevention Techniques (464)
Stress Reduction Techniques (465)
Time Management Strategies (470)
Nicknames of the States (504)
Countries and Capitals of South America (535)

B I N G O

		FREE		

MATCHING QUIZ

Stimulate interest by having pairs of students attempt to match pairs of items from lists.

Preparation:

Select a list that offers pairs of items such as vocabulary, nicknames, or achievements. Print or type the list on a sheet of paper as a matching quiz; for example, listing names in the left-hand column, and their accomplishments in scrambled order in the right-hand column. Duplicate a sufficient number for each pair of students.

Directions:

Form pairs either at random or using a technique such as Pairing Puzzles. Distribute a quiz sheet to each pair. Direct the students to connect each item from the left-hand list to the appropriate item on the right-hand list with a straight line. After 3–5 minutes, call time and score the results.

Suggested Lists (with List Numbers):

Occupations of the Nineteenth Century (53)
Slang of the 1920's (68)
Slang of the 1930's (71)
Slang of the 1950's (81)
U.S. Women's Firsts (106)
First Hits of Top Recording Artists (119)
Nicknames of Famous Americans (126)
Major Egyptian Deities (138)
Fathers of . . . (204)
Portraits on U.S. Currency (218)
Nicknames of the Presidents (239)
Presidential Trivia Quiz (242)
Household Measures (272)
Labor Unions (300)
Old Names for Illnesses (326)
Phobias (414)
Current Names of Old Places (496)
Nicknames of the States (504)
Countries and Capitals of South America (535)
Countries and Capitals of Europe (536)
Countries and Capitals of Asia (537)

CROSSWORD PUZZLES

Spark interest or review through crossword puzzles based on appropriate lists. An example based on List 229, "Presidents of the United States," is presented here.

Preparation:

Using an appropriate list, construct a crossword puzzle. A very useful computer program, "Crossword Magic," is available for the Apple GS or Macintosh computers from Mindscape, Inc., 3444 Dundee Road, Northbrook, IL 60062, or most major computer software mail-order houses. You may choose to give the students a list including the words used in the puzzle. Duplicate copies of the finished puzzle. You might challenge older students to construct their own puzzles.

Directions:

Distribute a copy of the puzzle for each student or to each pair. Crossword puzzles can be completed in pairs, in class, or as homework. It is generally best to permit students to use whatever resources they can as this reinforces information-gathering skills. Post the answers.

Crossword Puzzle Software:

Across
http://thinks.com

Crossword Compiler
http://www.crossword-puzzle-maker.com

Crossword Creator
http://www.centronsoftware.com

Crossdown
http://www.crossdown.com

CrossWorks
http://www.homeware.com

Sympathy—Crossword Construction
http://www.bryson.demon.co.uk

Presidential Crossword Puzzle

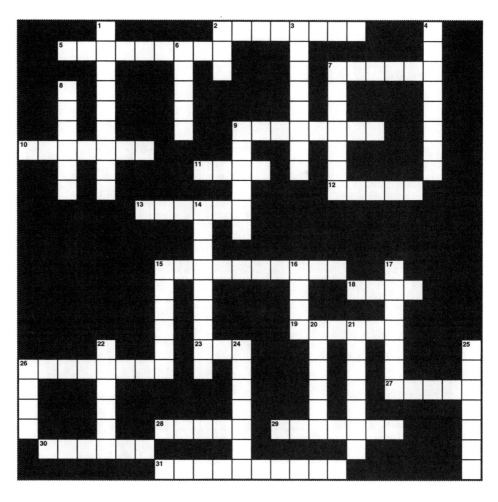

Across

2. Brokered The Compromise of 1850
5. Only Pres. to serve non-consecutive terms
7. Slogan was "A chicken in every pot and two cars in every garage"
9. "Silent Cal"
10. First Pres. to be impeached
11. Played football at Univ. of Michigan
12. West Point grad. & Civil War general
13. Completed the Gadsden Purchase
15. Only Pres. to receive 100% of electoral college votes
18. "Fifty-four, forty or fight" campaign
19. Ordered atomic bomb drop on Japan
23. Began the "War on Poverty"
26. Never married
27. Only Pres. to resign from office
28. Husband of "Lemonade Lucy"
29. First Republican Pres.
30. "Era of Good Feeling" President
31. WWII general

Down

1. Purchased the Louisiana Territory
2. Elected Pres. 4 times (initials)
3. Pres. during Spanish-American War
4. Shot July 2, 1881; died Sept. 19
6. First White House resident
7. Associated with Teapot Dome scandal
8. Pres. 1881–1885
9. Peanut farmer
14. "Rough Rider"
15. The League of Nations initiator
16. Later a U.S. Chief Justice
17. Wife elected to U.S. Senate
20. Star of "Bedtime for Bonzo"
21. "The Father of the Constitution"
22. "Old Rough & Ready"
24. On $20 bill
25. Created the Peace Corps
26. Former CIA Director

Presidential Crossword Puzzle Key

Suggested Lists (with List Numbers):

Patriot Leaders of the American Revolution (10)
The Transcendentalists (27)
Civil War Military Leaders (35)
Major Civil War Battles and Campaigns (40)
Occupations of the Nineteenth Century (53)
The Muckrakers (60)
Women's Rights Pioneers (61)
Notable Hispanic Americans (104)
Notable Arab Americans (105)
U.S. Women's Firsts (106)
Labor Leaders (108)
Entrepreneurs Who Shaped America (111)
American Inventors and Their Inventions (112)
Nicknames of Famous Americans (126)
Early Explorers of the Americas (157)
Nicknames of Various World Leaders (202)
Portraits on U.S. Currency (218)
Presidential Firsts (238)

Nicknames of the Presidents (239)
Eminent Pioneer Psychologists (412)
Common Defense Mechanisms (429)
Current Names of Old Places (496)
States and Their Capitals (502)
Geographic Nicknames (528)
Countries and Capitals of Asia (537)

WORD PUZZLES

Generate a variety of word puzzles to introduce new content, as sponge activities, to peak curiosity or to stimulate review. An example based on List 229, "Presidents of the United States," is presented here.

Preparation:

Using an appropriate list, construct a hidden word puzzle. While puzzles can be made by hand, several inexpensive computer programs create puzzles very quickly. (See list below.) You may want to give the students a list including the words used in the puzzle. Duplicate copies of the finished puzzle.

Directions:

Distribute a copy of the puzzle for each student or to each pair. Word puzzles can be completed in pairs, in class, or as homework. Some teachers distribute word puzzles before the students enter the room. A note on the board invites students to begin working on the puzzle—either individually or in pairs—as soon as they enter the room. This entices students into a learning mode, even before the class officially begins.

Word Puzzle Software:

The following computer software easily and quickly create a variety of word puzzles:

Word Search Construction Kit
http://www.wordsearchkit.com

Wordsearch Creator
http://www.centronsoftware.com

Word Splash Pro
http://wordsplashpro.chronasoft.com

Suggested Lists:

The same lists that would be appropriate for crossword puzzles could be used for word puzzles.

Presidents Word Puzzle

There are thirty-four names of U.S. Presidents in the word puzzle below. How many can you find? Names may appear horizontally, vertically, diagonally, forward, or backward. Circle each one as you find it.

```
C R C K C C I M P B U S H N X Z N A I K
C L O O V L X Y A I I H M M V H U B P N
J T E O O D I N D D E C X Y X T C P A C
J R R V S L L N O E I R C C Q G Q G A Q
V U W E E I E T S N S C I N R A R E E
Y M I G W L V D I O K N O E C E T F R B
B A L R P O A E G F N C E N R E A O U N
O N S A O B H N L E R Z A K R M M C T I
N J O N L E W N D T L A J J M L H G A X
S H N T K C N U E H Q F G C L A J H F O
M P H Q M O J D Z S I U K I N E W L T N
A D U G S H Z P G F I I F A F A I V L S
D M R P D B I M B O N E N F S N G M B L
A J J X Y T I L A L N H E H C U G N E Y
R T X M V U R E E O A R I O R F U T L E
O R M E Z I O Y S R S N L F Q E A H Z V
L E K S O R T N D O G N W K S P V B Z X
Y L H K N U H I N T Z Z E G A C G O P G
A Y J O B O N U O E C V D I M M N L O W
T T M A J G V N F O R D G T N I O Y C H
```

Presidents Word Puzzle Key

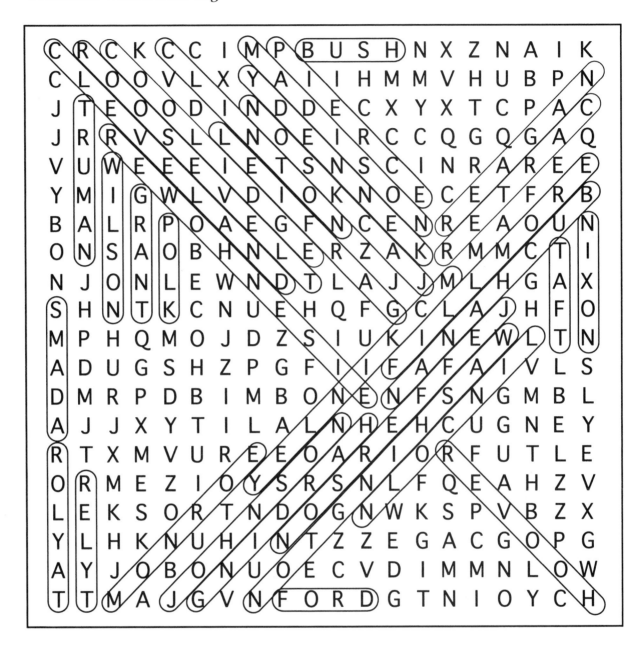

ANAGRAMS

Anagrams, or words with the letters scrambled, can be used to develop interest in a topic and to practice problem-solving skills.

Preparation:

Select a list comprised of one-word items. On a chalkboard, newsprint, or handout, rearrange the letters of the words on the list using all capital letters. For example, from the list of the states the anagram KASALA would unscramble ALASKA. A maximum of ten words is sufficient for all but the more advanced classes.

Directions:

Reveal or distribute the anagrams. Tell the students the topic of the lists (e.g., States of the Union). While the puzzles can be done individually either in class or as homework, it is probably best to randomly pair students. This encourages cooperation and minimizes the disadvantages of ability. If spelling may be a problem, a copy of the correctly spelled list might be posted. Anagrams may also be distributed as "fillers" to constructively occupy moments such as when students complete a list early.

Anagrams Software:

The following computer software programs easily and efficiently create an assortment of anagrams:

> *Anagrams Creator*
> http://www.centronsoftware.com
>
> *Anagram Genius*
> http://www.genius2000.com

Suggested Lists (with List Numbers):

North American Explorers (3)
Tools of the Pioneers (23)
Weaponry of the Civil War (36)
Nineteenth-Century American Authors (52)
Women's Rights Pioneers (61)
African American Firsts (101)
Clothing Timeline (118)
Wars Involving the United States (121)
Nicknames of Famous Americans (126)
The Seven Deadly Sins (155)
Early Explorers of the Americas (157)
Fathers of . . . (204)
Religious Symbols (339)
Holy Books (340)
Forms of Marriage (352)
Major World Religions (357)
Ivy League Colleges (380)
Psychological Needs (425)
Multiple-Intelligences: 8 Ways of Being Smart (452)
Forms of Propaganda (455)
Map Features (498)
Provinces and Territories of Canada (509)
Longest Rivers of the World (511)
Weather Terms (516)
Major Crops of the United States (517)
World Currencies (529)

DICTIONARY GAME

This is a variation of the old party game. The idea of the game is to guess the correct definition of an unfamiliar word. It works well with lists that include words that are entirely new to the students. You will need a sufficient supply of identical 3″ × 5″ cards or pieces of paper for each student to have six pieces.

Preparation:

Advance preparation consists of selecting a list related to the topic the class is studying. It is important that the students are unlikely to know the words on the list. For each item on the list, write the word and its definition on a card or paper. You will need one set of cards for every five students in the class.

Directions:

Break the class into groups of 5–6 students and have them gather in small circles. Each student will need the same number of cards as there are in the prepared deck. Place a set of prepared cards face down in the center of each group. One student begins by selecting at random one card from the deck and reading aloud the word from the card, but not its definition. The task is for each student to then make up a plausible definition and write it on one of their cards. They should not see each other's definitions. If they should know the real definition, they should not tell anyone and make up a phoney one. Encourage students to print neatly so that the definition can be easily read.

The cards are then given to the student who drew the original card. He or she will shuffle the cards, including the original one, and then read aloud all the definitions. After all the definitions have been read, the other students are to vote on which they believe is the correct one. Each time they guess correctly, they receive 1 point.

Rotating clockwise around the circle, the process is repeated until all the cards in the deck have been used.

Suggested Lists (with List Numbers):

Slang of the 1890's (49)
Occupations of the Nineteenth Century (53)
Slang of the 1920's (68)
The Alphabet of the New Deal (70)
Slang of the 1930's (71)
Slang of the 1940's (75)
Slang of the 1950's (81)
Slang of the 1960's (86)
Slang of the 1970's (93)
Women Inventors (107)
First Hits of Top Recording Artists (119)
"Hello" in Other Languages (192)
"Peace" in Other Languages (193)
"Love" in Other Languages (194)
Forms of Government (211)

Nautical Measurements (270)
Abbreviations of Academic Degrees (304)
Old Names for Illnesses (326)
Phobias (414)

INTERNET RESEARCH

Assign each student a different item from a relevant list to research on the Internet. In addition to enhancing content knowledge, the research activity develops research and critical-thinking skills.

Preparation:

Select a list related to the topic being taught (for example, List 539, Nations of Africa). Randomly assign each student (or pair of students) one item from the list. If access to a computer lab is available, take the class to the lab and guide their research.

Directions:

Students are asked to research their assigned items via the Internet. A distributed study guide listing specific web sites and relevant questions to answer in their research can help direct their search. (For example, with the nations of Africa list, students might seek the per capita income, average life expectancy, population, and type of government.) At the end of the allotted research period (or perhaps at the next class meeting), have students share their research findings in groups of four. Another option is for the small groups to prepare a brief class report summarizing their discussions.

Suggested Lists (with List Numbers):

Major Native American Leaders (1500–1900) (2)
Revolutionary War Battles (12)
Major Civil War Battles and Campaigns (40)
Important Roads, Trails, and Canals (43)
Major Events of 1876 (44)
The Alphabet of the New Deal (70)
Notable African Americans (102)
Notable Hispanic Americans (104)
Notable Arab Americans (105)
Women Inventors (107)
Entrepreneurs Who Shaped America (111)
American Inventors and Their Inventions (112)
Roman Deities (145)
Least Developed Countries (186)
Major World Philosophers (200)
Standing Congressional Committees (224)
Early Black Civil Rights Leaders (247)
Government's Greatest Endeavors (252)
U.S. Social Reformers (322)

Eminent Pioneer Psychologists (412)
Counseling Approaches (415)
States and Their Capitals (502)
Provinces and Territories of Canada (509)
Careers in Geography (520)
Countries and Capitals of Asia (537)
World's Most Populous Metropolises (541)

INTEREST BUILDERS

Posters

Design (or let students make) colorful posters that incorporate the lists. Add pictures, drawings, and designs related to the theme of the list. The posters can be displayed on the door or in the room as interest grabbers. Try hanging a new one each day or on random days. The element of surprise gets students' attention. They begin to read the posters before class begins. Save them for use next year.

Bulletin Board Displays

Challenge a group of students to design and construct an attractive bulletin board display (either in the classroom or in a hallway) that incorporates one of the lists. Photos, drawings, and color add to the interest.

Coming Attractions

As a homework assignment, announce the topic of one of the lists (e.g., Items Rationed During World War II (80), Fads and Fancies of the 1970's (94), Things from 1960 That Are Hard to Find Today (349), or Common Superstitions (445).

Have the students enlist the aid of their parents in listing as many items as they can. In the next class, have students call out their items as one student records them on the board. Add any from the published list that are not mentioned by the students.

Learning Centers

Incorporate lists into learning centers. Photos or drawings that illustrate the lists will add interest. The goal should not be to memorize the lists, but to use them to reinforce a concept, apply a skill, challenge assumptions, develop appreciation, or influence attitudes.

Handouts

Some of the lists make useful handouts that the students can read and take home. They will not only arouse students' interest but parents' as well.

Overhead Transparencies

Include some of the lists on overhead transparencies. Turn on the transparency before the class begins. Students who arrive early can enjoy the day's list. When the bell rings, turn off the transparency. This rewards students who are on time and increases the day's learning time, as well as arousing interest in the day's topic. If time permits at the end of class, you may put the transparency back on.

Addressing the Social Studies Standards: Ten Thematic Strands

THE NATIONAL COUNCIL FOR THE SOCIAL STUDIES, in its publication *Expectations of Excellence: Curriculum Standards for Social Studies*, lists ten thematic standards describing what every K–12 student should know and be able to do. The following descriptions of the ten strands specify the major areas of competence each student should master. All the lists included in *The Social Studies Teacher's Book of Lists* can be used to teach at least one of the ten strands. For examples, see the "Thematic Table of Contents" on pages 26–37.

CULTURE AND CULTURAL DIVERSITY

Social studies programs should include experiences that provide for the study of culture and cultural diversity.

People create, learn, and adapt culture. Culture helps us to understand ourselves as both individuals and members of various groups. Human cultures exhibit both similarities and differences. We all, for example, have systems of beliefs, knowledge, values, and traditions. Each system also is unique. In a democratic and multicultural society, students need to understand multiple perspectives that derive from different cultural vantage points. This understanding will allow them to relate to people in our nation and throughout the world.

Cultures are dynamic and ever-changing. The study of culture prepares students to ask and answer questions such as: What are the common characteristics of different cultures? How do belief systems, such as religion or political ideals of the culture, influence the other parts of the culture? How does the culture change to accommodate different ideas and beliefs? What does language tell us about the culture?

In schools, this theme typically appears in units and courses dealing with geography, history, and anthropology, as well as multicultural topics across the curriculum.

TIME, CONTINUITY, AND CHANGE

Social studies programs should include experiences that provide for the study of the ways human beings view themselves in and over time.

People seek to understand their historical roots and to locate themselves in time. Such understanding involves knowing what things were like in the past and how things change and develop. Knowing how to read and reconstruct the past allows one to develop a historical perspective and to answer questions such as: Who am I? What happened in the past? How am

I connected to those in the past? How has the world changed and how might it change in the future? Why does our personal sense of relatedness to the past change? How can the perspective we have about our own life experiences be viewed as part of the larger human story across time? How do our personal stories reflect varying points of view and inform contemporary ideas and actions?

This theme typically appears in courses that: (1) include perspectives from various aspects of history; (2) draw upon historical knowledge during the examination of social issues; and (3) develop the habits of mind that historians and scholars in the humanities and social sciences employ to study the past and its relationship to the present in the United States and other societies.

PEOPLE, PLACES, AND ENVIRONMENTS

Social studies programs should include experiences that provide for the study of people, places, and environments.

Technological advances connect students at all levels to the world beyond their personal locations. The study of people, places, and human–environment interactions assists learners as they create their spatial views and geographic perspectives of the world. Today's social, cultural, economic, and civic demands on individuals mean that students will need the knowledge, skills, and understanding to ask and answer questions such as: Where are things located? Why are they located where they are? What patterns are reflected in the groupings of things? What do we mean by region? How do landforms change? What implications do these changes have for people?

This area of study helps learners make informed and critical decisions about the relationship between human beings and their environment.

INDIVIDUAL DEVELOPMENT AND IDENTITY

Social studies programs should include experiences that provide for the study of individual development and identity.

Personal identity is shaped by one's culture, by groups, and by institutional influences. How do people learn? Why do people behave as they do? What influences how people learn, perceive, and grow? How do people meet their basic needs in a variety of contexts? Questions such as these are central to the study of how individuals develop from youth to adulthood. Examination of various forms of human behavior enhances understanding of the relationships among social norms and emerging personal identities, the social processes that influence identity formation, and the ethical principles underlying individual action. In schools, this theme typically appears in units and courses dealing with psychology and anthropology.

Given the nature of individual development and our own cultural context, students need to be aware of the processes of learning, growth, and development at every level of their school experience. In the early grades, for example, observing brothers, sisters, and older adults; looking at family photo albums; remembering past achievements and projecting oneself into the future; and comparing the patterns of behavior evident in people of different age groups are appropriate activities because young learners develop their personal identities in the context of families, peers, schools, and communities.

INDIVIDUALS, GROUPS, AND INSTITUTIONS

Social studies programs should include experiences that provide for the study of interactions among individuals, groups, and institutions.

Institutions such as schools, churches, families, government agencies, and the courts all play an integral role in our lives. These and other institutions exert enormous influence over us, yet institutions are no more than organizational embodiments to further the core social values of those who comprise them. Thus, it is important that students know how institutions are formed, what controls and influences them, how they control and influence individuals and culture, and how institutions can be maintained or changed.

Students should be assisted in recognizing the tensions that occur when the goals, values, and principles of two or more institutions or groups conflict—for example, when the school board prohibits candy machines in schools vs. a class project to install a candy machine to help raise money for the local hospital. They should also have opportunities to explore ways in which institutions, such as churches or health-care networks, are created to respond to changing individual and group needs.

POWER, AUTHORITY, AND GOVERNANCE

Social studies programs should include experiences that provide for the study of how people create and change structures of power, authority, and governance.

Understanding the historical development of structures of power, authority, and governance and their evolving functions in contemporary U.S. society, as well as in other parts of the world, is essential for developing civic competence. In exploring this theme, students confront questions such as: What is power? What forms does it take? Who holds it? How is it gained, used, and justified? What is legitimate authority? How are governments created, structured, maintained, and changed? How can we keep government responsive to its citizens' needs and interests? How can individual rights be protected within the context of majority rule?

By examining the purposes and characteristics of various governance systems, students develop an understanding of how groups and nations attempt to resolve conflicts, and seek to establish order and security. Through study of the dynamic relationships among individual rights and responsibilities, the needs of social groups, and concepts of a just society, students become more effective problem-solvers and decision-makers when addressing the persistent issues and social problems encountered in public life.

PRODUCTION, DISTRIBUTION, AND CONSUMPTION

Social studies programs should include experiences that provide for the study of how people organize for the production, distribution, and consumption of goods and services.

People have wants that often exceed the limited resources available to them. As a result, a variety of ways have been invented to decide upon answers to four fundamental questions: What is to be produced? How is production to be organized? How are goods and services to be distributed? What is the most effective allocation of the factors of production (land, labor, and capital management)?

Unequal distribution of resources necessitates systems of exchange, including trade, to improve the well-being of the economy, while the role of government in economic policy-making varies over time and from place to place.

SCIENCE, TECHNOLOGY, AND SOCIETY

Social studies programs should include experiences that provide for the study of relationships among science, technology, and society.

Technology is as old as the first crude tool invented by prehistoric humans, but today's technology forms the basis for some of our most difficult social choices. Modern life as we know it would be impossible without technology and the science that supports it. But technology brings with it many questions: Is new technology always better than that which it will replace? What can we learn from the past about how new technologies result in broader social change, some of which is unanticipated? How can we cope with the ever-increasing pace of change, perhaps even with the feeling that technology has gotten out of control? How can we manage technology so that the greatest number of people benefit from it? How can we preserve our fundamental values and beliefs in a world that is rapidly becoming one technology-linked village?

GLOBAL CONNECTIONS

Social studies programs should include experiences that provide for the study of global connections and interdependence.

The realities of global interdependence require understanding the increasingly important and diverse global connections among world societies. Analysis of tensions between national interests and global priorities contributes to the development of possible solutions to persistent and emerging global issues in many fields: health care, economic development, environmental quality, universal human rights, and others. Analyzing patterns and relationships within and among world cultures, such as economic competition and interdependence, age-old ethnic enmities, political and military alliances, and others, helps learners carefully examine policy alternatives that have both national and global implications.

CIVIC IDEALS AND PRACTICES

Social studies programs should include experiences that provide for the study of the ideals, principles, and practices of citizenship in a democratic republic.

An understanding of civic ideals and practices of citizenship is critical to full participation in society and is a central purpose of the social studies. All people have a stake in examining civic ideals and practices across time and in diverse societies as well as at home, and in determining how to close the gap between present practices and the ideals upon which our democratic republic is based. Students confront such questions as: What is civic participation and how can I be involved? How has the meaning of citizenship evolved? What is the balance between rights and responsibilities? What is the role of the citizen in the community and the nation, and as a member of the world community? How can I make a positive difference?

Source: Excerpted from *Expectations of Excellence: Curriculum Standards for Social Studies* (NCSS Publications, P.O. Box 2067, Waldorf, Maryland 20604–2067). Used with permission.

Thematic Table of Contents

THE NATIONAL COUNCIL FOR THE SOCIAL STUDIES established ten interdisciplinary thematic standards that encompass the subject areas of social studies. Here are examples of lists that can be used to augment instruction in each of the ten thematic standards.

Culture and Cultural Diversity

Time, Continuity, and Change

People, Places, and Environments

Individual Development and Identity

Individuals, Groups, and Institutions

Power, Authority, and Governance

Production, Distribution, and Consumption

Science, Technology, and Society

Global Connections

Civic Ideals and Practices

Academic Standards Bibliography

GENERAL ACADEMIC STANDARDS

The following is a listing of articles and books related to academic standards.

Blum, R.E. (2000). Standards-based Reform: Can it make a difference for students? *Peabody Journal of Education, 75*(4), 90–113.

Dodd, A.W. (2000). Are higher standards and students' needs compatible? *Principal Leadership, 1*(1), 28–32.

Doyle, D.P., & Pimentel, S. (1999). *Raising the standard: An eight-step action guide for schools and communities.* Thousand Oaks, CA: Corwin Press.

Frater, G. (June 2001). Thinking about standards. *Basic Skills,* 8–10.

Gandal, M., & Vranek, J. (2001). Standards: Here today, here tomorrow. *Educational Ledership, 59*(1), 6–13.

Gordon, D.W. (2000). Preparing students for rigorous standards. *Leadership, 30*(2), 8–10.

Guskey, T.R. (2001). Helping standards make the grade. *Educational Leadership, 59*(1), 20–27.

———. (2001). High percentages are not the same as high standards. *Phi Delta Kappan , 82*(7), 534–536.

———. (2001). Making standards work. *The School Administrator, 56*(9), 44.

Hall, S. (2001). Learning for all: Standards for racial equality in schools. *MCT, 19*(3), 19–20, 25.

Hardy, L. (2000). The trouble with standards. *American School Board Journal, 187*(1), 22–26.

Jennings, N.E. (2000). Standards and local curriculum: A zero-sum game? *Journal of Research in Rural Education, 16*(3), 193–201.

Jones, R. (2000). Making standards work. *American School Board Journal, 187*(1), 27–31.

Kannapel, P.J. (2000). Standards-based reform and rural school improvement: Finding the middle ground. *Journal of Research in Rural Education, 16*(3), 202–208.

Kluth, P., & Straut, D. (2001). Standards for diverse learners. *Educational Leadership, 59*(1), 43–46.

La Marca, P.M. (2001). *Alignment of standards and assessments as an accountability criterion.* ERIC Digest. ERIC Clearinghouse on Assessment and Evaluation, College Park, MD. (ERIC Document No. 458288)

Matlock, L., Fielder, K., & Walsh, D. (2001). Building the foundation for standards-based instruction for all students. *TEACHING Exceptional Children, 33*(5), 68–72.

Merrow, J. (2001). Undermining standards. *Phi Delta Kappan, 82*(9), 652–659.

Nevi, C. (2001). Saving standards. *Phi Delta Kappan, 82*(6), 460–461.

Quenemoen, R.F. (2001). IEPs within standards-based reform. *Assessment for Effective Intervention, 26*(2), 75–76.

Renzulli, J.S. (2001). Standards and standards plus: A good idea or a new cage? *Journal of Secondary Gifted Education, 12*(3), 139–140.

Schmoker, M., & Marzano, R.J. (1999). Realizing the promise of standards-based education. *Educational Leadership, 56*(6), 17–21.

Snow-Renner, R. (2001). *Teachers' perspectives on standards-based education: Initial findings from a high-performing, high-needs school district.* Mid-Continent Research for Education and Learning, Aurora, CO. (ERIC Document No. 457150)

Thompson, S. (2001). The authentic standards movement and its evil twin. *Phi Delta Kappan, 82*(5), 358–362.

Thompson, S.J., Thurlow, M.L., Esler, A., & Whetstone, P.J. (2001). Addressing standards and assessments on the IEP. *Assessment for Effective Intervention, 26*(2), 77–84.

Tomlinson, C.A. (2000). Reconcilable differences: Standards-based teaching and differentiation. *Educational Leadership, 58*(1), 6–11.

ACADEMIC STANDARDS FOR SOCIAL STUDIES

American Psychological Association. (2002). *National standards for the teaching of high school psychology: Promoting active learning.* Internet: http://www.apa.org/ed/natlstandards.html.

Arizona State Dept. of Education. (2000). Arizona Standards: Social Studies Standards. Phoenix: Arizona State Dept. of Education. (ERIC Document No. 449049)

Benjamin, L.T., Jr. (2001). American psychology's struggles with its curriculum: Should a thousand flowers bloom? *American Psychologist, 6*(9), 735–742.

Blanchard, R.A., Senesh, L., & Patterson-Black, S. (1999). The organic social studies curriculum and the 1994 NCSS standards: A model for linking the community and the world. *Social Studies, 90*(2), 63–67.

Bohn, A.P., & Sleeter, C.E. (2000). Multicultural education and the standards movement: A report from the field. *Phi Delta Kappan, 82*(2), 156–159.

Buckles, S., & Watts, M. (1998). National standards in economics, history, social studies, civics, and geography: Complimentarities, competition, or peaceful coexistence? *Journal of Economic Education, 29*(2), 157–166.

Center for Civic Education. (1994). *National standards for civics and government.* Calabasas, CA: Center for Civic Education.

Danker, A.C. (2000). Linking technology with social studies learning standards. *Social Studies, 91*(6), 253256.

Drake, S.M. (2001). Castles, kings . . . and standards. *Educational Leadership, 59*(1), 38–42.

Dynneson, T.L., & Gross, R.E. (1999). *Designing effective instruction for secondary social studies.* Old Tappan, NJ: Prentice Hall.

Geography Education Standards Project. (1994). *Geography for life: National geography standards.* Washington, DC: National Geographic Research & Exploration.

Guerra, L. (2000). Idaho State Board of Education K–8 Achievement Standards. Boise, ID: Idaho State Board of Education. (ERIC Document No. 456570)

Hilke, E. (1999). *Children's literature and the K–4 social studies standards.* Fastback 453. Bloomington, IN: Phi Delta Kappa Educational Foundation.

Lindquist, T. (1997) *Ways that work: Putting social studies standards into practice.* Portsmouth, NH: Heinemann.

National Board for Professional Teaching Standards. (1998). *Social studies-history standards (for teachers of students ages 7–18 +).* Southfield, MI: National Board for Professional Teaching Standards.

National Center for History in the Schools. (1996). *National standards for history.* University of California, Los Angeles.

National Council for the Social Studies. (1994). *Expectations of excellence: Curriculum standards for social studies.* Silver Spring, MD: National Council for the Social Studies.

———. (2000). *National standards for social studies teachers.* Washington, DC: National Council for the Social Studies.

National Council on Economic Education. (1997). *Voluntary national content standards in economics.* New York: National Council on Economic Education.

North Carolina State Dept. of Public Instruction. (2000). North Carolina Standard Course of Study and Grade Level Competencies: Social Studies K–12. Raleigh, NC: North Carolina State Dept. of Public Instruction. (ERIC Document No. 447025).

Scott, R. (2000). Developing storypath units for integrating social studies and the Michigan content standards. *Michigan Social Studies Journal, 12*(1), 7–12.

Wegner, G. (1996). The NCSS Curriculum Standards. *Social Education, 60*(2), 83–86.

Wilen, W.W. (2000). *Favorite lesson plans: Powerful standards-based activities.* Washington, DC: National Council for the Social Studies.

NATIONAL SOCIAL STUDIES STANDARDS

The following resources provide lists of academic standards for the various social studies disciplines.

Expectations of Excellence: Curriculum Standards for Social Studies
National Council for the Social Studies
http://www.ncss.org/standards/stitle.html

National Geography Standards
National Geographic Society
http://www.nationalgeographic.com/resources/ngo/education/standardslist.html

National Geography Standards
National Council for Geographic Education
http://www.ncge.org/standards/

National Standards for Civics and Government
Center for Civic Education
http://www.civiced.org/stds.html

National Standards for the Teaching of High School Psychology
American Psychological Association
http://www.apa.org/ed/natlstandards.html

National Standards for United States History for Grades K–4
National Standards for United States History for Grades 5–12
National Standards for World History
National Center for History
http://www.sscnet.ucla.edu/nchs/standards.html

Voluntary National Content Standards in Economics
The National Council on Economic Education (NCEE)
http://www.economicsamerica.org/standards/index.html

STATE SOCIAL STUDIES STANDARDS WEB ADDRESSES

Social studies standards can be found on the Internet. Use the web sites listed below to find the standards for your state.

Alabama
http://www.alsde.edu/html/sections/section_detail.asp?section=54&footer=sections

Alaska
http://www.eed.state.ak.us/qschools/standards.html

Arizona
http://www.eed.state.az.us/qschools/standards.html

Arkansas
http://arkedu.state.ar.us/standards/index.html

California
http://www.cde.ca.gov/cfir/index.html#4

Colorado
http://www.cde.state.co.us/index_stnd.htm

Connecticut
http://www.state.ct.us/sde/dtl/curriculum/currkey3.htm

Delaware
http://www.doe.state.de.us/DPIServices/DOE_Standards.htm

District of Columbia
http://www.k12.dc.us/dcps/standardsindex.html

Florida
http://www.firn.edu/doe/curric/prek12/frame2.htm

Georgia
http://www.glc.k12.ga.us/qstd-int/homepg.htm

Hawaii
http://doe.k12.hi.us/standards/

Idaho
http://www.sde.state.id.us/osbe/exstand.htm

Illinois
http://www.isbe.state.il.us/ils/

Indiana
http://ideanet.doe.state.in.us/standards/

Iowa
No standards linked March 2002.

Kansas
http://www.ksde.org/assessment/index.html

Kentucky
http://www.kde.state.ky.us/oapd/curric/

Louisiana
http://www.doe.state.la.us/DOE/asps/home.asp?I=CONTENT

Maine
http://www.state.me.us/education/lres/homepage.htm

Maryland
http://mdk12.org/mspp/index.html

Massachusetts
http://www.doe.mass.edu/frameworks/default.html

Michigan
http://cdp.mde.state.mi.us/

Minnesota
http://mecr.state.mn.us/

Mississippi
http://www.mde.k12.ms.us/curriculum/

Missouri
http://www.dese.state.mo.us/divimprove/curriculum/newwebpages/ss.html

Montana
http://www.opi.state.mt.us/standards/

Nebraska
http://www.nde.state.ne.us/Issu/AcadStand.html

Nevada
http://www.nde.state.nv.us/sca/standards/index.html

New Hampshire
http://www.ed.state.nh.us/CurriculumFrameworks/curricul.htm

New Jersey
http://www.state.nj.us/njded/stass

New Mexico
http://www.cesdp.nmhu.edu/standards/content/

New York
http://www.emsc.nysed.gov/deputy/Documents/learnstandards.htm

North Carolina
http://www.dpi.state.nc.us/curriculum/

North Dakota
http://www.dpi.state.nd.us/standard/

Ohio
http://www.ode.state.oh.us/academic_content_standards/

Oklahoma
http://www.sde.state.ok.us/home/home01_test.html

Oregon
http://www.ode.state.or.us/cifs/standards/

Pennsylvania
http://www.sde.state.ok.us/home/home01_test.html

Rhode Island
http://www.ridoe.net/standards/

South Carolina
http://www.myscschools.com/offices/cso/Standards_Page.htm

South Dakota
http://www.state.sd.us/deca/dacs/contentstandards/

Tennessee
http://www.state.tn.us/education/ci/cistandards.htm

Texas
http://www.tea.state.tx.us/teks/

Utah
http://www.uen.org/core/

Vermont
http://www.state.vt.us/educ/stand/framework.htm

Virginia
http://www.pen.k12.va.us/VDOE/Instruction/sol.html

Washington
http://www.k12.wa.us/reform/EAlr/

West Virginia
http://wvde.state.wv.us/igos/

Wisconsin
http://www.dpi.state.wi.us/standards/

Wyoming
http://www.k12.wy.us/publications/standards/

Lists for
United States History

1. American Indian Tribes of the Colonial Period

Apache
Arapaho
Caddo
Catawba
Cayuga
Cherokee
Cheyenne
Chickasaw
Chippewa
Choctaw
Commanche
Creek
Delaware
Herring Pond
Illinois
Iowa
Iroquois
Kansa
Kaskaskia

Kickapoo
Kiowa Apache
Mattaponi
Menomenee
Miami
Mohican
Munsee
Narragansett
Nottaway
Oneida
Onondaga
Osage
Oto
Ottawa
Pamunkey
Passamaquoddy
Pawnee
Penobscot
Peoria

Piankashaw
Ponco
Potawatomie
Quapuw
Sac
Saulk
Seminole
Seneca
Shawnee
Sopoonee
Tonkawa
Tuscarora
Wampanoag
Wichita
Winnebago
Wisconsin
Wyandot
Yuchi

2. Major Native American Leaders (1500–1900)

Leader	Lifespan	Tribe
American Horse	1801–1876	Oglala Sioux
Attakullakulla	1700? –1778	Cherokee
Big Bear	1825–1888	Plains Cree
Big Foot	1825–1890	Sioux
Black Elk	1863–1950	Oglala Sioux
Black Hawk	1767? –1838	Sac
Black Kettle	1803–1868	Cheyenne
Joseph Brant	1742–1807	Mohawk
Captain Jack	1840–1873	Modac
Chato	1860–1934	Chiricahua
Cochise	1812? –1874	Apache
Cornplanter	1735? –1836	Seneca
Crazy Horse	1842–1877	Sioux
Crow Dog	1835? –1910	Brule Sioux
Crowfoot	1821–1890	Blackfoot
Dull Knife	1810–1883	Cheyenne
Gall	1840–1894	Sioux
Geronimo	1829–1909	Apache
Joseph	1840–1904	Nez Perce
Kamiakin	1800? –1909	Apache
Little Crow	1810? –1863	Sioux
Little Turtle	1852–1912	Sioux
Lone Wolf	1820? –1879	Kiowa
Manuelito	1818–1894	Navajo
Massasoit	1580? –1661	Wampanoag
Mato-tope	1800–1837	Mandan
Oconostota	1710? –1785	Cherokee
Opothleyahoolo	1798–1862	Creek
Osceola	1804? –1838	Tallassees
Ouray	1820? –1880	Ute-Apache
Philip	1639? –1676	Wampanoag
Pontiac	1720–1769	Ottawa
Powhatan	1547? –1618	Powhatan
Quanah Parker	1847–1911	Comanche
Red Cloud	1822–1909	Oglala Sioux
Red Eagle	1780? –1824	Creek
Roman Nose	1830–1868	Cheyenne
Santanta	1820–1878	Kiowa
Sitting Bull	1831–1890	Sioux

2. *(continued)*

Leader	Lifespan	Tribe
Spotted Tail	1833? –1881	Brule Sioux
Standing Bear	1829? –1908	Ponca
Tall Bull	1815? –1869	Cheyenne
Tecumseh	1768–1813	Shawnee
Victorio	1825? –1880	Apache
Washakie	1804? –1904	Shoshoni

3. North American Explorers

Explorer	Area	Year(s)
Leif Ericson	North American coast	circa 1000
John Cabot	Newfoundland, Nova Scotia	1497–1498
Juan Ponce de Leon	Florida	1513
Jacques Cartier	St. Lawrence River	1534–1542
Hernando De Soto	Mississippi River	1539–1541
Francisco de Coronado	American Southwest	1540–1542
Samuel de Champlain	eastern coast of North America	1603–1616
Henry Hudson	Hudson Bay, Hudson River	1609–1611
Father Marquette, Louis Joliet	Northern Mississippi River	1672
Robert LaSalle	mouth of the Mississippi	1682

4. Original American Colonies

Colony	Date settled	Colony	Date settled
Virginia	1607	Delaware	1638
Plymouth	1620	North Carolina	1653
Maine & New Hampshire	1622	New York	1664
Massachusetts	1630	New Jersey	1664
Maryland	1634	South Carolina	1670
Connecticut	1636	Pennsylvania	1681
Rhode Island	1636	Georgia	1733

5. Founders of the American Colonies

Date	Colony	Founder
1585	Roanoke	Sir Walter Raleigh
1607	Virginia	John Smith
1620	Plymouth	William Bradford
1626	New York	Peter Minuit
1630	Massachusetts Bay	John Winthrop
1630	New Hampshire	John Mason
1634	Maryland	George Calvert
1636	Connecticut	Thomas Hooker
1636	Rhode Island	Roger Williams
1653	North Carolina	Group of proprietors
1660	New Jersey	Lord Berkeley
1682	Pennsylvania	William Penn
1733	Georgia	James Oglethorpe

6. Foods of Colonial Americans

apples
beans
berries
carrots
cheese
chickens
cider
cornbread
corn fritters
dumplings
fish
grapes
hoecake
hominy
honey

johnnycake
maize (Indian corn)
maple sugar mush
oysters
pears
peas
popcorn
pork
porridge
pumpkin
salt
shoofly pie
squash
stews
succotash

tea
turnips
wild game
wild plums
wine

7. Contributions of Ben Franklin

Clerk of the Philadelphia Assembly

Editor of *Pennsylvania Gazette*

Published *Poor Richard's Almanack*

First editor in America to publish a newspaper cartoon

First editor in America to use maps to illustrate news stories

Postmaster of *Philadelphia Deputy*

First proposed daylight savings time

Established first city mail delivery

Established first subscription library

Organized Philadelphia fire department

Raised money to build Pennsylvania Hospital in Philadelphia

Helped found academy which became University of Pennsylvania

Experiment that proved lightning was electricity

Discovered that diseases spread rapidly in poorly ventilated rooms

Invented lightning rod

Invented bifocal glasses

Invented the Franklin stove

Unofficial ambassador to England

Invented the rocking chair

Elected to Second Continental Congress

Organized national post office

Minister to France

Helped write the Treaty of Paris

President of the Executive Council of Pennsylvania

Delegate to the Constitutional Convention

President of America's first anti-slavery society

8. Witticisms and Quotations of Ben Franklin

"Early to bed and early to rise, makes a man healthy, wealthy, and wise."

"God helps them that help themselves."

"Little strokes fell great oaks."

"He that falls in love with himself will have no rivals."

"An ounce of prevention is worth a pound of cure."

"He's a fool that makes his doctor heir."

"Eat to live and not live to eat."

"Three may keep a secret if two of them are dead."

"Lost time is never found again."

"Remember that time is money."

"There never was a good war or a bad peace."

"Don't throw stones at neighbors if your own windows are glass."

"We must all hang together, or most assuredly, we shall hang separately."

"Fish and visitors stink after three days."

"You may delay, but time will not."

"Be slow in choosing a friend, slower in changing."

"There is no little enemy."

"He that lives upon hope will die fasting."

"They that can give up essential liberty to obtain a little temporary safety deserve neither liberty nor safety."

"I shall never ask, never refuse, not ever resign an office."

"Sin is not hurtful because it is forbidden, but it is forbidden because it is hurtful."

"Sell not virtue to purchase wealth, not liberty to purchase power."

"Laws gentle are seldom obeyed; too severe seldom executed."

"Our Constitution is in actual operation; everything appears to promise that it will last; but nothing in this world is certain but death and taxes."

9. Parts of a Revolutionary War General's Uniform

boots
coat skirt
crossbelt
epaulette
frock
coat
gloves

knee britches
infantry button
scabbard
sword
tricorn
waistcoat

10. Patriot Leaders of the American Revolution

John Adams
Samuel Adams
Silas Deane
Benjamin Franklin
John Hancock
Patrick Henry
John Jay
Thomas Jefferson

Richard Henry Lee
Robert Livingston
George Mason
Robert Morris
James Otis
Thomas Paine
Paul Revere
George Washington

11. American Military Leaders of the Revolutionary War

Ethan Allen
Benedict Arnold
George R. Clark
George Clinton
Horatio Gates
Nathanael Greene
Nathan Hale
John Paul Jones
Henry Knox
Charles Lee

Henry Lee
Francis Marion
Rufus Putnam
Arthur St. Clair
Philip Schuyler
Artemas Ward
Seth Warner
George Washington
Anthony Wayne

12. Revolutionary War Battles

1775	Apr. 19	Lexington & Concord	Massachusetts
	June 17	Bunker Hill	Massachusetts
	Nov. 13	Montreal	Quebec
	Dec. 31	Quebec	Quebec
1776	Aug. 27	Long Island	New York
	Dec. 26	Trenton	New Jersey
1777	Jan. 3	Princeton	New Jersey
	Aug. 16	Bennington	Vermont/New York
	Sept. 11	Brandywine	Pennsylvania
	Sept. 19	Freeman's Farm	New York
	Oct. 4	Germantown	Pennsylvania
	Oct. 7	Freeman's Farm	New York
1778	June 28	Monmouth	New Jersey
1779	Sept. 23	*Bonhomme Richard* vs. *Serapis*	North Sea
1780	Aug. 16	Camden	South Carolina
	Oct. 7	Kings Mountain	South Carolina
1781	Mar. 15	Guilford Courthouse	North Carolina
	Oct. 6-19	Yorktown	Virginia

13. The Ratification of the Constitution

Order	State	Date	Votes for	Votes against
1	Delaware	December 7, 1787	30	0
2	Pennsylvania	December 12, 1787	46	23
3	New Jersey	December 18, 1787	38	0
4	Georgia	January 2, 1788	26	0
5	Connecticut	January 9, 1788	128	40
6	Massachusetts	February 6, 1788	187	168
7	Maryland	April 28, 1788	63	11
8	South Carolina	May 23, 1788	149	73
9	New Hampshire	June 21, 1788	57	47
10	Virginia	June 25, 1788	89	79
11	New York	July 26, 1788	30	27
12	North Carolina	November 21, 1789	194	77
13	Rhode Island	May 29, 1790	34	32

14. Earliest Colleges

College	Founded	Location
Harvard College	1636	Cambridge, MA
William and Mary	1693	Williamsburg, VA
Yale	1700	New Haven, CT
College of New Jersey (Princeton)	1746	Princeton, NJ
Washington & Lee	1749	Lexington, VA
Kings (Columbia)	1754	New York
Philadelphia (Univ. of Pennsylvania)	1755	Philadelphia
Rhode Island College (Brown)	1764	Providence
Queen's College (Rutgers)	1766	New Brunswick, NJ
Dartmouth	1769	Hanover, NH

15. Largest U.S. Cities in 1790

Philadelphia	42,444
New York	33,131
Boston	18,038
Charlestown	16,359
Baltimore	13,503
Salem	7,921
Newport	6,716

Source: Bureau of the Census.

16. 1790 Slave Population

New Hampshire	157
Rhode Island	958
Connecticut	2,648
New York	21,193
New Jersey	11,423
Pennsylvania	3,707
Delaware	8,887
Maryland	103,036
Virginia	292,627
North Carolina	100,783
South Carolina	107,094
Georgia	29,264
Kentucky	12,430
Southwest Territory	3,417
United States	697,624

Source: Bureau of the Census.

17. Major Events of 1800

Library of Congress was established.

Land Act of 1800 spurred land speculation.

President John Adams fired Secretary of State Thomas Pickering.

Slave insurrection in Virginia thwarted; leader Gabriel hanged.

Congress moved to Washington, new national capital.

The Evangelical Church was founded.

Presidential campaign between John Adams, Federalist, and Thomas Jefferson, Democratic-Republican, resulted in electoral college tie.

Santee Canal in South Carolina was completed.

Second U.S. census was conducted.

The Federalist Party held the first secret congressional caucus.

First vaccination for smallpox was administered by Benjamin Waterhouse.

Sailors went on strike in New York City.

Eli Whitney made muskets with interchangeable parts.

The first book with color plates was printed.

New York City equipped the first fireboat used in the United States.

18. Achievements of Thomas Jefferson

Served in the Virginia House of Burgesses

Wrote the Declaration of Independence

Elected governor of Virginia

Served as minister to France

Secretary of State

Vice President of the United States

President of the United States

Orchestrated the Louisiana Purchase

Founded University of Virginia

Designed his mountaintop home, Monticello

19. Thomas Jefferson's Recipe for Ice Cream

Ice cream frequently appears in visitors' accounts of meals with Thomas Jefferson. One visitor commented: "Among other things, ice-creams were produced in the form of balls of the frozen material inclosed [sic] in covers of warm pastry, exhibiting a curious contrast, as if the ice had just been taken from the oven."

Jefferson was able to enjoy ice cream throughout the year because ice was "harvested" from the Rivanna River in winter and taken to the Monticello ice house, which held sixty-two wagon-loads. The ice house, located in Monticello's north dependency wing, was used throughout the year primarily to preserve meat and butter, but also to chill wine and to make ice cream. In 1815, Jefferson noted, the ice supply lasted until October 15.

While George Washington's papers contain a prior reference to an ice cream maker, the first American recipe for the dish is in Jefferson's hand:

ICE CREAM

2 bottles of good cream
6 yolks of eggs
½ lb. sugar

Mix the yolks & sugar.
Put the cream on a fire in a casserole, first putting in a stick of Vanilla.
When near boiling take it off & pour it gently into the mixture of eggs & sugar. Stir it well.
Put it on the fire again stirring it thoroughly with a spoon to prevent it's [sic]
    sticking to the casserole.
When near boiling take it off and strain it thro' a towel.
Put it in the Sabotiere (inner cannister).
Then set it in ice an hour before it is to be served. Put into the ice a handful of salt.
Put salt on the coverlid of the Sabotiere & cover the whole with ice.
Leave it still half a quarter of an hour.
Then turn the Sabotiere in the ice 10 minutes.
Open it to loosen with a spatula the ice from the inner sides of the Sabotiere.
Shut it & replace it in the ice.
Open it from time to time to detach the ice from the sides.
When well taken (prise) stir it well with the Spatula.
Put it in moulds, justling it well down on the knee.
Then put the mould into the same bucket of ice.
Leave it there to the moment of serving it.
To withdraw it, immerse the mould in warm water, turning it well till it will
    come out & turn it into a plate.

Source: Monticello Web site at http://www.monticello.org/. The original recipe is found in the Jefferson Papers collection at the Library of Congress.

20. Inventory of the Estate of Slaveholder Joseph Bell, Elbert County, Georgia, 1818

Joseph Bell (1750–1818) was a planter and Revolutionary War veteran who lived in northeast Georgia. He was an ancestor of the author. His estate inventory provides a unique insight into the lifestyle of early plantation owners.

18 head hogs @ $3.50 piece	45.50
24 head hogs @ @1.25 piece	30.00
2 cows & calves @ $16.00 each	32.00
5 cows & calves	40.00
1 Negro man Jack @	800.00
1 Negro named Britt @	850.00
1 Negro named Matt @	700.00
1 Woman Negro Fanny @	
½ child	600.00
1 Boy Negro David @	600.00
1 Negro Hal @	600.00
1 Negro Simion @	300.00
1 Horse Bay @	65.00
1 Sorrel Bay blaze @	30.00
1 Sorrel Horse Do @	75.00
1 Roan Horse @	100.00
1 young Sorrel Horse @	60.00
20 Barrels of Corn @ $4.00 per Bl	80.00
3 pair Gear @	7.50
1 lot ploughs $ plough hoes @	11.00
1 old wagon @	15.00
1 lot hoes @	4.50
5 axes @	7.00
1 lot of Iron @	.50
1 froe @	.50
1 wedge @	.50
1 cutting knife @	.50
1 pair Stilyards @	1.00
1 Handsaw @	1.00
1 auger, 1 drawing knife, 1 chisel	.50
1 claw hammer @	.50
700 lbs. Bacon @ 20 cts.	140.00
60 lbs. Lard @ 20 cts.	12.00
3 H Hg.d. @	2.00

1 Fat Tub and Butter Pot @	.75
6 Bushels Wheat @	4.50
1 Loom @	15.00
2 Spinning Wheels @	.50
1 Spinning Wheel & pr cotton	
cards @	3.75
1 cupboard & ware @	14.00
1 lot pewter @	7.00
1 lot tin ware @	.50
1 lot knives & forks @	2.50
½ Doz. table spoons	.37
1 lot water vessels, pail @	.50
1 pair waffle irons @	2.50
1 large pot @	15.00
1 oven & lid	2.50
1 oven & lid @	2.00
1 large pot injured	2.00
1 spider @	1.50
1 log chain @	4.00
1 pine table @	.50
1 walnut table @	4.00
1 spice mortar	1.50
1 small pine table	1.50
1 Shovel & tongs	.75
1 Doz. Setting Chairs	8.00
1 Candle & 9 blades	2.00
5 Bls. & winging blades	.75
20 lbs. clean cotton @ 25 cts.	5.00
1 feather bed stead & cord	
& furniture	30.00
1 feather bed @	35.00
2 feather beds @ $30 each	60.00
12 counter pins	36.00
1 walnut chest	4.00

(continued)

20. *(continued)*

1 walnut chest with drawers	7.00	4 cowhides @	5.00
1 trunk @	4.00	1 pair Dad Irons @	.69
1 small trunk	.25	1 pair spectacles	.75
2 large looking glasses	10.00	1 cross cut saw @	3.00
1 razor case & strop	.50	1 hive @	.25
1 lot books	6.00	1 meat tub & bread bag	.75
1 candle stick & comb case	.25	Saddle Bridle & leather	3.00
16 geese	8.00	4 wagon hubs	2.00
1 large jug & pitcher	1.75	one grind stone	2.92
1 Jar & 40 lbs. Sugar	7.00	one chamber pot	.50
67 lbs. soap @ 15 cts.	9.00	Cash on hand	20.00
3 gallons molasses	3.75		$5,627.60

We James Morrison, Francis M. Gilmer, & Nicholas Good do certify the above to be a just and true appaisment of all & singular the goods & chattels of Joseph Bell, Senr Deceased as shown us by Joseph Bell Exr. to said decease's estate. 1818 this 19th May.

21. Battles of the War of 1812

1812

Queenston Heights

1813

Lake Erie
Thames River

1814

Raisin River Massacre
Lake Champlain
Lundy's Lane

1815

New Orleans

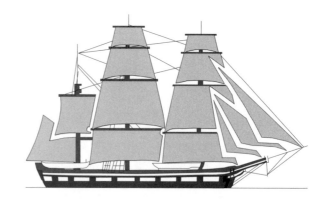

22. Early Firearms

blunderbuss
Colt Peacemaker
derringer
dueling pistols
flintlock
Kentucky long rifle
matchlock
percussion rifle
Remington revolver
wheellock pistol

23. Tools of the Pioneers

adze	froe	oxen yoke
anvil	grain cradle	pick
auger	grindstone	pitchfork
axe	hammer	plane
barrels	hand cultivator	potato digger
bellows	harrow	rake
branding iron	hatchet	sack needles
broad axe	hoe	saddles
buck saw	hog scraper	scythe
corn knife	hoof files	shovel
corn planter	knives	sickle
crosscut saw	mallet	spoke shavers
drawknife	mattock	wedges
flail	maul	whetstone
forge		

24. Household Implements of the Pioneers

apple peeler
bean pot
bed warmer
butter churn
butter mold
candle mold
candle snuffer
cider press
copper kettles
corn grater
crocks
fire screen
flatiron
foot stove
iron cooking pot
kettles

ladles
lard press
loom
milk strainer
quilting frame
razor strop
sausage gun
sieves
skin stretchers
spinning wheel
splint broom
tinderbox
washboard
whale oil lamp
wooden buckets
wooden trencher & spoons

25. Percentage of Slaveowners, 1850

	Percent of total white population
New England States	
Maine	0
New Hampshire	0
Vermont	0
Massachusetts	0
Rhode Island	0
Middle States	
New York	0
New Jersey	0.2
Pennsylvania	0
Delaware	6.5

25. (continued)

Southern States

Maryland & District of Columbia	21.9
Virginia	35.1
North Carolina	29.2
South Carolina	53.1
Georgia	42.0
Florida	42.5
Kentucky	28.7
Tennessee	25.5
Alabama	39.2
Mississippi	44.6
Louisiana	46.1
Texas	28.7
Arkansas	21.1
Missouri	18.5
United States	10.1

Source: U.S. Census Bureau. *A Century of Population Growth.* Washington, D.C.: Government Printing Office, 1909.

26. Firsts of the 1850's

The following pioneering efforts all occurred during the 1850's:

First female college graduate, Oberlin College
Private railroad car used by Jenny Lind
School for mentally retarded opened, Boston
National Women's Rights Convention
Condensed milk produced
YMCA organized in Boston
Stereoscope invented
College to prevent discrimination in race, color, or creed, Cooper Union
Safety elevator manufactured
Commercial oil well drilled at Titusville, Pennsylvania
Oil refinery constructed
Compulsory school attendance law enacted, Massachusetts
Railroad suspension bridge built
Veterinary school founded, Boston
Woman's college founded, Elmira, New York
Discovery of borax
Gold used in dental fillings
Trans-Atlantic cable laid

(continued)

26. *(continued)*

School band formed
Toilet paper manufactured
College for blacks founded, Chester County, Pennsylvania
School for the blind formed in St. Louis
Rotary washing machine manufactured
Electric stove invented
Railroads expand west of the Mississippi
Cable street car invented
Roll-top desk manufactured
Intercollegiate baseball game
Typesetting machine built
Pencil with attached eraser manufactured
Bloomers introduced
Braille taught to blind students
U.S. Navy bans flogging
United States population surpasses 25 million
New York Times begins publication
Walter Hunt patents disposable paper collar
U.S. Army buys pack camels for the desert southwest
Mardi Gras parades held in New Orleans
California, Oregon, and Minnesota are admitted as states
Cast iron frame building constructed
Longfellow writes "The Song of Hiawatha"
Matthew C. Perry negotiates first American-Japanese treaty
First spinal anesthesia used by J.L. Corning

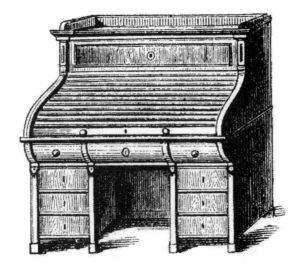

27. The Transcendentalists

Bronson Alcott
Orestes A. Brownson
Emily Dickinson
Ralph Waldo Emerson
Margaret Fuller
Nathaniel Hawthorne
Fredric Hedge

Joseph Palmer
Theodore Parker
Elizabeth Palmer Peabody
George Ripley
Henry David Thoreau

Emerson

28. Famous Abolitionists

James Gillespie Birney
Antoinette (Brown) Blackwell
John Brown
Olympia Brown
Elizabeth Buffum Chase
William Ellery Channing
Lydia Maria Child
George William Curtis
Frederick Douglass
William Lloyd Garrison
Robert Ingersoll

Elijah Lovejoy
Samuel Joseph May
Lucretia Mott
Wendell Phillips
Elizabeth Cady Stanton
Lucy Stone
Sojourner Truth
Harriet Tubman
John Woolman
Elizur Wright

29. Underground Railroad Song: "Follow the Drinking Gourd"

Runaway slaves seeking freedom knew they had to travel north. The words of this song provided an oral "road map" to guide them safely in their journey. The song and its translation are as follows:

When the sun comes back and the first quail calls,
Follow the Drinking Gourd.
For the old man is waiting for to carry you to freedom,
If you follow the Drinking Gourd.

"When the sun comes back" means winter and spring, when the altitude of the sun at noon is higher each day. Quail are migratory birds that winter in the South. The Drinking Gourd is the Big Dipper. The old man is Peg Leg Joe. The verse tells slaves to leave in the winter and walk towards the Drinking Gourd. Eventually they will meet a guide who will escort them for the remainder of the trip.

Most escapees had to cross the Ohio River, which is too wide and too swift to swim. The Underground Railroad struggled with the problem of how to get escapees across, and with experience came to believe the best crossing time was winter. Then the river was frozen, and escapees could walk across on the ice. Since it took most escapees a year to travel from the South to the Ohio, the Railroad urged slaves to start their trip in winter in order to be at the Ohio the next winter.

The river bank makes a very good road, / The dead trees show you the way,
Left foot, peg foot, traveling on / Follow the Drinking Gourd.

This verse taught slaves to follow the bank of the Tombighee River north, looking for dead trees that were marked with drawings of a left foot and a peg foot. The markings distinguished the Tombighee from other north-south rivers that flow into it.

The river ends between two hills, / Follow the Drinking Gourd.
There's another river on the other side, / Follow the Drinking Gourd.

These words told the slaves that when they reached the headwaters of the Tombighee, they were to continue north over the hills until they met another river. Then they were to travel north along the new river, which is the Tennessee River. A number of the southern escape routes converged on the Tennessee.

Where the great big river meets the little river, / Follow the Drinking Gourd.
For the old man is awaiting to carry you to freedom, / If you follow the Drinking
Gourd.

This verse told the slaves the Tennessee joined another river. They were to cross that river (i.e., the Ohio River) and on the north bank meet a guide from the Underground Railroad.

Source: NASA Quest Web site at http://quest.arc.nasa.gov.

30. Slaveholders and Slaves in the U.S.: 1860

	Slaveholders	*Slaves*
Alabama	33,730	435,080
Arkansas	11,481	111,115
Delaware	587	1,798
Florida	5,152	61,745
Georgia	41,084	462,198
Kansas	2	2
Kentucky	38,645	225,483
Louisiana	22,033	331,726
Maryland	13,783	87,189
Mississippi	30,943	436,631
Missouri	24,320	114,931
Nebraska	6	15
North Carolina	34,658	331,059
South Carolina	26,701	402,406
Tennessee	36,844	275,719
Texas	21,878	182,566
Virginia	52,128	490,865
TOTAL	393,975	3,950,528

Source: 1860 Slave Schedule, U.S. Census Bureau.

31. The Confederate States

Alabama	North Carolina
Arkansas	South Carolina
Florida	Tennessee
Georgia	Texas
Louisiana	Virginia
Mississippi	

32. Rights Under the Confederate Constitution

While modeled after the United States Constitution, the Constitution of the Confederate States also included the following rights:

- Slavery was legal, although foreign slave trade was banned.
- The terms of the President and the Vice President were six years, and the President was prohibited from serving consecutive terms.
- Congress was not permitted to levy protective tariffs, make appropriations for internal improvements, or to award bounties.
- Cabinet members received non-voting seats in Congress.
- A two-thirds vote of Congress was needed to admit new states.
- The President had the power of the line-item veto in appropriation bills.

33. Northern Advantages During the Civil War

- superior railway system
- ³/₄ of the national wealth
- control of the sea
- industrial capacity
- access to overseas supplies and markets
- twice as many people
- larger army

34. Southern Advantages During the Civil War

- large territory
- well-trained officers
- expert leadership of Robert E. Lee
- fighting for independence
- did not need a victory, but only to endure until the North lost determination
- defensive strategy

35. Civil War Military Leaders

North

Burnside, Ambrose
Butler, Benjamin F.
Doubleday, Abner
Farragut, David
Foote, Andrew
Fremont, John C.
Grant, Ulysses S.
Halleck, Henry W.
Hancock, Winfield S.
Hooker, Joseph
Logan, John
McClellan, George
Meade, George
Miles, Nelson
Porter, Fitz-John
Rosecrans, William S.
Sheridan, Philip
Sherman, William T.
Thomas, George
Wallace, Lew
Wilkes, Charles

South

Beauregard, Pierre G. T.
Bragg, Braxton
Breckinridge, John C.
Buckner, Simon Bolivar
Early, Jubal
Ewell, Richard
Forrest, Nathan
Hampton, Wade
Hood, John
Jackson, Stonewall
Johnston, Albert S.
Johnston, Joseph E.
Lee, Robert E.
Longstreet, James
Morgan, John
Mosby, John
Pickett, George
Polk, Leonidas
Semmes, Raphael
Smith, Edmund K.
Stuart, James E. B.
Watie, Stand
Wheeler, Joseph

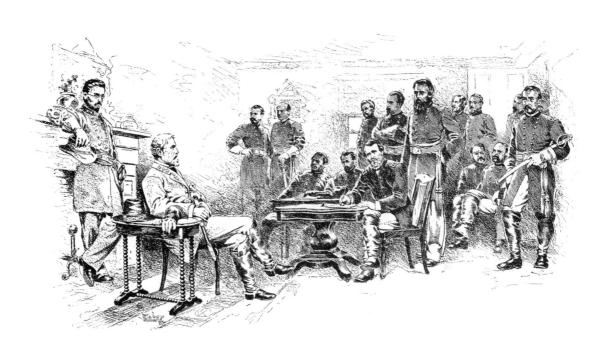

36. Weaponry of the Civil War

bayonet
Bowie knife
field cannon
garrison cannon
Gatling gun
grenades
land mines
minié rifle
musket

naval mines
naval swivel cannon
pistol
revolver
revolving rifle
rocket
sabre
smoothbore guns

37. Civil War Firsts

aerial photograph
aerial reconnaissance
ambulance corps
battle photography
cigarette tax
flame throwers
hospital ships
income tax
ironclad ships

machine gun
military draft
night flares
nursing corps
ready-made clothing factory
repeating rifles
smoke screen
U.S. Navy Admiral

38. Songs Popular During the Civil War

"Abide With Me"
"All Quiet on the Potomac"
"Annie Lisle"
"Aura Lee"
"Battle Cry of Freedom"
"Battle Hymn of the Republic" (North)
"Beautiful Dreamer"
"The Bonnie Blue Flag"
"Choosing a Man Is a Delicate Thing"
"Dixie" (South)
"Flag of Columbia"
"Goober Peas"
"Holy! Holy! Holy! Lord God Almighty"
"John Brown's Body" (North)
"Johnny Schmoker"
"Just Before the Battle, Mother"
"Killarney"
"Kingdom Coming"
"La Paloma"
"Marching Through Georgia" (North)
"Maryland, My Maryland" (South)
"Oh Where, Oh Where Has My Little Dog Gone?"
"Old Black Joe"
"Parade"
"Shenandoah"
"Streets of Laredo"
"Sweet and Low"
"Tenting on the Old Camp Ground" (North)
"Tramp, Tramp, Tramp" (North)
"The Vacant Chair"
"Weeping Sad and Lonely"
"When Johnny Comes Marching Home"

39. Black Soldiers in the Civil War

By the end of the Civil War, approximately 179,000 black men (10% of the Union Army) had served as soldiers in the U.S. Army and another 19,000 in the Navy.

Nearly 40,000 black soldiers died during the course of the war—30,000 from infection or disease.

Nearly 80 black men served as commissioned officers.

The July 1863 assault on Fort Wagner, SC, in which the 54th Regiment of Massachusetts Volunteers lost two-thirds of their officers and half of their troops, was memorialized in the film *Glory*.

Sixteen black soldiers were awarded the Medal of Honor for bravery.

Pay for black soldiers began at $10 per month from which $3 was automatically deducted for clothing. In contrast, white soldiers received $13 per month with no clothing allowance withheld. In June 1864 Congress granted equal pay to the "U.S. Colored Troops" and made the action retroactive. Black soldiers received the same rations and supplies.

Source: TEACHING WITH DOCUMENTS, National Archives and Records Administration. Online at: http://www.nara.gov/education/teaching/usct/home.html.

40. Major Civil War Battles and Campaigns

1861	Fort Sumter	Apr.
	Bull Run	July
1862	Ft. Donaldson	Feb.
	Monitor and *Merrimack*	Mar.
	Shiloh	April
	Fair Oaks	May–June
	Seven Days	June–July
	Second Bull Run	Aug.
	Antietam	Sept.
	Perrysville	Oct.
	Fredericksburg	Dec.
1863	Murfreesboro	Jan.
	Vicksburg	Apr.–July
	Chancellorsville	Apr.–May
	Gettysburg	July
	Chickamauga	Sept.
	Chattanooga	Nov.
1864	The Wilderness	May
	Spotsylvania Court House	May
	Cold Harbor	June
	Petersburg	June–July
	Mobile Bay blockade	Aug.
	Atlanta Campaign	May–Aug.
	Sherman's March	Nov.–Dec.
	Nashville	Dec.

41. Terms Popularized by the Civil War

antebellum

A.W.O.L.

copperhead

doughboy

draftee

ensign

federal income tax

greenbacks

Ironclads

kit

The Medal of Honor

pup tent

skedaddle

Springfields (rifles)

Tarheel

unconditional surrender

war correspondent

42. Flags Flown over Texas

Spain—1519–1685; 1690–1821

France—1685–1690

Mexico—1821–1836

Republic of Texas—1836–1845

Confederate States—1861–1865

United States—1845–1861; 1865–present

43. Important Roads, Trails, and Canals

Appalachian Trail

Boston Post Road

Bozeman Trail

Braddock's Road

California Trail

Champlain Canal

Chesapeake and Delaware Canal

Chisholm Trail

Cumberland Road

El Camino Real

Erie Canal

Lancaster Pike

Mohawk Trail

Mormon Trail

Natchez Trace

National Road

Old Spanish Road

Oregon Trail

Santa Fe Trail

Santee Canal

Wilderness Road

44. Major Events of 1876

Sioux Indians ordered to return to reservations

National League of Professional Baseball formed

Secretary of War, William Belknap, resigns in kickback scandal

Alexander Graham Bell patents the telephone

Centennial Exposition to celebrate 100th anniversary of the Declaration of Independence begins in Philadelphia

Mimeograph invented by Thomas Edison

Gen. George Custer defeated at Little Bighorn

First female admitted to the American Medical Association (S. H. Stevenson)

Colorado admitted as 38th state

First crematory built (in Washington, D.C.)

Controversial election of Rutherford B. Hayes over Samuel Tilden

Boss Tweed, convicted of fraud, caught in Spain and returned to New York City

First American cooking school opened (New York City)

Railroad bridge collapse in Ohio kills 84 *Pacific Express* passengers

Baseball catcher's mask invented

Johns Hopkins University opened in Baltimore

First Ph.D. awarded to a black (by Yale)

American Chemical Society founded

Greenback Party holds its first national convention

First tennis court built in the United States (Boston)

189 killed in New York City theatre fire

Dewey Decimal System for libraries initiated

First intercollegiate track meet

First cantilever bridge built (Kentucky River)

First tennis tournament in the U.S. held

45. American Folk Heroes and Heroines

John Alden
Johnny Appleseed
Clara Barton
Daniel Boone
Jim Bowie
John Brown
Kit Carson
"Buffalo Bill" Cody
Davy Crockett
Amelia Earhart
Wyatt Earp
Mike Fink
Benjamin Franklin
Barbara Fritchie
Nathan Hale

Ira Hayes
"Wild Bill" Hickock
Sam Houston
Casey Jones
John Paul Jones
Charles Lindbergh
Annie Oakley
Sam Patch
Zebulon Pike
Pocahontas
Betsy Ross
Capt. John Smith
Jim Thorpe
Sergeant York

46. Infamous Outlaws of the West

Apache Kid
Sam Bass
William Bonney (Billy the Kid)
Rube Burrow
Dalton brothers (Emmett, Gratton, William & Robert)
Billy Doolin
King Fisher
John Wesley Hardin
Doc Holliday
Frank James
Jesse James
Henry Plummer
John Reno
Cole Younger

47. Jim Crow Laws

Jim Crow Laws were enacted primarily, but not exclusively in southern and border states, between 1877 and the mid-1960s. They enforced segregation between the Blacks and Whites, affecting all aspects of life.

- **Nurses:** No person or corporation shall require any white female nurse to nurse in wards or rooms in hospitals, either public or private, in which Negro men are placed. (Alabama)

- **Buses:** All passenger stations in this state operated by any motor transportation company shall have separate waiting rooms or space and separate ticket windows for white and colored races. (Alabama)

- **Railroads:** The conductor of each passenger train is authorized and required to assign each passenger to the car or the division of the car, when it is divided by a partition, designated for the race to which such passenger belongs. (Alabama)

- **Pool and Billiard Rooms:** It shall be unlawful for a Negro and white person to play together or in company with each other at any game of pool or billiards. (Alabama)

- **Toilet Facilities, Male:** Every employer of white or Negro males shall provide for such white or Negro males reasonably accessible and separate toilet facilities. (Alabama)

- **Intermarriage:** The marriage of a person of Caucasian blood with a Negro, Mongolian, Malay, or Hindu shall be null and void. (Arizona)

- **Intermarriage:** All marriages between a white person and a Negro person or between a white person and a person of Negro descent to the fourth generation inclusive, are hereby forever prohibited. (Florida)

- **Juvenile Delinquents:** There shall be separate buildings, not nearer than one fourth mile from each other, one for white boys and one for Negro boys. White boys and Negro boys shall not, in any manner, be associated together or worked together. (Florida)

- **Mental Hospitals:** The Board of Control shall see that proper and distinct apartments are arranged for said patients, so that in no case shall Negroes and white persons be together. (Georgia)

- **Barbers:** No colored barber shall serve as a barber [to] white women or girls. (Georgia)

(continued)

47. *(continued)*

- **Burial:** The officer in charge shall not bury, or allow to be buried, any colored persons upon ground set apart or used for the burial of white persons. (Georgia)

- **Restaurants:** All persons licensed to conduct a restaurant, shall serve either white people exclusively or colored people exclusively and shall not sell to the two races within the same room or serve the two races anywhere under the same license. (Georgia)

- **Amateur Baseball:** It shall be unlawful for any amateur white baseball team to play baseball on any vacant lot or baseball diamond within two blocks of a playground devoted to the Negro race, and it shall be unlawful for any amateur colored baseball team to play baseball in any vacant lot or baseball diamond within two blocks of any playground devoted to the white race. (Georgia)

- **Parks:** It shall be unlawful for colored people to frequent any park owned or maintained by the city for the benefit, use and enjoyment of white persons, and unlawful for any white person to frequent any park owned or maintained by the city for the use and benefit of colored persons. (Georgia)

- **Wine and Beer:** Any person licensed to conduct the business of selling beer or wine shall serve either white people exclusively or colored people exclusively and shall not serve to the two races within the same room at any time. (Georgia)

- **Circus Tickets:** All circuses, shows and tent exhibitions, to which the attendance of more than one race is invited or expected to attend shall provide for the convenience of its patrons not less than two ticket offices with individual sellers, and not less than two entrances to the said performance, with individual ticket takers and receivers, and in the case of outside or tent performances, the said ticket offices shall not be less than twenty-five feet (25) apart. (Louisiana)

- **The Blind:** The board of trustees shall maintain a separate building on separate ground for the admission, care, instruction, and support of all blind persons of the colored or black race. (Louisiana)

- **Education:** Separate schools shall be maintained for the children of the white and colored races. (Mississippi)

- **Telephones:** Telephone companies must maintain separate booths for white and colored patrons when there is a demand for such separate booths. (Oklahoma)

47. *(continued)*

- **Recreation:** No black citizen shall be found playing any recreational activity with a white person such as, pool, dominoes, cards, checkers, dice, billiards, softball, basketball, football, golf, track, or associate or swim together at a swimming pool. [state not available]

- **Textbooks:** Books shall not be interchangeable between the white and colored schools, but shall be continued to be used by the race first using them. (North Carolina)

- **Transportation:** The Utilities Commission is empowered and directed to require the establishment of separate waiting rooms at all stations for the white and colored races. (North Carolina)

- **Bibles:** Negroes could not "swear to tell the truth" on the same Bible used by White witnesses. (Atlanta)

Source: Martin Luther King, Jr., National Historic Site. Online at http//www.nps.gov/malu/documents/jim crowlaws.htm.

48. Jim Crow Guide

Stetson Kennedy, the author of *Jim Crow Guide*, offered these simple rules that Blacks were supposed to observe in conversing with Whites:

1. Never assert or even intimate that a White person is lying.
2. Never impute dishonorable intentions to a White person.
3. Never suggest that a White person is from an inferior class.
4. Never lay claim to, or overly demonstrate, superior knowledge or intelligence.
5. Never curse a White person.
6. Never laugh derisively at a White person.
7. Never comment upon the appearance of a White female.

Source: Kennedy, Stetson. *Jim Crow Guide: The Way It Was.* Boca Raton: Florida Atlantic University Press, 1959/1990, pp. 216–117.

49. Slang of the 1890's

Slang	Meaning	Slang	Meaning
ankle	walk	pipe down	be quiet!
bindle	blanket roll	plug	a silver dollar
cheek	boldness	plunk	a dollar
chew the fat	to talk	plute	rich person
chin	to talk	rat	an informer, spy
close shave	narrow escape	sand	bravery, courage
crush	infatuation	shake a leg	hurry
daily bread	household wage earner	shantytown	poor neighborhood
doggy	well groomed	shove off	leave
dough	money	simoleon	a dollar
fink	scab, strikebreaker	slam	a cutting comment
foot-slogger	foot soldier	small-bore	unimportant
geezer	man, guy	smooth	very good
glad rags	best clothes	snap, a	easy
good-looker	attractive person	sneakers	athletic shoes
grandstand	to show off	spinach	a beard
gunboats	shoes	steady	boy/girl friend
gun moll	female criminal	step out	go to a party
hardtack	money	stone broke	without any money
hoity-toity	snobbish, uppity	stuck on	in love with
hornswoggle	to cheat	swivet	heated rage
hot	fast, speedy	tacky	in poor taste
jim-dandy	good, satisfactory	tad	a young boy
jitney	a nickel	take the cake	win
loco	crazy	tightwad	miserly person
long green	money	well-heeled	wealthy
mitt	hand	willies, the	very anxious
piffle	nonsense!		

50. Fads and Fancies of the 1890's

And Her Name Was Maud
  (comic strip)
bicycling
cakewalk (dance)
chewing gum
comic pictures
commemorative spoons
croquet
floral parades for automobiles
Foxy Grandpa comic strips
hootchy kootchy tie
huge hats for women
Gibson girl

lavendar gloves for men
magic lantern shows
minstrels
ouija board
petticoats
Pigs-in-Clover puzzles
roller skates
skirt dance
stereoptician
Sunday funnies
trade cards
vaudeville

51. Famous Performers of the Nineteenth Century

Maurice Barrymore
John Wilkes Booth
Junius Booth
Edwin Booth
William "Buffalo Bill" Cody
Lotta Crabtree
Charlotte Cushman
Louisa Lane Drew
Robert G. Ingersoll
Scott Joplin
Jumbo the Elephant
Jenny Lind
Annie Oakley

John Philip Sousa
Sitting Bull
Gen. Tom Thumb

Lind

52. Nineteenth-Century American Authors

Henry Adams
Jane Addams
Louisa May Alcott
Horatio Alger
Gertrude Atherton
George Bancroft
Ambrose Bierce
Ann Bradstreet
William Cullen Bryant
Kate Chopin
James Fenimore Cooper
Stephen Crane
Margaret Deland
Emily Dickinson
Ralph Waldo Emerson
Mary Wilkins Freeman
Margaret Fuller
Horace Greeley
Harlan F. Halsey
Joel Chandler Harris
Bret Harte
Nathaniel Hawthorne
Oliver Wendell Holmes
William Dean Howells
Washington Irving
Henry James
Sidney Lanier

James Russell Lowell
Herman Melville
Clement C. Moore
Petroleum V. Nasby
Edgar Allan Poe

Poe

William Sidney Porter (O. Henry)
James Whitcomb Riley
George Ripley
Harriet Beecher Stowe
Booth Tarkington
Henry David Thoreau
Mark Twain
Lewis Wallace
Artemus Ward
Noah Webster
Walt Whitman
John Greenleaf Whittier

53. Occupations of the Nineteenth Century

Accomptant	Accountant
Amanuensis	Secretary, stenographer
Aurifaber	Goldsmith
Boniface	Innkeeper
Bookmonger	Seller of books
Brazier	One who works with brass
Brightsmith	Metal worker
Chaisemaker	Carriage maker
Chiffonnier	Wig maker
Coachmaker	Maker of coaches
Cobbler	Shoemaker
Collier	Coal miner
Cooper	One who makes or repairs barrels or casks
Crocker	Potter
Docker	A dock worker who loads and unloads cargo, a stevedore
Dowser	One who finds water using a rod or witching stick
Draper	A dealer in dry goods
Drayman	One who drives a low sturdy cart
Drover	One who drives cattle, sheep to market
Farrier	A blacksmith, one who shoes horses
Gaoler	A jailer, keeper of the "gaol"
Hatcheler	One who carded (combed out) flax
Hillier	Roof tiler
Husbandman	A farmer who cultivates the land
Lamp Lighter	Street lamp lighter
Lavender	Washer woman
Mason	Bricklayer
Muleskinner	Teamster
Peruker	A wig maker
Porter	Door keeper
Quarrier	Quarry worker
Saddler	One who sells, makes, or repairs saddles
Shipwright	Builder of wooden ships
Tanner	One who tans (cures) animal hides into leather
Teamster	One who drives a team for hauling
Thatcher	Roofer
Tide waiter	Customs inspector
Tinker	An itinerant tin pot and pan seller and repairman
Turnkey	Prison warden or jail keeper
Wainwright	Wagon maker
Wheelwright	One who made or repaired wheels or carriages
Vineroon	Wine grower

54. Immigration to the U.S., 1820–1880

German Empire	3,000,000
Ireland	2,800,000
Britain	2,000,000
Austro-Hungarian Empire	1,000,000
Canada	750,000
China	230,000
Africa	50,000

Source: American Family Immigration Center at Ellis Island. Online at http://www.ellisislandrecords.org

55. Immigration to the U.S., 1880–1930

Between 1880 and 1930 over 27 million people entered the United States—about 20 million through Ellis Island.*

Italy	4,600,000
Austro-Hungarian Empire	4,000,000
Russian Empire	3,300,000
German Empire	2,800,000
Britain	2,300,000
Canada	2,300,000
Ireland	1,700,000
Sweden	1,100,000

Source: American Family Immigration Center at Ellis Island. Online at http://www.ellisislandrecords.org.

*See also List 74, Immigration to the U.S., 1931–2000.

56. Inventions of Thomas Edison

vote recorder
phonograph
electric incandescent light
motion-picture machine
peep show
talking picture machine
storage battery
cement mixer
dictaphone
duplicating machine
electric lighting plant
electric company

57. Popular Songs of 1900

"A Bird in A Gilded Cage"
"Because"
"The Bridge of Sighs"
"Creole Belle"
"De Cake Walk Queen"
"Down By the Riverside"
"Give Me the Good Old Fashioned Girl"
"I Can't Tell You Why I Love You, But I Do"
"I'd Still Believe You True"
"It's Just Because I Love You So"
"Jimmy, the Pride of Newspaper Row"
"Just One Kiss"
"Lift Every Voice and Sing"
"Lucinda, I Am Waiting for You"
"Ma Tiger Lily"
"Mandy Lee"
"Midnight Fire Alarm"
"My Automobile Girl"
"Nobody Sees Us but the Man in the Moon"
"Tell Me, Pretty Maiden"
"The Voodoo Man"
"When Chloe Sings a Song"
"When I Think of You"
"When the Harvest Days Are Over, Jennie Dear"
"When You Were Sweet Sixteen"
"You Can't Keep a Good Man Down"

58. Prices in 1900

baseball bat 35¢
bathtub $7.25
bicycle $10.50
box camera $3.50
brass bed $3.00
corn 43¢ a bushel
dozen eggs 12¢
Edison phonograph $19.00
eggs 10¢
electric light bulb 30¢
guitar $3.00
ice box $7.00
kerosene lantern 65¢
ladies' hose 15¢ pr.
men's neckties 18¢
men's tailor-made suit $9.00

mixed open buggy $26.00
nuts 15¢ lb.
roll-top desk $18.50
safety pins 2¢ doz.
set of false teeth $5.00
sewing machine $12.60
shave and a haircut 25¢ (2 bits)
shirt 23¢
silk 50¢ yd.
Smith & Wesson revolver $10.75
stereoscope 25¢
tin can 10¢
trombone $15.00
turkey dinner 20¢
white dress shirt 60¢
work shirts 18¢

59. Turn-of-the-Century Patent Medicines

Ayer's Cherry Pectoral
Carbonium Rheumatism Cure
Castoria
Chichester's Pennyroyal Pill
Dr. Bell's Pine-Tar-Honey
Dr. Hammond's Nerve and Brain
    Pills
Dr. M. Bain's Blood Pills
Dr. Rose's Obesity Powder
Electric Liniment
German Liquor Cure
Kid-ne-oids
Lydia E. Pinkham's Vegetable
    Compound
Mexican Headache Neuralgia and
    Cure
Mother's Friend
Nectarine
Nervita Pills

Peruna
Sapolio
St. Jacob's Oil
Tonsiline Throat Medicene
Wonderful Little Liver Pills

60. The Muckrakers

Writer	Areas of Influence
Ray Stannard Baker	labor abuses, unions
William Hard	child labor
Thomas Lawson	stock market manipulation
Charles Edward Russell	tenement living conditions
Upton Sinclair	food processing safety, monopolies
Lincoln Steffens	corrupt city government
Ida Tarbell	abuses of big business
George Kibbe Turner	corruption and vice

61. Women's Rights Pioneers

Susan B. Anthony
Alice Blackwell
Harriot Blatch
Amelia Bloomer
Lucy Burns
Carrie Chapman Catt
Paula Wright Davis
Crystal Eastman
Isabella Beecher Hooker
Esther Morris
Lucretia Mott
Emmeline Pankhurst
Alice Paul
Anne Smith Peck
Lucy Stone
Elizabeth Cady Stanton
Victoria Woodhull

62. Automobile Brands of 1906

Auburn
Autocar
Berkshire
Buick
Cadillac
Cannon
Columbia
Compound
Corbin
Crawford
Dolson
Duquesne
Duryea
Elmore
Ford
Franklin
Gale
Glide
Jackson
Knox
Lambert
Logan
Marion
Maxwell
Michigan
Mitchell
Moline
Monarch
Northern

Oldsmobile
Orient
Oxford
Pierce
Premier
Queen
Rambler
Reo
St. Louis
Stanhope
Stoddard-Dayton
Walker
Wayne
Wolverine
York
Zent

63. Terms Contributed by World War I

A.E.F.	dogfight	KP
Allies	dog tag	overseas
basket case	doughboys	red tape
Big Bertha (gun)	draft dodger	rookie
blimp	dud	sabotage
buck private	entente	shell shock
buddy	flame thrower	slacker
chemical warfare	goldbrick	sound off
chief of staff	hand grenade	strafe
chow	hitch	tank
civvies	khaki	trench warfare
C.O.	kingpin	U-boat
convoy		

64. World War I Campaigns Involving the U.S.

1917	Cambrai	Nov.-Dec.
1918	Somme	Mar.-July
	Lys	April
	Aisine	May-June
	Noyon-Montdidier	June
	Champagne-Maine	July
	Aisne-Marne	July
	Somme	Aug.
	Oise-Aisne	Aug.-Nov.
	Ypres-Lys	Aug.-Nov.
	Saint-Mihiel	Sept.
	Meuse-Argonne	Sept.-Nov.
	Vitono-Vento	Oct.-Nov.

65. Woodrow Wilson's Fourteen Points

1. Open covenants of peace, openly arrived at.

2. Freedom of navigation on the seas.

3. Removal of economic barriers and equality of trade conditions.

4. Guaranteed reduction in armaments.

5. Impartial adjustment of colonial claims.

6. Evacuation of occupied Russian territories and fair treatment of Russia.

7. Evacuation and restoration of Belgium.

8. Evacuation and restoration of all French territory.

9. Readjustment of Italy's border.

10. Guarantee autonomous development for Austria-Hungary.

11. Restoration of territories of Rumania, Serbia, and Montenegro.

12. Assure sovereignty to Turkish portions of Ottoman Empire and assure autonomy to other nationalities under Turkish rule. Free passage through Straits of Dardanelles.

13. Establish an independent Poland.

14. Formation of an association of nations to guarantee political independence and territorial integrity of all nations.

66. Model T Ford Production and Cost

Year	Cars Produced	Price*
1909	10,660	$850
1910	19,050	$950
1911	34,858	$780
1912	68,773	$690
1913	170, 211	$600
1914	202,667	$550
1915	308,162	$490
1916	501,462	$440
1917	735,020	$360
1918	664,076	$450
1919	498,342	$525
1920	941,042	$575
1921	463,451	$415
1922	971,610	$348
1923	1,301,067	$295
1924	2,011,125	$295
1925	1,922,048	$290
1926	1,554,465	$310
1927	399,725	$380

*Price of the popular touring model

Source: Model T Ford Club of America at http://www.mtfca.com.

67. Membership Growth of the Woman's Christian Temperance Union

Year	Number of Local Auxiliary Unions	Aggregate Membership
1879	1,118	26,843
1883	2,580	73,176
1890	7,126	149,527
1900	7,067	168,324
1910	12,000	248,343
1921	12,000	345,949

Source: Norton Mezvinsky, "The White Ribbon Reform, 1874–1920" (Ph.D. dissertation, University of Wisconsin, 1959): 68.

68. Slang of the 1920's

Slang	Meaning
all my whiskers	nonsense!
all wet	wrong, incorrect
and how!	definitely!
audies	sound movies
banana oil	nonsense
barnstorm	tour the country doing airplane shows
bathtub gin	homemade gin
bee's knees	great!
berries, the	the best
between a rock and a hard place	in a difficult situation
big cheese	an important person
bim	girl friend
blind dragon	chaperone
blind pig	a speakeasy
blotto	drunk
bootleg	make or sell illegal liquor
breeze in	drop in unexpectedly
bug wash	hair oil
bull session	group discussion
bunk	nonsense!
caper	a robbery
carhop	waitress at a drive-in restaurant
cat's, the	outstanding
cat's meow	outstanding
cat's pajamas	good, super
cheaters	eyeglasses
chopper	submachine gun
crush	being infatuated with
darb	excellent
dig dirt	to gossip
divine	nice, enjoyable
do in	to exhaust
fat cat	wealthy person

Slang	Meaning
flapper	uninhibited woman, a style of dressing
flick	movie
fridge	refrigerator
gaga	crazy, silly
get hot!	Dance! Go for it!
giggle-water	whiskey, liquor
goon	a thug, ruffian
governor	father, one's superior
grand	good
ham-and-egger	ordinary person
high hat	to snub someone
hoof	to dance
horsefeathers	nonsense!
hotsie-totsie	very good
hyper	excited, thrilled
jalopy	an old car
Jane	a plain girl
jinny	a speakeasy
juice-joint	a speakeasy
keen	attractive, good
kisser	the mouth
lickety-split	quickly
lousy	bad, inferior
lug	a dull man
main drag	main street
malarkey	lies, nonsense
nitwit	idiot
nuts	nonsense!
park	made out in a car
pash	passion
pip-squeak	a useless person
rah-rah	overly enthusiastic
raspberries	nonsense!
ricky tick	ragtime music of 20's
ritzy	elegant
rock	a dollar

68. *(continued)*

Slang	*Meaning*	*Slang*	*Meaning*
sad sack	an odd person	**swell**	fine
sheba	girl friend	**talkie**	movie with sound
sheik	handsome man	**tin Lizzie**	Model T Ford
sloppy	messy	**white cow**	vanilla milkshake
smooch	kiss/hug	**wise up**	become aware, learn
speakie	a movie with sound	**wish book**	catalog
struggle buggy	car	**wowser**	prude, self-righteous
stuffy	prudish		

69. Fads and Fancies of the 1920's

art deco
auto camping
baggy knickers
bathtub gin
bobbed hair for women
Burma Shave road signs
center-parted,
    patent-leather hair
the Charleston
cloche hats
crossword puzzles
dance marathons
flagpole sitting
flappers
Florida land boom
hip flasks
jazz
King Tut hats
Mah Jong
mascara
neon lights

Oxford bag (pants)
pajamas as daily wear
peekaboo hats
raccoon coats
radio
silent movies
speakeasies
Stutz Bearcat
tams
turned-down hose

70. The Alphabet of the New Deal

CCC	Civilian Conservation Corps
FERA	Federal Emergency Relief Act
FHA	Federal Housing Administration
HOLO	Home Owners' Loan Corporation
NRA	National Recovery Administration
NYA	National Youth Administration
PWA	Public Works Administration
REA	Rural Electrification Administration
SEC	Securities and Exchange Commission
TVA	Tennessee Valley Authority
USHA	United States Housing Authority
WPA	Works Progress Administration

71. Slang of the 1930's

Slang	Meaning
alligator	a fan of jive/swing music
back burner	to postpone
body and soul	girl/boy friend
boog	to dance
boondoogle	project wasting public funds
buttinski	nosey person
cannon fodder	regular soldier
crabber	nagging critic
creep	obnoxious person
cut a rug	dance
dinger	telephone
dizzy	odd, strange
doodle-bug	jalopy, buggy
doozy	wonderful person or thing
Dust Bowl	Great Plains states
G-man	FBI agent
grease	a bribe
have kittens	to get excited
high hat	arrogant, superior
Hoover blanket	newspaper used as blanket by homeless
jam session	musicians improvising as a group

Slang	Meaning
jerk	a fool, disliked person
lovebirds	sweethearts
nervous Nellie	anxious person
one and only	sweetheart
phooey	nonsense!
sad sack	unpopular student
screwball	an odd person
scuttlebutt	rumor
session	a party
Shangri La	paradise
smart Alec	wise guy
smoke eater	a firefighter
snooty	snobbish
spinach	nonsense!
threads	clothing
tops	the best
twerp	silly person
unlax	relax
up the wall	crazy
wacko!	great!
whodunit	detective story
with bells on	definitely
woof	to chat
zombie	weird person

72. Fads and Fancies of the 1930's

Betty Boop
big apple (dance)
bingo
boogie (dance)
broomstick dresses
Buck Rogers Disintegrator Ray guns
candid camera photography
contract bridge
Eugenie hat
fox trot (dance)
handies (game)
jigsaw puzzles
jitterbug (dance)
Lindy hop (dance)
Lambeth walk (dance)

memory games
Mickey Mouse
miniature golf
Monopoly®
pickle (dance)
roller skating
rumba (dance)
saddle shoes
shag (dance)
Shorty George (dance)
skiing
softball
swing
tent dress
two-piece swim suits (women)

73. American Automobiles of the 1930's

Auburn
American Austin
American Bantum
Buick
Cadillac
Chevrolet
Chrysler
Cord
DeSoto
Doble
Dodge
Duesenberg
Erksine
Essex
Ford
Franklin
Graham
Hudson
Hupmobile
LaFayette

LaSalle
Lincoln
Marmoin
Marquette
Nash
Oakland
Oldsmobile
Packard
Pierce-Arrow
Plymouth
Pontiac
Reo
Rockne
Roosevelt
Studebaker
Stutz
Terraplane
Whippet Viking
Willys

74. Immigration to the U.S., 1931–2000

Between 1931 and 2000 over 31 million people entered the United States. The leading countries of origin for legal immigrants 1931–2000 were:

Mexico	5,977,739
Philippines	1,530,598
Germany	1,301,856
China	1,112,975
United Kingdom	1,081,552
India	947,206
Korea	861,246
Vietnam	744,422
Soviet Union	717,687

The leading countries of origin for legal immigrants in 2000:

Mexico	173,919
People's Republic of China	45,652
Philippines	42,474
India	42,046
Vietnam	26,747

These five countries represented 39 percent of all immigrants in 2000.

Source: Immigration and Naturalization Service at http://www.ins.usdoj.gov.

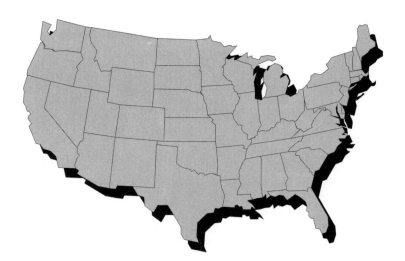

75. Slang of the 1940's

Slang	Meaning
ameche	to telephone
b.y.t.	bright young things
bag	to shoot down a plane
barouche	car, jalopy
brainchild	someone's creative idea
bunny	to chat
city slicker	dandy from the city
corny	unimportant, passe
cozy	comfortable
creep	despicable person
eager beaver	enthusiastic helper
fuddy-duddy	old-fashioned person
gobbledygook	double talk, long speech
gone with the wind	run off (with the money)
grandstand	to show off
grotty	new but useless
hi-de-ho	hello
in cahoots with	conspiring with
lettuce	money
old hat	out-dated
pass the buck	pass responsibility for
pennies from heaven	easy money

76. Fads and Fancies of the 1940's

bebop
bubble gum blowing contests
fast gun clubs
flying saucers
jitterbug
"new look" women's fashion
pinafore dresses
Rosie the Riveter
Slinky®
tutti-frutti
victory gardens
zoot suit

77. Popular Radio Shows of the 1940's

"The Abbott and Costello Show"
"The Adventures of Bulldog
    Drummond"
"The Adventures of Father Brown"
"The Adventures of Topper"
"Amos and Andy Show"
"Arthur Godfrey's Talent Scouts"
"Beulah"
"The Bickersons"
"Bing Crosby Show"
"Blackstone the Magic Detective"
"Calamity Jane"
"Captain Midnight"
"The Carters of Elm Street"
"Challenge of the Yukon"
"The Cisco Kid"
"Colonel Stoopnagle and Budd"
"Death Valley Days"
"The Dinah Shore Show"
"Dr. IQ"
"Duffy's Tavern"
"Edgar Bergen and Charlie McCarthy
    Show"
"Fibber McGee and Molly"
"Gene Autrey's Melody Ranch"
"The George Burns and Gracie Allen
    Show"
"The Grand Ole Opry"
"The Great Gildersleeve"
"The Green Hornet"
"Inner Sanctum Mysteries"
"It Pays to Be Ignorant"
"The Jack Benny Show"
"Leave It to the Girls"

"The Life of Riley"
"The Lone Ranger"
"Ma Perkins"
"Major Hoople"
"Maudie's Diary"
"The Mercury Wonder Show"
"Mrs. Miniver"
"Nick Carter, Master Detective"
"Our Miss Brooks"
"Perry Mason"
"Queen for a Day"
"Red Ryder"
"The Red Skelton Show"
"The Roy Rogers Show"
"The Saturday Morning Vaudeville
    Theatre"
"Scattergood Baines"
"Sherlock Holmes"
"Sky King"
"Stage Door Canteen"
"Stella Dallas"
"The Thin Man"
"20 Questions"
"Uncle Walter's Dog House"
"What's the Name of That Tune?"
"The Whistler"
"You Bet Your Life"
"Young Dr. Malone"
"Your Hit Parade"

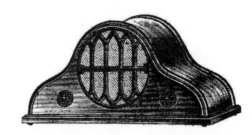

78. Terms Contributed by World War II

amphibious landing	gizmo	PX
atomic bomb	gobbledygook	Quonset hut
Axis	gremlin	radar
bazooka	gung ho	R and R
black market	home front	rationing
blitz	Jeep	Rosie the Riveter
blitzkrieg	Johnny-come-lately	saturation bombing
boondocks	kamikaze	scorched earth policy
commando	Lend Lease	snorkel
concentration camp	Liberty Ship	storm troopers
cover for	Nazi	USO
D-Day	ninety-day wonder	V.D.
Dear John letter	nylon	WAACS
draft dodger	Panzers	WAFS
ersatz	PFC	WAVES
fascist	pinup	walkie-talkie
five-star general	POW	war bonds
flak	propaganda	war brides
GI Joe	PT boat	

79. Five-Star Generals of World War II

Omar N. Bradley
Dwight D. Eisenhower
Douglas MacArthur
George C. Marshall
Henry "Hap" Arnold

80. Items Rationed During World War II

butter	gasoline
canned foods	meats
cheese	oils
coffee	shoes
fats	sugar

See also Lists 166–172 in the World History section for more on World War II.

81. Slang of the 1950's

Slang	Meaning	Slang	Meaning
a gas	great; super	funny money	counterfeit bills
a groove	superb	get it together	straighten out one's life
beat	tired		
beatnik	person indifferent to society	get-up-and-go	energy, pep
		glitch	obstacle
birdie biker	female motorcyclist	goof	to make a mistake
blast	a good time	greaser	person with long oily hair
blast off	scram		
boo	excellent	hardeeharhar	false laughter at a bad joke
bread hooks	hands		
buddy buddy	very friendly	hairy	difficult
buddy seat	motorcycle sidecar	hep or hip	enlightened
bug	bother	hoo-boy	Oh, boy!
bug out	to leave	hood	small-time criminal
burp gun	sub-machine gun	hot dog	a show-off
chiller-diller	a very scary movie	howdy doody	hello
chintzy	cheap, low quality	idiot box	televison
cool	superb; acceptable	iggle	to persuade
cowabunga	hello	in the groove	enjoying jazz
cut out	to leave	jumbo size	large, huge
daddy-o	man, dad	kicks	thrills; fun
dead head	dunce, a bore	klutz	clumsy person, nerd
deb's delight	eligible bachelor		
deepie	3-D movie	lose your cool	get angry
deke	to renege, back out	make the scene	arrive; attend
dicey	risky	nerf-bar	car's bumper
dig	understand, appreciate	nowhere	not hep; square
		off the wall	strange
dingaling	odd person, nerd	out of sight	great, unbelievable
disc jockey	radio show host	passion pit	drive-in theatre
disco	a discotheque	pad	home
do your own thing	express yourself	payola	bribe money
downer	an unpleasant experience	rip off	take advantage of
		rumble	fight; brawl
drag	anyone or anything dull or boring	scaggy	disgusting
		sends me	excites me
dream-boat	an attractive male	shag	to leave
dullsville	boring	shim	one who dislikes rock and roll music
far out	outstanding		
flip	get very excited	shook up	excited, alarmed
flaked out	exhausted; tired	shrink	psychiatrist

81. *(continued)*

Slang	*Meaning*	*Slang*	*Meaning*
sick	deranged, mentally ill	**tired blood**	without energy
skins	tires	**turf**	territory
slay	to impress	**twist**	a kind of dance
sock hop	a dance	**vibes**	aura a person projects
space cadet	a strange person	**way out**	excellent
spaced out	high on drugs	**whirly-bird**	helicopter
split	to leave	**wig out**	go crazy
square	old-fashioned person	**with it**	in style, hip
teenager	person 13–19 years old	**yoyo**	nerd
		yuck!	expression of disgust
the end	tops; the very best	**zorch**	super

82. Fads and Fancies of the 1950's

ankle bracelets
apaches (male's haircuts)
automobile stuffing
beatniks
Bermuda shorts
black leather jackets
black stockings
blue suede shoes
bomb shelters
bop (dance)
bowling
bunny hop (dance)
bucket purses
calypso (dance)
chemise dresses
circle, the (dance)
come-as-you-are parties
coonskin caps
crew cut (haircut)
crinolines
cufflinks, huge
doe eyes
droodles
ducktails (haircuts)
false eyelashes
felt skirts with appliqued
    poodles

fender skirts for cars
flat tops (haircuts)
garrison belts
hand jive (dance)
horse operas (westerns)
Hollywood exhaust pipes
Howdy Doody
hula-hoops
Indian moccasins
jukebox
jumbo-sized
jungle jackets
knock-knock jokes
long sideburns
mohawks (males' haircuts)
moon hub caps
motorcycle jackets
Mouseketeers
paint-by-number kits
panty raids
paste-on rhinestones
pegged pants
phone booth stuffing
picture windows
pizza
pompadour haircut
pony tails

(continued)

82. *(continued)*

poodle cut (haircut)
pop beads
"post office"
propeller-topped beanies
sack dresses
saddle shoes
Scrabble®
shirttails out
short shorts
Silly Putty®
sideburns
Slinky®
slop, the (dance)
soap operas
sock hops
"spin the bottle"
suburbia
sword pins
tail fins on cars

3-D movies
waxed hair
white bucks (shoes)
white lipstick
white socks
white sportcoats

83. Popular Singers of the 1950's

Paul Anka
Frankie Avalon
Chuck Berry
Big Bopper
Pat Boone
Freddy Cannon
Chubby Checker
Dee Clark
Eddie Cochran
Floyd Cramer
Bobby Darin
Jimmy Dean
Bo Diddley
Duane Eddy
Everly Brothers
Fabian (Forte)
Fats Domino
Connie Francis
Bobbie Freeman

Bill Haley
Buddy Holly
Tab Hunter
Jerry Lee Lewis
Little Anthony
Little Richard
Sal Mineo
Ricky Nelson
Sandy Nelson
Roy Orbison
Carl Perkins
Elvis Presley
Lloyd Price
Marty Robbins
Jimmie Rodgers
Bobby Rydell
Tommy Sands
Jack Scott
Neil Sedaka

Frank Sinatra
Johnny Tillotson
Conway Twitty
Richie Valens
Bobby Vee
Gene Vincent

84. Top Music Groups of the 1950's

The Blue Notes
The Browns
The Champs
The Chantels
The Cleftones
The Coasters
The Crescendos
The Crests
The Crew Cuts
The Crickets
Danny & the Juniors
The Dells
The Diamonds
Dion & the Belmonts
The Del Vikings
Dickey Doo & the
  Don'ts
Drifters

The Dubs
The Fireballs
The Five Satins
The Flamingos
The Fleetwoods
The Four Coins
The Four Freshmen
The Four Lads
The Four Preps
Frankie Lymon & the
  Teenagers
The Heartaches
The Isley Brothers
Jan & Dean
The Jesters
Joe Bennett & the
  Sparktones

Johnny & the
  Hurricanes
Little Anthony and
  the Imperials
The Miracles
The Moonglows
The Platters
The Playmates
The Shirelles
The Skyliners
The Turbans

85. Hit Television Shows of the 1950's

"Gunsmoke"
"Walt Disney"
"Red Skelton"
"I Love Lucy"
"Dragnet"
"You Bet Your Life"
"The Jack Benny Show"
"Ed Sullivan Show"
"Danny Thomas Show"
"Wagon Train"
"I've Got a Secret"
"General Electric Theatre"
"The Jackie Gleason Show"
"Colgate Comedy Hour"
"Candid Camera"
"Lassie"
"Have Gun, Will Travel"
"December Bride"

"Perry Mason"
"Perry Como Show"
"The Millionaire"
"$64,000 Question"
"The Real McCoys"
"Mama"
"What's My Line?"
"Lawrence Welk Show"
"Ford Theatre"

86. Slang of the 1960's

Slang	Meaning	Slang	Meaning
ankle biters	little children	**for real**	truly; indeed
bad scene	an unpleasant event	**freedom riders**	civil rights protesters
bat phone	police officer's phone	**funny money**	counterfeit bills
beach buggy	open vehicle driven on the sand	**funky**	excellent
		gasser	the very best
beach bunny	non-surfing girl at the beach	**generation gap**	difference between youth and their parents
birdie biker	female motorcyclist		
boss	super	**get it together**	straighten out one's life
boxes	guitars		
brain drain	emigration of a country's scientists	**get-up-and-go**	energy; pep
		glitch	an obstacle
bum trip	an unpleasant event	**go ape**	lose control
		go-go	of discotheques or a style of music
bummer	unpleasant experience		
bug	to annoy someone	**go with the flow**	to relax, be passive
catch some rays	sunbathe	**greaser**	person with long oily hair
chick	a young woman	**grody**	disgusting
clanked	tired	**gross**	repulsive
cool it	calm down	**grossed out**	disgusted
copping out	renege; break a promise	**groovy**	outstanding
		hack	cope
crash pad	place to sleep	**hang a left**	make a left turn
deb's delight	eligible bachelor	**hang loose**	relax
dingaling	an odd person; nerd	**hang-up**	problem
		happening	special event
do your own thing	do it your way	**hawk**	war supporter
dove	peace lover	**heavy**	powerful
downer	an unpleasant experience	**hood**	small-time, petty criminal
dropout	nonconformist	**hot dog**	show-off
dullsville	boring	**hustle**	to persuade or pressure
fab	attractive; exciting		
far out	great; outstanding	**klutz**	awkward person
fink out	to back out, quit	**mod**	modern; in fashion
flake off	scram		
flower child	hippie, member of the counterculture	**mop-top**	one with a Beatle haircut

86. *(continued)*

Slang	Meaning	Slang	Meaning
mover	influential person	straight	not using drugs
		street people	the homeless or poor
nifty	useful; good		
No way!	Definitely not!	sweat	to worry
now	fashionable	teenie bopper	young teen rock fan
off the wall	strange		
out of sight	great; unbelievable	tell it like it is	talk candidly
		the man	anyone in authority
pad	bed, place to sleep		
		threads	clothes
payola	money; a bribe	together	free of anxiety
pits	disgusting, unpleasant	total	completely demolish
plastic	artificial, fake	tough toenails	too bad
psychedelic	bright, dreamy patterns of light or color	trash	to destroy
		tuff	excellent
		tune in	pay attention
rag top	convertible	tune out	ignore
rap	to talk, chat	turn off	to repulse someone
rap session	discussion		
rat fink	detestable person	uncool	bad; tense
right on	yes, okay	unreal	outstanding
rip off	robbery, theft	uptight	nervous, tense
shades	sunglasses	vibes	person's aura
shot down	rejected	whiz kid	intelligent child
shrink	psychiatrist	wow	fantastic!
shuck	a phony	yuck!	expression of disgust
sit in	to take over an area in protest		
		zap	wipe out; defeat
spaced out	high on drugs	zilch	zero
spiffy	neat; good	zit	pimple
squaresville	a dull place	zot	zero

87. Fads and Fancies of the 1960's

acid rock
Alligator (dance)
Arab kaftans
astrology
Barbie® dolls
bare feet
Batman merchandise
beards
The Beatles
beehive hairdos
bell-bottom pants
body painting
bouffant hair-do
circle pins
communes
computer dating
cosmic consciousness
dune buggy
Eskimo muk luks
flower power
flowers on jeans
Frisbees™
Frug (dance)
Funky Chicken (dance)
go-go dancing
granny glasses
Haight Ashbury
hair ironing

harmonicas
hippie costumes
hootenannies
huge sunglasses
Hully-Gully (dance)
incense
"instant insanity" puzzles
ironing hair
Jerk (dance)
leather pants
light shows
love beads
love chains
Mickey Mouse watches
mini-skirts
mop-top haircut (males)
Monkey (dance)
multicolor painted vans
navy pea coats
Nehru collars
new math
paisley clothing
panty hose
paper clothes
piano wrecking
pigtails on men
pillbox hat

pop art
Princeton haircut (males)
protest buttons
psychedelic posters
rocking chairs
skateboarding
spike heels
Superball®
surfer styles
surfing
TP'ing (toilet papering)
tarot fortune-telling cards
teased hair
thigh high boots
toe rings
trampolines
transcendental meditation
trivia contests
Twist (dance)
underground newspapers
unisex clothing
very long hair
Volkswagen beetles
Watusi (dance)
wet-look fabrics
Woodies (station wagons)
worry beads

88. Hit Records of 1960

"Alley Oop"
"Are You Lonesome Tonight?"
"Cathy's Clown"
"El Paso"
"Exodus"
"Everybody's Somebody's Fool"
"I'm Sorry"
"It's Now or Never"
"Itsy Bitsy Teeny Weeny Yellow Polka Dot Bikini"
"I Want to Be Wanted"
"Mister Custer"
"My Heart Has a Mind of Its Own"
"Running Bear"
"Save the Last Dance for Me"

"Sink the Bismark"
"The Sound of Music"
"Stay"
"Stuck on You"
"Teen Angel"
"Theme From a Summer Place"
"Why"

89. Best-Selling Fiction of 1968

Airport by Hailey
Couples by Updike
The First Circle by Solzhenitsyn
The Hurricane Years by Hawley
Preserve and Protect by Drury
The Queen's Confession by Holt
Red Sky in the Morning by Bradford
The Senator by Pearson
Tell Me How Long the Train's Been Gone by Baldwin
Testimony of Two Men by Caldwell
The Tower of Babel by West
The Triumph by Galbraith
True Grit by Portis
Tunc by Durrell
Vanished by Knebel
A World of Profit by Auchincloss

90. Major Events of 1968

Southern California defeated Indiana 14–3 in the Rose Bowl.

Synthetic DNA was first produced.

USS *Pueblo* seized by the North Koreans.

Tet offensive was initiated in South Vietnam.

Super Bowl II was won by the Green Bay Packers.

Martin Luther King, Jr. was assassinated.

Riots broke out in 125 cities.

Nixon and Humphrey were nominated for president.

Poor People's March held in Washington, D.C.

Peace talks with North Vietnam began in Paris.

Robert Kennedy was assassinated.

Nuclear nonproliferation treaty was signed.

U.S. Open tennis championship was won by Arthur Ashe.

Democratic National Convention resulted in violent clash between anti-war protestors and Chicago police.

Bombing of North Vietnam began.

Helen Keller, John Steinbeck, Upton Sinclair, and Edna Ferber died.

Students struck at San Francisco State College.

The first woman was added to the FBI's most wanted list.

Films *2001: A Space Odyssey*, *Rosemary's Baby*, and *Yellow Submarine* were released.

Olympic games were held in Mexico City.

Peggy Fleming won the Olympic gold medal for figure skating.

Oliver! won the Academy Award for best picture.

Jackie Kennedy married Aristotle Onassis.

Richard Nixon was elected President.

First American astronauts oribited the earth.

First NFL-AFL football draft was held.

Pete Maravich's 44.2 points per game won the NCAA Division I basketball scoring title.

Freeze-dried coffee was introduced.

Shirley Chisholm, first black female U.S. Representative, was elected.

Simon and Garfunkel won a Grammy Award for *Mrs. Robinson*.

First U.S. heart transplant performed by Dr. Denton Cooley.

Southern California's O. J. Simpson won the Heisman Trophy.

91. Performers at Woodstock

In 1969 the Woodstock Music and Art Fair attracted 450,000 people to a pasture in Sullivan County, New York. For four days, the site became the counterculture's biggest bash for peace and music.

Joan Baez
The Band
Jeff Beck Group
Blood, Sweat and Tears
Canned Heat
Creedence Clearwater Revival
Joe Cocker
Crosby, Stills and Nash
Grateful Dead
Arlo Guthrie
Tim Hardin
Keef Hartley
Richie Havens
Jimi Hendrix
Incredible String Band
Iron Butterfly
Janis Joplin
Jefferson Airplane
Mountain
Quill
Santana
Ravi Shankar
Sly and the Family Stone
Bert Sommer
Sweetwater
Ten Years After
The Who
Johnny Winter

92. Terms Contributed by the Vietnam War

defoliate	protective reaction
DMZ	Viet Cong
fire fight	dove
Green Berets	Silent Majority
grunt	teach-in
Ho Chi Minh trail	peacenik
MIA	Yippies
Napalm	

93. Slang of the 1970's

Slang	Meaning	Slang	Meaning
-aholic	suffix for any addiction	**flea market**	street sale
		flat-out	totally
antsy	nervous	**flick**	movie
awesome	great	**-gate**	suffix for any scandal
biggie	important event or person	**get your act together**	straighten out one's life
boss	excellent	**get down**	to dance freely
burnout	exhausted from drugs, or stress	**get into**	become interested
		gig	job
bust	arrest for drug use	**go bananas**	get excited
buy the farm	to die	**gofer**	lackey, errand runner
cheapie	low-quality merchandise	**hang-up**	a mental or emotional resistance
come on like gangbusters	over-zealous	**hassle**	to annoy
		hatchet man	one brought in to fire employees
cost an arm and a leg	expensive		
		head up	to lead; organize
decent	nice; very good	**humongous**	very large
dig	understand	**hype**	big promotional effort
dirty pool	unfair tactics	**jet set**	the super-wealthy
do a number on	try to deceive	**jive**	nonsense
dork	a fool, nerd	**jock**	any athlete
downer	bad experience	**judgment call**	a close choice
empowerment	taking control of one's life	**keep on truckin'**	hang in there
		laid back	easy going
even-handed	fair	**life style**	way of life
fall guy	scapegoat	**make waves**	to cause trouble

93. *(continued)*

Slang	*Meaning*	*Slang*	*Meaning*
-mania	suffix for craze	**take care of business**	to commence
match-up	a competition	**totally awesome**	wonderful!
megabucks	large amount of money	**totally gross**	disgusting
narc	tattletale	**track record**	past achievements
old fogey	old-fashioned person	**trash**	waste; destroy
out-of-pocket	unreimbursed	**truck**	walk
preppy	dress like a prep-school student	**turkey**	a nerd
punk	form of rock and roll	**up front**	honest
right on	yes, that's right	**WASP**	white, Anglo-Saxon protestant
scuttlebutt	gossip	**whole nine yards**	full commitment; all the way
shtick	act; show	**widget**	mechanical contraption
square one	beginning	**workaholic**	person compelled to work
step-by-step	in a sequence	**zit**	pimple
suave	well-poised		
superstar	a major media idol		

94. Fads and Fancies of the 1970's

afro (haircut)
backgammon
Ben Franklin glasses
bean bag chairs
bell-bottom pants
bib overalls
biorhythms
CB's
chokers
"chopper" bicycles
clacker balls
cybernetics
denim jackets
disco dancing
dreadlocks
earth shoes
8-track tapes
Farrah Fawcett-Majors posters
55-mile-per-hour speed limit
frizzy hair
flip-flops
G.I. fatigues
gypsy look
hang-gliding
headbands
health food stores
hot pants
hot tubs
Indian jewelry
"Jaws" T-shirts at the beach
jogging outfits
kissathon
macramé

maxi-skirt
mechanics' jump suits
mood rings
mutton-chop sideburns
peace symbol
pet rocks
pie killing
puka shell necklaces
punk fashions
punk purple hair
roller disco
skateparks
"Space Invaders" video game
spandex garments
streaking
string bikinis
Susan B. Anthony dollar
tarot cards
tattoos
think tanks
toga parties
"Trekkies"
unisex look
velveteen jackets
waterbeds
white stockings
wigs

95. Movies of Ronald Reagan

Accidents Will Happen
An Angel from Texas
Angels Wash Their Faces
The Bad Man
Bedtime for Bonzo
Boy Meets Girl
Brother Rat
Brother Rat and a Baby
Cattle Queen of Montana
Code of the Secret Service
Cowboy from Brooklyn
Dark Victory
Desperate Johnny
The Girl from Jones Beach
Girls on Probation
Going Places
The Hasty Heart
Hellcats of the Navy
Hell's Kitchen
Hollywood Hotel
Hong Kong
International Squadron
It's a Great Feeling
John Loves Mary
Juke Girl
The Killers
Kings Row

Knute Rockne—All American
The Last Outpost
Law and Order
Louisa
Love Is on the Air
Million Dollar Baby
Murder in the Air
Naughty but Nice
Night Unto Night
Nine Lives Are Not Enough
Prisoner of War
Santa Fe Trail
Secret Service of the Air
Sergeant Murphy
*She's Working Her Way Through
    College*
Smashing the Money Ring
Stallion Road
Storm Warning
Swing Your Lady
Tennessee's Partner
That Hagen Girl
This Is the Army
Tugboat Annie Sails Again
The Voice of the Turtle
The Winning Team
Tropic Zone

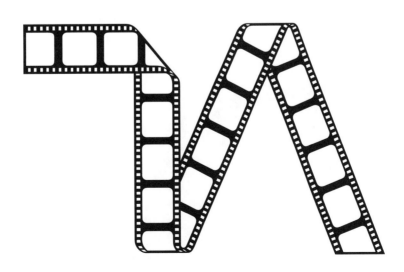

96. Fads and Fancies of the 1980's

acid-washed jeans
aerobic dancing
argyle checked socks
baggy sweaters
"Baby on Board" signs
beepers
blackened redfish
BMW
bottled water
break dancing
button-fly denim jeans
Cabbage Patch™ dolls
call waiting
charm bracelets
ceiling fans
clog shoes
comedy clubs
computer games
deck shoes
designer sweats
Dungeons and Dragons®
E.T. dolls
fanny packs
fifties clothing
flat-top haircut
flotation tanks
gourmet ice cream
Hacky Sack®
hand weights
home answering machines
jelly bean shoes
jogging
joysticks

lazer tag
leather bomber jackets
legwarmers
macramé friendship bracelets
music videos
Mutant Ninja Turtles®
New Wave music
oat bran
Pac Man™
pasta
rap music
ripped jeans
Rollerblade skates
Rubik's® Cube
sequined T-shirts
skateboarding
slam dancing
Smurfs™
snowboarding
square-framed glasses
stress management seminars
sun porches
Susan B. Anthony dollar
suspenders
Swatch watches
Trivial Pursuit®
tube dresses
valley girls
video dating services
walking shoes
wave, the
YUPPIES

97. Slang of the 1980's

Term	*Meaning*
bean counter	numbers person, accountant
beltway bandit	Washington, D.C., consultant
boom box	large portable radio
bow heads	girls wearing ribbons
break dance	style of gymnastic dance
CD	compact disk
casual	fashionable, good
chill	calm down
clonked out	broken
Clydesdale	handsome guy
couch potato	persistent television viewer
dancercise	aerobics to music
ditsy	goofy, silly
dude	guy, man
dweeb	nerd
fast-tracker	person moving up the corporate ladder
fine tune	to adjust, perfect
floppies	computer disks
freezenik	person for a nuclear freeze
fresh	cool, nice
fuzzify	to muddle
gag me with a spoon	disgusting!
golden parachute	big severance pay agreement for executives of companies merging
groovy	old-fashioned
hacker	one who breaks into computer files
hands-on manager	boss who gets directly involved
happening	an important event
happy camper	satisfied person
have a cow	get excited, over-react
I'm so sure.	Right. (sarcastically)
major league	important
make a run for the border	skip school
make my day	don't mess with me
maxed out	credit cards charged to the limit
networking	using personal contacts for career gain
PC	personal computer
photo op	chance for pictures of a politician
plastic	phony

(continued)

97. *(continued)*

Term	*Meaning*
power tie	dress-for-success necktie
prioritizing	establishing priorities
proactive	taking preventive action
quality time	giving attention to loved ones
radical	outstanding; excellent
rank	good looking
red eye	late-night flight
rock-jock	a mountain climber
slammin'	enjoyable
sound bite	political quote for television broadcast
streamlining	making more aero-dynamic, simplifying
stretch	a long limo
totally gross	disgusting!
twisted grill	crooked teeth
VJ	video jockey
up-scale marketing	advertising targeted at wealthy consumers
upside potential	opportunity for a profit
verbal	to harass, rib
What's shakin'?	What's happening?
Where's the beef?	Where's the result?
yo	hey; hello
YUPPIE	young urban professional
zapping	using fast forward on VCR to skip commercials
zedwig	nerd

98. Innovations of the 1980's

air bags
answering machines
autofocus cameras
automatic teller machines
BMX bicycles
boombox
cable television
cable TV shopping
call forwarding
call waiting
camcorders
cellular telephones
compact discs
computer spelling checkers
cordless telephones
curb recycling
disposable cameras
electronic mail
EPCOT
fax machines
food processors
frequent flyer programs
front wheel drive cars
frozen yogurt
gourmet frozen dinners
hair mousse
home computers
junk bonds
laser discs
laser printers
liposuction
"lite" everything
living wills
microcassettes
microwave ovens
miniature portable televisions
minivans
modems

mouse (computer control)
mandatory seat belt laws
New Coke®
911 emergency phone service
Nintendo™
non-smoking
nursery monitors
patriot missiles
personal computers
Post-it® notes
quality circles
radar detectors
return of the 65 mph speed limit
solar calculators
space shuttle
space telescope
state lotteries
stealth bombers
tomahawk missiles
unisex clothing
universal bar code
videocassette recorders
voice mail
Walkman™
wireless remote control

99. Fads and Fancies of the 1990's

Air Jordans
ATMs
Barney
Beanie Babies®
beepers
body piercing
butterfly clips
call waiting
cargo pants
cell phones
competency testing
day trading
dot-com craze
extreme sports
Gameboys
gansta rap
Grunge
Hip-hop
home computers
infomercials
inline skates
laser pointers
MTV
Pokemon®
political correctness (PC)
proficiency testing
rap music

soccer moms
sports utility vehicles (SUVs)
Starbucks
starter jackets
Tae-Bo
talk radio
tattoos for men and women
team building
telecommuting
torn jeans
virtual reality
World Wide Web

DIVERSITY IN THE U.S.

100. Ten (Self-)Critical Things I Can Do to Be a Better Multicultural Educator

By Paul Gorski

1. I can engage in self-reflective writing or journaling to explore my own process of identity development and how I react to different events or people.

2. I can invite critique from colleagues and accept it openly. Though it's easy to become defensive in the face of critique, I can thank the person for their feedback, remembering that people may experience me differently from how I see and experience myself.

3. I can understand the relationship between INTENT and IMPACT. Many times, especially when I'm in a situation in which I experience a level of privilege, I have the luxury of referring and responding only to what I intended, no matter what impact I have on somebody. I must take responsibility for impact, recognizing that I can never be totally aware of the biases and prejudices I carry into the classroom and how my students or colleagues experience me.

4. I can reject the myth of color-blindness. As painful as it is to admit sometimes, I know that I react differently when I'm in a room full of people who share many dimensions of my identity than I do in a room full of people who are very different from me. I have to be open and honest about that, because those shifts inevitably inform the experiences of people in my classes or workshops. In addition, color-blindness denies people validation of their whole person.

5. I can recognize my own social identity group memberships and how they may affect my students' experiences and learning processes. People do not always experience me the way I intend them to, even if I am an active advocate for all my students.

6. I can build coalitions with teachers who are different from me (in terms of race, ethnicity, sexual orientation, gender, religion, first language, disability, and other identities). These can be valuable relationships of trust and honest critique.

7. I can invite critique from my students, and when I do so, I can dedicate to listening actively and modeling a willingness to change if necessary.

8. I can reflect on my own experiences as a student and how that informs my teaching. The practice of drawing on these experiences, the positive and the negative, provide important insights regarding my teaching practice.

(continued)

100. *(continued)*

9. I can challenge myself to take personal responsibility before looking for fault elsewhere. For example, if I have one student who is falling behind and misbehaving, I will consider what I am doing or not doing that may be contributing to their disengagement.

10. I can celebrate myself as an educator and total person. I can, and should, also celebrate every moment I spend in self-critique, however difficult and painful, because it will make me a better educator.

Source: From the Multicultural Pavilion: http://curry.edschool.virginia.edu/go/multicultural. Used with permission.

101. African American Firsts

First African American . . .

child born in America	William Tucker	1621
founder of Chicago	Jean Baptiste du Sable	1772
poet	Phillis Wheatley	1774
presidential appointee	Benjamin Banneker	1791
minister of a white congregation	John Morront	1795
bishop in the U.S.	Richard Allen	1816
college graduate	Alexander L. Twilight	1823
patent holder	Henry Blair	1834
to publish a novel	W. W. Brown	1853
elected to an office	John Mercer	1854
chaplin of U.S. Army	Henry M. Turner	1863
major in U.S. Army	Martin Delany	1865
United States senator	Hiram Rhodes Revels	1870
Kentucky derby winner	Oliver Lewis	1875
Ph.D. recipient (Yale)	E. A. Bouchet	1876
graduate of West Point	Henry O. Flipper	1877
baseball player	Moses Fleetwood	1883
professional baseball team	Cuban Giants	1884
millionaire	Jonathan Wright	1885
Harvard Ph.D. recipient	W. E. B. Du Bois	1895
rodeo bulldogger	Bill Pickett	1900
Medal of Honor winner	William Harvey Carney	1900
female bank president	Lena Walker	1902
sorority	Alpha Kappa Alpha	1908
heavyweight champion	Jack Johnson	1908
to set foot on North Pole	Matthew Henson	1909
Rhodes scholar	Alan Leroy Locke	1910
female millionaire	C. J. Walker	1914
All-American football player	"Fritz" Pollard	1916

101. *(continued)*

First African American . . .

professional football player	"Fritz" Pollard	1919
basketball team	Renaissance	1923
woman state legislator	Crystal Fauset	1938
woman judge	Jane M. Bolin	1939
to perform at the White House	Marian Anderson	1939
Oscar winner	Hattie McDaniel	1940
to play in baseball major leagues	Jackie Robinson	1947
Naval Academy graduate	Wesley Brown	1949
U.S. Naval Aviator	Jessie Brown	1949
Pulitzer prize winner	Gwendolyn Brooks	1950
Nobel Peace prize winner	Dr. Ralph Bunche	1950
NBA basketball player	Charles H. Cooper	1950
Air Force General	Benjamin O. Davis, Jr.	1954
Wimbledon competitor	Althea Gibson	1957
professional hockey player	Willie O'Ree	1958
airline stewardess	Ruth Carol Taylor	1958
Heisman trophy winner	Ernie Davis	1961
student at University of Mississippi	James Meredith	1962
warship commander	Samuel Gravely	1962
major league umpire	Emmett Ashford	1966
Cabinet member	Robert C. Weaver	1966
on Federal Reserve Board of Governors	Andrew Brimmer	1966
Supreme Court justice	Thurgood Marshall	1967
professional sports coach	Bill Russell	1967
man to win tennis U.S. Open	Arthur Ashe	1968
orchestra conductor	Henry Lewis	1968
professional football quarterback	Marvin Briscoe	1968
woman in House of Representatives	Shirley Chisholm	1969
to win "Mr. America" contest	Chris Dickerson	1970
major league baseball manager	Frank Robinson	1975
woman armed services pilot	Loren Monroe	1979
in space on *Challenger*	Gulon Bluford	1983
to win "Miss America"	Vanessa Williams	1983
Texas Ranger	Lee Roy Young	1988
Roman Catholic archbishop	Eugene Marino	1988
chairman of Joint Chiefs of Staff	Gen. Colin Powell	1989
head of a major political party	Ronald Brown	1989
Nobel Prize for literature	Toni Morrison	1993
Tony Award winners	George Wolfe & Savior Glover	1996
to win golf's Masters championship	Tiger Woods	1997
woman to win U.S. Open tennis finals	Serena Williams	1999

102. Notable African Americans

Directions: Fill in the correct name next to their achievements. Answers are below.

1. Founder of the Rainbow Coalition: _____

2. Winner of an Emmy Award, over 20 Grammy Awards, and several Oscar nominations: _____

3. Author of *Beloved* and *Song of Solomon* who was awarded the Nobel Prize for Literature in 1993: _____

4. Appointed Ambassador to New Zealand after being the first African-American woman to serve in the U.S. Senate: _____

5. First African-American actor to win an Oscar (for *Lilies of the Field*, 1963): _____

6. First African American to hold the office of United States Secretary of State: _____

7. Poet who read her poem "On the Pulse of Morning" at the inauguration of Bill Clinton: _____

8. The Pulitzer Prize-winning author who wrote *The Autobiography of Malcolm X* and *Roots*: _____

9. One of the most famous jazz singers of all time: _____

10. The 1960s Calypso singer who became the leader of the Nation of Islam in America: _____

Answers:

1. Rev. Jesse Jackson, Sr.
2. Quincy Jones
3. Toni Morrison
4. Carol Moseley-Braun
5. Sidney Poitier
6. General Colin Powell
7. Maya Angelou
8. Alex Haley
9. Billie Holiday
10. Louis Farrakhan

103. Famous Native Americans

John Louis Clarke	wood sculptor
Charles Curtis	U.S. vice president
Sacajawea	interpretor for Lewis and Clark
Ira Hayes	Marine who helped raise flag at Iwo Jima
Hiawatha	founder of Iroquois Confederacy
Pocahontas	legendary lifesaver of Captain John Smith
Will Rogers	humorist
Mitchell Silas	Navajo sand painter
Squanto	interpreter in negotiations between the Pilgrims and Massasoit
Jim Thorpe	Olympic champion, pro football player
Clarence Tinker	U.S. Army General in World War II
Annie Dodge Wauneka	Navajo spokesperson
Sara Winnemucca	Piute translator and peacemaker

104. Notable Hispanic Americans

Jerry Apodaca	New Mexico Governor, 1974–79
Donna Alvardo	Director of ACTION, government agency
Herman Badillo	U.S. Congressman from New York
Joan Baez	popular protest song recording artist
Romana A. Bañuelos	U.S. Treasurer, 1971–74
Raymond Barrio	author
Nash Candelaria	author
Vickki Carr	popular singer
Lauro Cavazos	Secretary of Education
César Chavez	labor leader
Henry G. Cisneros	Mayor of San Antonio
Roberto Clemente	baseball player
Jaime Escalante	Los Angeles teacher who inspired the movie *Stand and Deliver*
Freddy Fender	singer
Hector Garcia	U.S. Civil Rights Commissioner
Henry B. Gonzales	First Mexican-American congressman
Rodolfo "Corky" Gonzales	boxing champion, Democratic party leader
José Gutiérrez	organized "La Rasa Unida," political third party
Marf-Luci Jaramillo	U.S. ambassador to Honduras
Luis Jiménez	muralist, sculptor
Joe Kapp	professional football player
Nancy Lopez	women's professional golfer
Trini Lopez	popular singer

(continued)

104. *(continued)*

Manuel Lujan, Jr.	U.S. Representative, Secretary of Interior
Bob Martinez	Governor of Florida
Elba Molina	prominent Arizona businesswoman
Joseph Montoyo	first Mexican-American Senator (New Mexico)
Katherine Davalos Ortega	U.S. Treasurer
Anthony Quinn	actor
Belinda Cárdenas Ramírez	first woman appointed to the Civil Rights Commission
Diego Rivera	muralist
Linda Ronstadt	singer
Gary Soto	writer
Manuel Hernández Trujillo	artist
Richie Valens	singer
Richard Vásquez	author of *The Plain Plum Pickers*
Esteban Villa	painter
José Antonio Villareal	author of *Poncho* and other works

105. Notable Arab Americans

Paula Abdul	singer
James Abourezk	former U.S. Senator
F. Murray Abraham	actor, won Oscar for *Amadeus*
Spencer Abraham	U.S. Energy Secretary
George Addes	secretary-treasurer of United Auto Workers
Michael DeBakey	heart surgeon
Mansour Farah	clothing manufacturer (Farah Company)
Jamie Farr	actor; Corporal Klinger from *M*A*S*H*
Doug Flutie	pro football player
Kahlil Gibran	author of *The Prophet*
Theodore Gontos	clothing retailer
Phillip Habib	undersecretary of state for political affairs
Joseph Haggar	clothing manufacturer (Haggar Company)
John Kacere	artist
Casey Kasem	radio and television personality
George Mitchell	former Senate Majority Leader
Ralph Nader	consumer advocate
Rosa Lee Nemir	medical researcher
Naomi Shihab Nye	children's author and poet
Mary Rose Qakar	U.S. Congresswoman
Donna Shalala	college president; former U.S. Secretary of Health and Human Services
Marlo Thomas	actress and author
Helen Thomas	former White House press corps journalist

106. U.S. Women's Firsts

Name	First U.S. Female . . .	Year
Ann Bradstreet	author in America	1640
Ann Franklin	newspaper editor	1762
Mary Kies	granted a patent	1809
Susan G. Bagley	telegrapher	1846
Frances B. Whitcher	humorist	1846
Elizabeth Blackwell	awarded a medical degree	1849
Antoinette B. Blackwell	ordained minister	1853
E. R. Jones	dentist	1855
Mary Surratt	hanged by U.S. government	1865
Mary Edwards Walker	Medal of Honor recipient	1866
Esther Hobart	justice of the peace	1870
Frances E. Willard	college president	1871
Victoria Woodhull	presidential candidate	1872
Helen Magill	awarded a Ph.D.	1877
Susanna Salter	mayor (Argonia, Kansas)	1887
Naggie L. Walker	bank president	1903
Bessica Raiche	solo flight	1910
Alice Wells	policewoman (Los Angeles)	1910
Harriet Quimby	licensed airplane pilot	1911
Annette A. Adams	federal prosecutor	1914
Jeanette Rankin	member of U.S. House of Representatives	1916
Annette Adams	U.S. district attorney	1918
Opha May Johnson	Marine	1918
Marie Luhring	automotive engineer	1920
Nellie Taylor Ross	elected governor of a state	1925
Phoebe Omlie	licensed pilot	1927
Jane Addams	Nobel Peace Prize recipient	1931
Amelia Earhart	transatlantic solo flight	1932
Hattie Caraway	elected to U.S. Senate	1932
Frances Perkins	cabinet member (Labor)	1933
Helen Richey	commercial airline pilot	1934
Gretchen Schoenleber	stock exchange member	1935
Georgia N. Clark	Treasurer of the United States	1949
Eugenie M. Anderson	United States ambassador	1949
Jerrie Mock	solo flight around the world	1964
Diane Crump	jockey in Kentucky Derby	1970
Billie Jean King	athlete to earn $100,000 a year	1971
Janet Gray Hayes	mayor of major city (San Jose)	1974

(continued)

106. *(continued)*

Name	First U.S. Female . . .	Year
Sandra Day O'Connor	member of U.S. Supreme Court	1981
Dr. Sally K. Ride	astronaut to ride in space	1983
Geraldine A. Ferraro	candidate for vice president	1984
Kathryn D. Sullivan	astronaut to walk in space	1984
Libby Riddles	winner of Iditarod dogsled race	1985
Robin Ahrens	FBI agent killed on duty	1985
Lynette Woodard	member of Harlem Globetrotters	1985
Capt. Linda Bray	to lead American troops in combat	1989

107. Women Inventors

Sybilla Masters	cornmeal-making process	1715
Tabitha Babbit	circular saw	1812
Nancy Johnson	hand-cranked ice cream freezer	1843
Margaret Knight	paper bag machine	1868
Amanda Jones	vacuum method of canning	1873
Mary Anderson	windshield wiper	1904
Mary Phelps Jacob	brassiere	1913
Madeline Turner	fruit press	1916
Marjorie Joyner	permanent wave machine	1926
Beulah Henry	bobbinless sewing machine	1940
Marion Donovan	disposable diaper	1950
Grace Hopper	computer compiler	1952
Patsy Sherman	Scotchgard™ fabric protector	1955
Bette Nesmith Graham	White Out™	1956
Ruth Handler	Barbie® Doll	1959
Stephanie Kwolek	Kevlar™	1964
Rachel Brown, Elizabeth Hazen	Nystatin antifungal antibiotic	1994
Randi Altschul	disposable cell phone	1999

Sources: Inventors Museum at www.inventorsmuseum.com; 400 Years of Women in Science at www.astr. ua.edu/4000WS.

BUSINESS, INDUSTRY, AND TRANSPORTATION

108. Labor Leaders

Henry Bridges	George Meany
Cesar Chavez	Frances Perkins
Eugene Debs	Terrence Powderly
Elizabeth Flynn	A. Phillip Randolph
Samuel Gompers	Rose Schneiderman
Jimmy Hoffa	Albert Shanker
Mary "Mother" Jones	Uriah Stephens
John L. Lewis	William H. Sylvis
Charles Litchman	William S. Townsend

109. Union Membership in the United States

Percent of private, non-agricultural work force:

1900	6.5
1910	10.5
1920	19.2
1930	13.3
1940	24.3
1950	34.6
1960	37.0
1970	31.0
1980	20.6
1990	12.1
2000	9.0

Source: U.S. Department of Labor Bureau of Labor Statistics.

110. Farm Machinery and Technology Timeline

1790's	Cradle and scythe introduced
1793	Invention of cotton gin
1794	Thomas Jefferson's moldboard of least resistance tested
1797	Charles Newbold patented first cast-iron plow
1819	Jethro Wood patented iron plow with interchangeable parts
1819–25	U.S. food-canning industry established
1834	McCormick reaper patented
1837	John Deere and Leonard Andrus began manufacturing steel plows
1837	Practical threshing machine patented
1841	Practical grain drill patented
1842	First grain elevator, Buffalo, NY
1844	Practical mowing machine patented
1847	Irrigation begun in Utah
1849	Mixed chemical fertilizers sold commercially
1854	Self-governing windmill perfected
1856	2-horse straddle-row cultivator patented
1868	Steam tractors were tried out
1870's	Silos came into use
1870's	Deep-well drilling first widely used
1874	Glidden barbed wire patented
1890–95	Cream separators came into wide use
1910–15	Big open-geared gas tractors came into use in areas of extensive farming
1918	Small prairie-type combine with auxiliary engine introduced
1926	Cotton-stripper developed for High Plains
1926	Successful light tractor developed
1930's	All-purpose, rubber-tired tractor with complementary machinery came into wide use
1941–45	Frozen foods popularized
1942	Spindle cottonpicker produced commercially
1970's	No-tillage agriculture popularized

Source: "A History of American Agriculture 1776–1990," Economic Research Service, USDA.

111. Entrepreneurs Who Shaped American History

Elizabeth Arden	cosmetics
Philip Armour	meat packing
John Jacob Astor	furs and real estate
P. T. Barnum	entertainment
Alexander G. Bell	telephones
Clarence Birdseye	frozen foods
Asa Candler	soft drinks
Andrew Carnegie	steel
William Colgate	soap, toothpaste
Samuel Colt	guns
Peter Cooper	railroads
Ezra Corwell	telegraph
Robert de Graft	pocket paperbacks
Cecil B. De Mille	movies
John Deere	plows
Eleutbére Irénée Du Pont	gunpowder
William C. Durant	automobiles
George Eastman	photographic equipment
Thomas Edison	electrical equipment, phonograph
Harvey Firestone	tires
Henry Ford	automobiles
Bill Gates	computer software
J. Paul Getty	oil
Fred Harvey	fast food
H. J. Heinz	food
Howard Hughes	movies, aviation
Henry J. Kaiser	shipbuilding
Will Kellogg	breakfast cereal
Joseph P. Kennedy	banking, entertainment, real estate
Ray Kroc	fast food, McDonald's
Donald McKay	shipbuilding
Sarah McWilliams	cosmetics
J. Pierpont Morgan	banking, steel
Ransom E. Olds	automobiles
Elisha Otis	elevators
John D. Rockefeller	oil
David Sarnoff	broadcasting
R.W. Sears & A.C. Roebuck	mail order sales
Samuel Slater	textiles
Leland Stanford	railroads
Levi Strauss	denim pants

(continued)

111. *(continued)*

Cornelius Vanderbilt	steamboats, railroads
Charles Walgreen	drugstores
John Wanamaker	department stores
A. Montgomery Ward	mail order sales
Eli Whitney	cotton gin, guns, clocks
Frank W. Woolworth	department stores
Frank & Orville Wright	airplane
William Wrigley, Jr.	chewing gum

112. American Inventors and Their Inventions

Invention	*Inventor*	*Year*
Lightning rod	Benjamin Franklin	1752
Bifocal glasses	Benjamin Franklin	1760
Steam boat	John Fitch	1787
Cotton gin	Eli Whitney	1793
Cotton sewing thread	Mrs. Samuel Slater	1793
Comb cutting machine	Phineas Pratt	1799
Aerosol spray gun	Alan de Vilbiss	1803
Screw propeller	John Stevens	1804
Reaper	Cyrus McCormick	1834
Threshing machine	Hiram and John Pitts	1834
Revolver	Samuel Colt	1835
Morse code	S. B. Morse	1836
Steel plow	John Deere	1837
Rubber vulcanization	Charles Goodyear	1839
Life preserver	Napoleon Guerin	1841
Sewing machine	Elias Howe	1846
Commercial chewing gum	John Bacon Curtis	1848
Baby carriage	Charles Burton	1848
Safety pin	Walter Hunt	1849
Device to buoy vessels over shoals	Abraham Lincoln	1849
Roll-top desk	Abner Cutler	1850
Bloomers	Amelia Bloomer, E. Smith	1851
Cylinder lock	Linus Yale, Jr.	1851
Safety elevator	Elisha Otis	1854
Accordian	Anthony Faas	1854
Calliope	Joshua Stoddard	1855
Machine gun	Charles Barnes	1856
Mason jar	J. Mason	1858
Cable car	Eleazer Gardner	1858

112. *(continued)*

Invention	Inventor	Year
Paper dress patterns	Eleanor Butterick	1863
Sleeping car	George M. Pullman	1865
Typewriter	Christopher Sholes	1867
Air brake	George Westinghouse	1868
Plywood	John Mayo	1868
Brown paper bags	Margaret Knight	1870
Stock ticker	Thomas Edison	1870
Gasoline engine	George Brayton	1872
Jeans	Oscar Levi Strauss	1873
Barbed wire	Joseph Glidden	1874
Telephone	Alexander Graham Bell	1876
Carpet sweeper	Melville Bissell	1876
Mimeograph	Thomas Edison	1876
Phonograph	Thomas Edison	1877
Catamaran	Nathaneal Herreschoff	1877
Incandescent lamp	Thomas Edison	1879
Cash register	John Ritty	1879
Electric fan	Schuyler Wheeler	1882
Fountain pen	Lewis Waterman	1884
Roller skate	Levant Richardson	1884
Adding machine	William Burroughs	1885
Linotype	Ottmar Mergenthaler	1885
Motorcycle	Gottlieb Daimler	1885
Coca-Cola®	John S. Pemberton	1886
Kodak box camera	George Eastman	1888
Ballpoint pen	John H. Land	1888
Pneumatic hammer	Charles King	1890
Submarine	John P. Holland	1891
Zipper	Whitcomb Judson	1893
Movie machine	Thomas Edison	1893
Corn flakes	John H. Kellogg	1894
Safety razor	King C. Gillette	1895
Electric stove	William Hadaway	1896
Pencil sharpener	J. L. Love	1897
Golf tee	George Grant	1899
Tractor	Benjamin Holt	1900
Mouse trap	Charles Nelson	1900
Hair straightener	Sarah Breedlove Walker	1905
Radio amplifier	Lee De Forest	1907

(continued)

112. *(continued)*

Invention	Inventor	Year
Electric vacuum cleaner	Spangler	1907
Kewpie doll	Rose O'Neill	1907
Drip coffee	Melitta Bentz	1908
Electric auto starter	Charles Kettering	1911
Air conditioning	Willis Camer	1911
Crossword puzzle	Arthur Wynne	1913
Vacuum cleaner	James Kirby	1916
Arc welder	Elihu Thomson	1919
Lie detector	John Larsen	1921
Talking movie	Warner brothers	1927
Snowmobile	Carl Eliason	1927
Iron lung	Lewis Slaw & Philip Drinker	1928
Rocket engine	Robert H. Goddard	1929
Analog computer	Vannevar Bush	1930
Electric razor	Jacob Schick	1931
Cyclotron	Ernest O. Lawrence	1931
Chocolate chip cookie	Ruth Wakefield	1933
Launderette	J. F. Cantrell	1934
Nylon	Edwin Armstrong	1935
Parking meter	Carlton Magee	1935
Xerography	Chester Carlson	1938
Helicopter	Igor Ivan Sikorsky	1939
Radar	Robert Page	1940
Polaroid camera	Edwin H. Land	1947
Long playing record	Goldmark	1947
Microwave oven	Percy LeBaron Spencer	1947
Transistor	John Bardeen	1948
Disposable diaper	Marion Donovan	1950
Computer compiler	Grace Murray Hopper	1952
Panoramic movie	Fred Waller	1952
Polio vaccine	Jonas Salk	1953
Heart-lung machine	John Gibbon	1953
Calculator	George Stibitz	1954
Liquid Paper®	Belle Nesmith Graham	1956
Barbie doll	Ruth Handler	1959
Integrated circuit	Jack S. Kilby	1959
Laser	Theodore Maiman	1960
Music synthesizer	Robert A. Moog	1964
Noise reduction system	Ray Dolby	1966
Solar powered aircraft	Paul Macready	1980
Artificial heart	Robert Jarvik	1982

113. U.S. Transportation Timeline

1794	Lancaster Turnpike opened, first successful toll road.
1807	Robert Fulton demonstrated practicability of steamboats.
1825	Erie Canal finished.
1830	Peter Cooper's railroad steam engine, the Tom Thumb, ran 13 miles.
1830	30,000 miles of railroad track had been laid.
1868	George Westinghouse invented the compressed air locomotive brake
1869	Union Pacific, first transcontinental railroad, completed.
1903	Orville Wright and Wilbur Wright flew the first motor-driven airplane.
1908	Henry Ford developed assembly line automobile manufacturing.
1904	On October 27 the New York City Subway opened.
1947	First supersonic flight.
1960	Interstate Highway Act passed.
1969	First manned mission to the Moon.
1980	Railroad and trucking industries were deregulated.
1981	First flight of the space shuttle.

Source: U.S. Department of Agriculture, http://www.usda.gov/history2/text6.htm.

114. Historic Types of Sailing Vessels

bark	galleon
barkentine	junk
brig	ketch
brigantine	merchantman
catamaran	schooner
clipper	sloop
cutter	wherry
frigate	yawl

115. Automobile Firsts

1769	steam truck
1824	four-wheel drive vehicle
1860	2-stroke gas engine
1875	gas-powered motor car
1877	4-stroke gas engine
1885	pneumatic car tire
1887	electric car
1894	U.S. automobile company (Duryea)
1895	automobile race
1897	magneto ignition
1901	auto license plate (NY)
1905	AAA founded
1907	supercharged engine
1907	Model-T Ford introduced
1913	drive-in gas station
1914	water-cooled V-8 engine
1922	car radio (Marconiphone)
1924	motel (San Luis Obispo)
1933	drive-in theater
1935	parking meters (Oklahoma City)
1936	pop-up headlights (Cord)
1939	air-conditioned auto (Packard)
1940	superhighway (Pennsylvania)
1948	tubeless tires
1950	tinted windows
1955	front-wheel disk brakes (Citroen)
1955	drive-in restaurant (McDonald's)
1955	solar-powered car
1973	air bag safety cushion (GM)

ENTERTAINMENT AND CULTURE

116. Timeline of Games

1869	Parcheesi™ was copyrighted in the United States by E. G. Selchow & Co.
1890's	Tiddlywinks was an incredible craze throughout the United States.
1890's	Snakes and Ladders™ was introduced in England. The American version, known as "Chutes and Ladders," first appeared in the U.S. in 1943.
1903	Parker Brothers first introduced the game of Pit in 1903.
1913	Arthur Wynne, an immigrant from England who worked for the *New York World,* invented the crossword puzzle.
1916	Uncle Wiggily™ was introduced by the Milton Bradley Company.
1929	BINGO™ marketed by a toy salesman named Edwin Lowe.
1930's	Battleship™, a popular paper and pencil game, was first produced as a commercial game.
1934	Sorry™ was licensed to Parker Brothers, though it was introduced in England earlier.
1935	Parker Brothers began production of the game of Monopoly™. Charles Darrow, an unemployed engineer, created the game and sold the rights to Parker Brothers for an undisclosed sum.
1944	Andrew Pratt, a solicitor's clerk before his retirement, invented the classic "who dunnit" game, CLUE™.
1948	Scrabble™ trademarked by Alfred Mosher Butts. The game is now found in 1 of 3 homes in the U.S.
1949	Candyland™ marketed by the Milton Bradley Company.
1956	Edwin S. Lowe purchased the rights to Yahtzee™, from a wealthy Canadian couple who invented the game to play aboard their yacht.
1958	Milton Bradley Company introduced Concentration™, based upon a popular television program of the same name.
1959	Risk™ was introduced by Parker Brothers; earlier marketed in France as Conquest of the World.

(continued)

116. *(continued)*

1960   Milton Bradley released The Game of Life™, which was loosely beased upon Mr. Milton Bradley's 1860 "The Checkered Game of Life."

1966   Milton Bradley's Twister™ game caught on when introduced by Johnny Carson on the "Tonight Show."

1968   Goro Hasegawa published Othello™, an adaptation of the game of Reversi, which had been popular in England from 1888 until the 1920's.

1980   Rubik's Cube, introduced in Budapest, Hungary in the 1970's by Erno Rubik, was distributed in North America in 1980.

1982   Trivial Pursuit® is introduced in the United States at the American International Toy Fair after its invention in Canada by Scott Abbott, Chris Haney, John Haney, and Ed Werner.

1985   Parker Brothers market Pictionary™.

1985   Dave Arneson and Gary Gygax invented Dungeons & Dragons™.

117. Timeline of Toys

1769	Roller skates are invented by Joseph Merlin.
1865	The first embossed ABC wooden blocks were manufactured.
1886	The first BB gun was created.
1901	Twenty-two-year-old Joshua Lionel Cowen created a battery-powered train engine as an "animated advertisement" for a store's display window. The interest of customers spurred the creation of Lionel Trains.
1902	Inspired by a Theodore Roosevelt hunting incident, Morris Michtom, had his wife sew several plush toy bears for sale in the family's novelty store. Michtom sent Roosevelt a bear and received his permission to use the president's name on the bears.
1903	The first Crayola crayons appeared in the United States. They were packaged in a box of eight and sold for about five cents. The eight original colors were brown, red, green, black, blue, yellow, orange, and violet.
1913	A. C. Gilbert, winner of a gold medal for pole vaulting in the 1908 Olympics, developed the Erector Set.
1913	Nearly one million Tinkertoy sets have been sold since its introduction at the American Toy Fair in New York.
1915	John Gruelle created Raggedy Ann to entertain his sick daughter. Raggedy Andy followed five years later.
1916	John Lloyd Wright, the son of architect Frank Lloyd Wright invented Lincoln Logs. Wright's inspiration came from watching his father design the earthquake-proof Imperial Hotel in Tokyo.
1917	The Radio Flyer wagon was conceived. Today the Radio Flyer wagon factory produces 5,000 wagons per day.
1943	Mechanical engineer Richard James observed a torsion spring fall off a shelf. He and is wife, Betty, transformed that concept into the Slinky—80 feet of coiled wire that became a national craze in 1946. More than 250 million Slinkys have been sold.
1944	Ole Kirk Christiansen, a Danish carpenter and toy maker, created a plastic brick that could be locked together in different configurations. The name LEGO, comes from the Danish leg godt, meaning "play well." Coincidentally, in Latin the word means "I study" or "I put together."

(continued)

117. *(continued)*

1945	Binney & Smith, Inc. began manufacture of Silly Putty®.
1952	Mr. Potato Head was born. It became the first toy to be advertised on television.
1956	Play-Doh was introduced by Rainbow Crafts in Cincinnati. It was available only in one color: an off-white.
1957	The Tonka truck was developed by a group of Minnesota teachers. The word Tonka means "great" in the language of the Dakota Sioux.
1958	Wham-O introduced the Hula Hoop. It quickly became the most successful toy (up to that time) with over 20 million sold in one year.
1958	California surf shop owner Bill Richards and his son Mark popularized the skateboard. In 1971 Richard Stevenson of Los Angeles gave the skateboard a tail, called a "kicktail," at the back of the board, making it more maneuverable. Two years later Frank Nasworthy added polyurethane wheels. These two refinements spurred a national "sidewalk surfing" craze.
1959	Barbie was first marketed. The best-selling doll was created by Elliot Handler, the founder of Mattel, Inc., and his wife, Ruth. The doll was named after the Handlers' daughter, Barbie. Ken was the name of the creator's son.
1960	Ohio Art introduces the first Etch-a-Sketch. Invented by Arthur Granjean in the late 1950s, the toy was originally called L'Ecran Magique. Over one hundred million sets have been sold.
1963	Hasbro, Inc. introduced the Easy Bake Oven.
1968	Hot Wheels Cars and Racing Sets hit the market.
1969	Parker Brothers' Nerf ball, a polyurethane foam ball for indoor play, first appeared in the stores. The first year more than four million Nerf balls were sold.
1972	Atari was formed to market Pong, the high-tech computer game. Atari's 40th employee was Steve Jobs, who later collaborated with Steve Wozniak to found Apple Computer.
1993	Toy inventor H. Ty Warner marketed plush bean bag toys called Beanie Babies.

118. Clothing Timeline

1733	James (or John) Kay invented the flying shuttle.
1764	James Hargreaves invented the spinning jenny.
1784	Edmund Cartwright developed the power loom.
1793	Eli Whitney patented the cotton gin.
1801	Joseph Marie Jacquard made the first successful automatic drawloom using a punched card system to weave complex patterns.
1840	First lady's boot was designed at the request of Queen Victoria.
1846	Elias Howe patented the lock-stitch sewing machine.
1849	Safety pin invented.
1851	First trousers for women introduced in U.S. by Amelia Bloomer.
1865	The bustle became fashionable for women.
1869	First baseball caps introduced by the Cincinnati Red Stockings.
1872	Levi Strauss, a California dry goods merchandiser, and Jacob Davis, a Nevada tailor, patent the first blue jeans. The pants featured metal rivets at the points of pocket corners and the base of the fly.
1886	The dinner jacket, later termed the tuxedo, made its first official appearance at the Tuxedo Club.
1910	Rayon invented as the first artificial fiber.
1913	New York socialite Mary Phelps Jacob developed the first modern bra.
1917	Keds® became the first mass-marketed canvas-top "sneakers."
1937	Automatic home washing machine invented.
1939	DuPont Company, using a new fabric "as strong as steel, as fine as a spider's web," introduced nylon stockings at the New York World's Fair in 1939. The "ny" in nylon is for New York.
1946	French designer Jean Reard introduced the bikini.
1953	Polyester introduced to the textile market.
1955	Steam iron introduced.
1972	Nike® brand jogging shoes debuted.
1978	First designer jeans were fashioned by Gloria Vanderbilt.

119. First Hits of Top Recording Artists Over the Past 50 Years

1939	Frank Sinatra	"All or Nothing at All"
1950	Fats Domino	"The Fat Man"
1955	Pat Boone	"Two Hearts"
1956	Elvis Presley	"Heartbreak Hotel"
1957	Ray Charles	"Swanee River Rock"
1957	Ricky Nelson	"A Teenager's Romance"
1958	James Brown	"Try Me"
1961	Aretha Franklin	"Won't Be Long"
1962	Marvin Gaye	"Stubborn Kind of Fellow"
1962	The Beach Boys	"Surfin' USA"
1962	The Supremes	"Your Heart Belongs to Me"
1963	Stevie Wonder	"Fingertips, Pt 2"
1964	The Rolling Stones	"Not Fade Away"
1964	The Beatles	"I Want to Hold Your Hand"
1964	The Temptations	"The Way You Do the Things You Do"
1966	Neil Diamond	"Solitary Man"
1970	Elton John	"Border Song"
1970	Chicago	"Questions 67 and 68"
1971	Michael Jackson	"Got to Be There"
1971	Rod Stewart	"Maggie May"
1971	Paul McCartney	"Another Day"
1980	Prince	"I Wanna Be Your Lover"
1983	Madonna	"Holiday"
1990	Celine Dion	"Where Does My Heart Beat Now?"
1990	Mariah Carey	"Vision of Love"
1991	Boyz II Men	"Motownphilly"

120. American Media Firsts

1638	Printing press in America (Cambridge)
1704	Successful newspaper: *Boston Newsletter*
1784	Daily newspaper: *Pennsylvania Packet and Daily Advertiser*
1741	Magazine in America: *The American Magazine*
1823	American novel (*The Pioneers,* James F. Cooper)
1828	American dictionary (Noah Webster)
1869	First journalism course (Washington University)
1875	Newspaper comic strip
1886	Book set by linotype
1890	Newspaper photograph
1894	Movie theater (New York City)
1903	Moving picture story: *The Great Train Robbery*
1903	Movie star (Max Aronson)
1906	Radio broadcast
1906	Animated cartoon: *Humorous Phases of Funny Faces*
1907	Female movie star (Florence Lawrence)
1920	Commercial radio station
1921	Play-by-play baseball game radio broadcast (Pittsburgh)
1928	Television receiver
1929	Color television demonstration
1929	Color talking picture: *On with the Show*
1939	Regular television broadcast made
1941	Commercial television station: WNBT, New York City
1953	National color television broadcast: "Colgate Comedy Hour"
1976	Videocassette recorders sold in United States
1984	FCC approves television broadcasting in stereo

MILITARY AND POLITICAL HISTORY

121. Wars Involving the United States

Revolutionary War
War of 1812
Mexican War
Civil War
Spanish-American War
World War I
World War II
Korean War
Vietnam War
Persian Gulf War
Afghanistan War

122. Significant Ships in American History

Alabama

Arizona

Bon Homme Richard

Clermont

Constitution (Old Ironsides)

Cutty Sark

Essex

Intrepid

Lawrence

Luisitania

Maine

Mayflower

Merrimac

Missouri

Monitor

Nautilus

Niagara

Oklahoma

PT *109*

Pueblo

Savannah

United States

123. Major Treaties Signed by the U.S.

Treaty	Date	Main Provisions
Treaty of Paris	1783	U.S. and Great Britain following Revolutionary War. American independence recognized.
Jay Treaty	1794–1795	U.S. and Britain each agreed to arbitrate financial claims of their citizens.
Pinckney Treaty	1795	Spain recognized the Mississippi as the western boundary of the U.S.
Louisiana Purchase	1803	France sold territory to U.S., doubling U.S. area.
Treaty of Ghent	1814	U.S. and Great Britain following War of 1812. Reestablished pre-war boundaries of the U.S.
Rush-Bagot Treaty	1817	Limited U.S. and British armaments on Great Lakes.
Adams-Onis Treaty	1819	Spain agreed on sale of Florida and the boundary between Mexico and Oregon country.
Webster-Ashburton Treaty	1842	U.S. and Great Britain settled boundary dispute over Maine.
Guadalupe Hildago	1848	Treaty following Mexican War by which Mexico recognized Rio Grande as border of Texas and gave up claim to California and New Mexico.
Treaty of Paris	1898	Treaty with Spain following Spanish-American War in which Puerto Rico was ceded to U.S. and Philippine Islands sold to U.S.
Treaty of Versailles	1919	U.S. and other Allies' treaty with Germany following World War I, by which Germany ceded border territories and colonies, agreed to disarm and pay reparations, and League of Nations was created. (Not ratified by Senate.)

(continued)

123. *(continued)*

Treaty	Date	Main Provisions
Nine-Power Treaty at the Washington Conference	1921–1922	U.S., Japan, Britain, France, and 5 other countries agreed to outlaw poison gas and respect China's integrity.
Kellogg-Briand Pact	1928	U.S. with Germany, Japan, and others agreed to outlaw war.
North Atlantic Treaty	1949	Established NATO.
Treaty of Peace with Japan	1952	Treaty following World War II, by which Japan lost its conquests, agreed to help countries hurt during war, and was recognized as independent nation (49 signatures).
Southeast Asia Treaty Organization	1954	Established SEATO.
Limited Nuclear Test Ban Treaty	1963	U.S., Britain, and Russia agreed not to test in atmosphere, space, or under water without onsite inspection.
Nuclear Non-Proliferation Treaty	1968	U.S., Russia, and Britain with U.N. General Assembly, by which nations not having nuclear weapons agree not to develop them, effected 1970.
SALT I Accords	1972	U.S. and Russia agreed to limit ABM sites and to freeze size of offensive missile systems.
Panama Canal	1978	Canal returned to Panama.
SALT II Treaty	1979	Proposed U.S.-Soviet ceiling on strategic nuclear delivery vehicles. (Not ratified by Senate.)
Intermediate Nuclear Force Treaty	1987	U.S. and Soviet Union agreed to begin dismantling intermediate range nuclear weapons.
World Trade Agreement	1994	Establishing the World Trade Organization and including the General Agreement on Tariffs and Trade (GATT).

124. Political Assassinations

Abraham Lincoln	President	1865
Charles Caldwell	Black Senator from Mississippi	1875
James Garfield	President	1881
William Goebel	Kentucky gubernatorial candidate	1900
William McKinley	President	1901
Huey P. Long	Louisiana Senator	1935
Medgar Evers	NAACP field representative	1963
John F. Kennedy	President	1963
Malcolm X	Black spokesman	1965
George Lincoln Rockwell	founder, American Nazi Party	1967
Martin Luther King, Jr.	civil rights leader	1968
Robert Kennedy	New York Senator	1968
John Gorden Mein	U.S. Ambassador to Guatemala	1968
Joseph Yablonski	labor leader	1970
Leo Ryan	U.S. Representative	1978
George Mosone	Mayor of San Francisco	1978
Harvey Milk	San Francisco board of supervisors	1978
Adolph Dubs	U.S. Ambassador to Afghanistan	1979

125. Popular Mottoes and Slogans in U.S. History

Join or die.
Liberty or death.
No taxation without representation.
Liberty and no excise.
Free trade and sailors' rights.
Millions for defense but not one cent for tribute.
In God we trust.
Remember the Alamo.
Fifty-four Forty or Fight.
California or Bust.
Death before Dishonor.
Remember the Maine.
Loose lips sink ships.
The war to end all wars.
Better dead than Red.
America, love it or leave it.
WIN (Whip Inflation Now).
Just say no.

MISCELLANEOUS

126. Nicknames of Famous Americans

Sam Adams	Father of American Revolution
John James Audubon	American Woodsman
P. T. Barnum	Greatest Showman on Earth
Clara Barton	Angel of the Battlefield
Chuck Berry	Father of Rock and Roll
James G. Blaine	The Plumed Knight
William H. Bonney	Billy the Kid
Daniel Boone	Long Knife
Omar Bradley	Doughboy's General
William Jennings Bryan	The Peerless Leader of the Democratic Party
John C. Calhoun	Father of States' Rights; Onslow
Wilton Chamberlain	Wilt the Stilt
Lon Chaney	Man of a Thousand Faces
Charles Chaplin	The Little Tramp
John Chapman	Johnny Appleseed
Henry Clay	The Great Pacificator
Samiel Langhorne Clemens	Mark Twain
William F. Cody	Buffalo Bill
Stephen Douglas	The Little Giant
Thomas Edison	Wizard of Menlo Park
Adm. David Farragut	Hero of Mobile Bay
Benjamin Franklin	The American Socrates
Lou Gehrig	The Iron Man
Ernest Hemingway	Papa
James Butler Hickock	Wild Bill Hickock
Gen. Joseph E. Hooker	Fighting Joe
Sam Houston	Father of Texas
Washington Irving	Diedrich Knickerbocker
Claudia Johnson	Lady Bird
Mary Harris Jones	Mother Jones
Cherilyn LaPierre	Cher
Henry Lee	Lighthorse Harry
Robert E. Lee	Uncle Robert
Jenny Lind	The Swedish Nightingale
Charles Lindberg	Lucky Lindy; Lone Eagle
Henry P. Long	The Kingfish
Gen. George McClellan	Little Mac
John Naismith	Father of Basketball
Thomas Paine	Humanus
Gen. George Patton	Old Blood and Guts

126. *(continued)*

Gen. John J. Pershing	Blackjack Pershing
Elvis Presley	The King; The Pelvis
George Herman Ruth	Babe Ruth
Gen. Norman Schwarzkopf	Stormin' Norman
Gen. Winfield Scott	Old Fuss and Feathers
Gen. William T. Sherman	Old Tecump
Al Smith	The Happy Warrior
Harriet Tubman	Moses

127. Famous Americans Who Also Taught School

John Adams	U.S. President
Madeleine Albright	Secretary of State
Louisa May Alcott	author
Chester A. Arthur	U.S. President
Clara Barton	Founder of American Red Cross
Alexander Graham Bell	inventor
Dan Blocker	"Hoss," in "Bonanza"
Clarence Darrow	attorney
Amelia Earhart	aviator
Geraldine Ferraro	vice presidential candidate
Abigail Fillmore	First Lady
Roberta Flack	singer
Margaret Fuller	transcendentalist author; social reformer
Art Garfunkel	singer
John Wesley Hardin	outlaw
Lyndon B. Johnson	U.S. President
Janis Joplin	rock star
William McKinley	U.S. President
Anne Murray	singer
Carry Nation	temperance leader
Pat Nixon	First Lady
Thomas Paine	colonial patriot
Gen. John Pershing	chief of World War I American Expeditionary Force
William Quantrill	Confederate guerilla leader
Dixie Lee Ray	governor of Washington
Eleanor Roosevelt	First Lady, author, lecturer
Gene Simmons	member of rock group "KISS"
Margaret Chase Smith	U.S. Senator from Maine
Mary Church Terrell	social reformer

128. Sources for Genealogical Research

birth certificates
cemetery records
census records
church record
city directories
county histories
criminal records
death certificates
diaries
family Bibles
immigration records
land deeds
living relatives

marriage records
military records
naturalization records
newspaper files
probate court records
published family histories
school records
tax roles
telephone directories
tombstones
veteran pension records
wills

129. Helpful Resources for Online Genealogy Research

The following all offer valuable tutorials and resources for beginning and advanced family history researchers. Increasingly, access to actual historical documents are being made available through such portals.

Ancestry.com
http://www.ancestry.com

Cyndi's List of Genealogy Sites on the Internet
http://www.cyndislist.com

Family Search
http://www.familysearch.org

Family Tree Maker
http://familytreemaker.genealogy.com/index.html

Genealogy.com
http://www.genealogy.com

National Archives and Records Administration
http://www.nara.gov/

RoostsWeb.com
http://www.rootsweb.com/

Ultimate Family Tree
http://www.uftree.com/UFT/Nav/howtossetting.html

130. Naming Traditions

Many American and European groups followed this traditional pattern for naming their children.

1st son = father's father
2nd son = mother's father
3rd son = father
4th son = father's oldest brother
5th son = father's 2nd oldest brother or mother's oldest brother
1st daughter = mother's mother
2nd daughter = father's mother
3rd daughter = mother
4th daughter = mother's oldest sister
5th daughter = mother's 2nd oldest sister or father's oldest sister

131. History-Oriented Periodicals

American Heritage
American Historical Review
American History Illustrated
American Jewish Historical Review
American Quarterly
The America West
Art and Archaeology Newsletter
British Heritage
Canada West
Chicago History
Civil War Times Illustrated
Genealogical Helper
Historic Preservation
Indian Historian
Journal of American History
Journal of Interdisciplinary History
Journal of Southern History
Journal of the History of Ideas

Journal of Genealogy
Mankind: The Magazine of Popular History
Military Review
North Carolina Historical Review
North South Trader
Old West
Persimmon Hill
Social Education
Social Studies Review
Theory and Research in Social Education
True West
Virginia Cavalcade
Virginia Magazine of History and Biography
Wisconsin Magazine of History

132. Online Resources for Teaching U.S. History

American Colonist's Library
http://personal.pitnet.net/primarysources/

American Cultural History: The Twentieth Century
Kingwood College Library
http://www.nhmccd.edu/contracts/lrc/kc/decades.html

American Indian History
http://www.csulb.edu/projects/ais/index.html

American Memory, Library of Congress
http://memory.loc.gov/ammem/amhome.html

American Social History Project
http://www.ashp.cuny.edu/

ERIC Clearinghouse for Social Studies/Education
http://www.indiana.edu/ ~ ssdc/eric_chess.htm

Library of Congress Exhibitions
http://lcweb.loc.gov/exhibits/

Making of America
University of Michigan
http://moa.umdl.umich.edu/

National Center for History in the Schools
http://www.sscnet.ucla.edu/nchs/

National Council for History Education
http://www.history.org/nche/

National Museum of American History
http://www.si.edu/activity/planvis/museums/i-nmah.htm

Society for History Education
http://www.csulb.edu/ ~ histeach/#AboutSHE

Teaching Early American Topics
http://www.lehigh.edu/ ~ ejg1/topics.html

United States Historical Census Data Browser
University of Virginia
http://fisher.lib.virginia.edu/census/

Women's History in America
Women's International Center
http://www.wic.org/misc/history.htm

Lists for
World History

133. The Seven Wonders of the Ancient World

The Temple of Artemis at Euphesus on the west coast of present day Turkey, was built around 550 B.C. Except for the wooden roof this massive temple was built entirely of marble. The ornately decorated temple was dedicated to the Greek goddess Artemis. The original temple was destroyed and rebuilt several times. In 262 A.D. Goths destroyed the final structure. Today only the foundation and parts of the second temple survive.

The Statue of Zeus at Olympia, Greece, was built around 435 B.C. by the sculptor Phidias. It was dedicated to the king of gods, Zeus. The 40 foot high statue depicted Zeus on a golden throne. His robe and ornaments were made of gold and his skin of ivory. It was probably destroyed by invading armies.

The Lighthouse of Alexandria, Egypt, was built during the reign of Ptolemy (283–246 B.C.) on the island of Pharos. It rose approximately 440 feet. It stood on a massive platform of three sections; the bottom one was square, the middle octagonal, and the top circular. The fire at the top guided ships into the harbor for over a thousand years before it was brought down by an earthquake.

The Mausoleum at Halicarnassus was a massive marble tomb built for King Mausolus, a Persian Empire ruler who died in 353 B.C. Located in present-day southwestern Turkey it was built by his widow Artemisia, who was also his sister. The fame of the tomb provided the source of the term "mausoleum." While the tomb survived 1900 years, it was finally toppled by an earthquake.

The Colossus of Rhodes was erected at the Harbor of Rhodes on the Aegean Sea in the early 200's B.C. The huge bronze statue was built in honor of the sun god Helios. The hollow statue was built of stone blocks and iron support bars with thin copper plating. It stood 1200 feet tall. It was destroyed by an earthquake in 224 B.C. In 667 A.D. its remains were sold for scrap.

The Hanging Gardens of Babylon were built by King Nebuchadnezzar II near modern day Baghdad in Iraq. Historians speculate that the gardens were built by the king for one of his wives. The garden was laid out on a massive brick terrace approximately 400 feet square and 75 feet high. An elaborate irrigation system brought water from the Euphrates River.

The Pyramids of Egypt are the only Wonder of the Ancient World still standing. They were also the oldest of the Ancient Wonders. They were built as tombs for the Egyptian kings. One of the most famous of the pyramids is the Great Pyramid of Cheops built around 2600 B.C. It stands 4821 feet high near Cairo.

134. Ancient Units of Measurement

cubit	length of a man's arm from the end of the middle finger to the elbow (about 18 to 22 inches)
hand	the breadth of the human palm (about 4 inches)
foot	length of a man's foot
yard	distance from a man's nose to the tip of his middle finger
dinar	.15 ounce (Arabia)
stadium	606 feet
drachma	.154 ounces
mina	100 drachmas
swan	100 minas
shekel	about $\frac{1}{2}$ oz.
amphora	6.84 gallons (Rome)
ephah	1.1 bushels

135. The Code of Hammurabi (circa 1780 B.C.)

Translated by L. W. King (1915)

The Code of Hammurabi, proclaimed by sixth king of the Amorite Dynasty of Old Babylon, is recognized as the earliest-known example of a ruler declaring publicly a complete body of laws. A few examples of rules dictated in the code:

15. If any one take a male or female slave of the court, or a male or female slave of a freed man, outside the city gates [to escape], he shall be put to death.

16. If any one receive into his house a runaway male or female slave of the court, or of a freedman, and does not bring it out at the public proclamation of the [police], the master of the house shall be put to death.

21. If any one break a hole into a house (break in to steal), he shall be put to death before that hole and be buried.

22. If any one is committing a robbery and is caught, then he shall be put to death.

25. If fire break out in a house, and some one who comes to put it out cast his eye upon the property of the owner of the house, and take the property of the master of the house, he shall be thrown into that self-same fire.

53. If any one be too lazy to keep his dam in proper condition, and does not so keep it; if then the dam break and all the fields be flooded, then shall he in whose dam the break occurred be sold for money, and the money shall replace the [grain] which he has caused to be ruined.

110. If a "sister of a god" open a tavern, or enter a tavern to drink, then shall this woman be burned to death.

135. *(continued)*

127. If any one "point the finger" (slander) at a sister of a god or the wife of any one, and can not prove it, this man shall be taken before the judges and his brow shall be marked (by cutting the skin, or perhaps hair).

138. If a man wishes to separate from his wife who has borne him no children, he shall give her the amount of her purchase money and the dowry which she brought from her father's house, and let her go.

142. If a woman quarrel with her husband, and say: "You are not congenial to me," the reasons for her prejudice must be presented. If she is guiltless, and there is no fault on her part, but he leaves and neglects her, then no guilt attaches to this woman, she shall take her dowry and go back to her father's house.

162. If a man marry a woman, and she bear sons to him; if then this woman die, then shall her father have no claim on her dowry; this belongs to her sons.

195. If a son strike his father, his hands shall be [cut] off.

196. If a [noble-]man put out the eye of another [noble-]man, his eye shall be put out.

197. If he break another [noble-]man's bone, his bone shall be broken.

198. If he put out the eye of a freed man, or break the bone of a freed man, he shall pay one gold mina.

199. If he put out the eye of a man's slave, or break the bone of a man's slave, he shall pay one-half of its value.

200. If a man knock out the teeth of his equal, his teeth shall be knocked out.

229. If a builder build a house for some one, and does not construct it properly, and the house which he built fall in and kill its owner, then that builder shall be put to death.

230. If it (a house) kill the son of the owner, the son of that builder shall be put to death.

231. If it (a house) kill a slave of the owner, then he shall pay slave for slave to the owner of the house.

136. Innovations and Contributions of Ancient Sumer

adoption	jewelry	tuition
drug catalog	literature	universities
elementary schools	pear	wheel
harp	schools	wheeled vehicles
jacks (game)	theater	writing

137. Innovations and Contributions of Ancient Egypt

advertisements
books
bowling
bread
candy
checkers
clarinet
dice
domestic cats
embalming
football
gambling

ink
masonry
oboe
paper
papyrus
pens
postal system
sailing
sundial
tapestry
tunnel
water clocks

138. Major Egyptian Deities

Amon	king of the gods
Anubis	god of the dead
Geb	god of the earth
Horus	god of heaven and light
Isis	goddess of fertility
Ptah	god of fertility
Re or **Ra**	sun god, ruler of the world
Set	god of evil; god of the desert
Shu	god of light, air, supporter of the sky
Thoth	moon god; god of learning and wisdom

139. Innovations and Contributions of Ancient Greece

Archimedean screw
boxing
column
drama
encyclopedia

geometry
libraries
lighthouses
mime
mosaic floors

philosophy
public education
sculpture
shorthand

140. Authors of Ancient Greece

Aeschylus   Homer
Aristophanes   Plato
Demosthenes   Sophocles
Euripides   Thucydides
Herodotus

141. Greek Deities

Aeolus	gods of the winds
Aesculapius	god of healing
Aphrodite	goddess of love
Apollo	god of music, purity, and poetry
Ares	god of war
Artemis	goddess of hunting and childbirth
Asclepius	god of healing
Athena	goddess of wisdom and war
Chloris	goddess of flowers
Cronus	ruler of the Titans
Demeter	goddess of growing things
Dionysus	god of wine, fertility, and wild behavior
Eris	goddess of strife and discord
Eros	god of love
Hades	god of the underworld
Hephaestus	god of fire
Hermes	god of commerce and science
Hestia	goddess of the hearth
Hygeia	goddess of health
Hypnos	god of sleep
Morpheus	god of dreams
Nemesis	goddess of vengeance
Nike	goddess of victory
Nyx	goddess of night
Pan	god of the forest and pastures
Plutus	god of wealth
Poseidon	god of the sea, horses, and earthquakes
Rhea	mother of the Olympian goddesses and gods
Selene	goddess of the moon
Thantos	god of death
Uranus	god of heaven
Zeus	ruler of heaven; chief of the deities

142. The Greek Alphabet

Alpha	A	α	**Nu**	N	ν
Beta	B	β	**Xi**	Ξ	ξ
Gamma	Γ	γ	**Omicron**	O	o
Delta	Δ	δ	**Pi**	Π	π
Epsilon	E	ε	**Rho**	P	ρ
Zeta	Z	ζ	**Sigma**	Σ	σ
Eta	H	η	**Tau**	T	τ
Theta	Θ	θ	**Upsilon**	Υ	υ
Iota	I	ι	**Phi**	Φ	φ
Kappa	K	κ	**Chi**	X	χ
Lamda	Λ	λ	**Psi**	Ψ	ψ
Mu	M	μ	**Omega**	Ω	ω

143. Innovations and Contributions of Ancient Rome

bilingual education
circus
concrete
Julian calendar
newspapers

one-way streets
paved roads
state-supported schools
stone bridges
stop signs

144. Authors of Ancient Rome

Cattullus
Cicero
Gate the Elder
Gaius Lucilius
Gnaeus Naevius
Horace
Juvenal
Livy
Lucan
Lucius Accius
Lucius Aurelius
Lucretius

Marcus Aurelius
Martial
Marcus Pacuvius
Ovid
Pliny the Elder
Quintus Ennius
Sallust
Seneca
Tacitus
Varro
Virgil

145. Roman Deities

Aurora	goddess of the dawn
Bacchus	god of wine, fertility, and wild behavior
Ceres	goddess of growing things
Coelus	god of heaven
Cupid	god of love
Diana	goddess of hunting and childbirth
Dis	god of the underworld
Faunus	god of fields and shepherds
Janus	god of entryways
Juno	queen of the gods; Jupiter's wife
Jupiter	ruler of the gods
Juventas	goddess of youth
Luna	goddess of the moon
Mars	god of war
Mercury	god of commerce and science
Minerva	goddess of crafts, war, and wisdom
Mors	god of death
Neptune	god of the sea
Nox	god of night
Picus	god who foretold the future
Pluto	god of the underworld
Pomona	goddess of fruits and trees
Psyche	goddess of the soul
Salacia	goddess of the oceans
Saturn	god of agriculture
Somnus	god of sleep
Terminus	god of boundries
Tiberinus	god of the Tiber River
Venus	goddess of love
Vesta	goddess of the hearth
Victoria	goddess of victory
Vulcan	god of fire

146. Roman Numerals

1	I	90	XC
2	II	100	C
3	III	200	CC
4	IV	300	CCC
5	V	400	CD
6	VI	500	D
7	VII	600	DC
8	VIII	700	DCC
9	IX	800	DCCC
10	X	900	CM
11	XI	1,000	M
12	XII	1,100	MC
13	XIII	1,200	MCC
14	XIV	1,300	MCCC
15	XV	1,400	MCD
16	XVI	1,500	MD
17	XVII	2,000	MM
18	XVIII	2,100	MMC
19	XIX	3,000	MMM
20	XX	4,000	$M\overline{V}$
30	XXX	5,000	$\overline{V}$
40	XL	10,000	$\overline{X}$
50	L	20,000	$\overline{XX}$
60	LX	50,000	$\overline{L}$
70	LXX	100,000	$\overline{C}$
80	LXXX	500,000	$\overline{D}$

Note: The numerals V, X, L, C, D, or M shown with a horizontal line above denote 1,000 times the original value.

MCXVIII

147. Romance Languages

French
Italian
Portuguese
Romanian
Spanish

148. Contributions and Innovations of China

brandy
cannon
cast iron
chess
collar harness
compass
cross bow
decimal mathematics
drive belt
fireworks
fishing reel
flame thrower
grenades
gun powder
guns
hot air balloon
immunology
iron plowshare
kite
lacquer
liquor
Mandarin orange
mechanical clock
moldboard plow
mortars
multi-stage rocket
negative numbers

paddle wheel
paper
paper money
parachutes
playing cards
poison gas
porcelain
printing
relief maps
rocket
rotary fan
row planting
seed drill
seismograph
ship's rudder
sliding caliper
soybean
spinning wheel
stirrup
suspension bridge
tea
tear gas
umbrella
underwater mine
water power
wheelbarrow
whiskey

149. The Analects of Confucius

(selected examples)

"To study and not think is a waste. To think and not study is dangerous."

"Reviewing what you have learned and learning anew, you are fit to be a teacher."

"If a person lacks trustworthiness, I don't know what s/he can be good for. When a pin is missing from the yoke-bar of a large wagon, or from the collar-bar of a small wagon, how can it go?"

"If you do everything with a concern for your own advantage, you will be resented by many people."

"When you see a good person, think of becoming like her/him. When you see someone not so good, reflect on your own weak points."

"If you are virtuous, you will not be lonely. You will always have friends."

"If everybody hates something, you'd better check into it. If everybody loves something, you'd better check into it."

"To make a mistake and not correct it: this is a real mistake."

Source: Charles Muller, Resources for the Study of East Asian Language and Thought, www.human.toyogakuen-u.ac.jp/~ acmuller/contao/analects.htm.

150. Early Weapons

articulated club	crossbow	slingshot
axe	dagger	spear
blowgun	flail	sword
boomerang	gauntlet	throwing club
bow and arrow	halberd	tomahawk
catapult	mace	war hammer
chakram	rapier	whip
club		

151. The Signs of the Zodiac

Capricorn	goat	Dec. 22–Jan. 19
Aquarius	water bearer	Jan. 20–Feb. 18
Pisces	fishes	Feb. 19–Mar. 20
Aries	ram	Mar. 21–Apr. 19
Taurus	bull	Apr. 20–May 20
Gemini	twins	May 21–June 20
Cancer	crab	June 21–July 22
Leo	lion	July 23–Aug. 22
Virgo	virgin	Aug. 23–Sept. 22
Libra	scales	Sept. 23–Oct. 22
Scorpio	scorpion	Oct. 23–Nov. 21
Sagittarius	archer	Nov. 22–Dec. 21

152. Hebrew Months

Tishri (September–October)

Heshvan, or Marheshvan (October–November)

Kislev (November–December)

Tevet (December–January)

Shevat (January–February)

Adar (February–March)

Nisan (March–April)

Iyyar (April–May)

Sivan (May–June)

Temmuz (June–July)

Av (July–August)

Elul (August–September)

153. Jewish Holidays

Pesach	(Passover)
Shavuos	(Pentecost)
Fast of Tisha B'Av	(Ninth of Av)
Rosh Hashana	(New Year)
Yom Kippur	(Day of Atonement)
Sukkot	(Tabernacles)
Hanukka	(Feast of Dedication)
Purim	(Feast of Lots)

154. The Ten Commandments

1. I am the Lord your God.
2. You shall take no other gods before me. You shall not make for yourself a sculptured image.
3. You shall not swear falsely by name of the Lord your God.
4. Remember the sabbath and keep it holy.
5. Honor your father and mother.
6. You shall not murder.
7. You shall not commit adultry.
8. You shall not steal.
9. You should not bear false witness against your neighbor.
10. You should not covet your neighbor's house or wife or anything that is your neighbor's.

155. The Seven Deadly Sins

avarice
pride
wrath
lust
gluttony
sloth
envy

156. Fifteenth-Century English Recipe

Take fair pork, the fore quarter, and take off the skin; and put the pork on a fair spit, and roast it half enough; then take it off and smite it in fair pieces, and cast it on a fair pot; then take onions and shred them and peel them, and not too small, and fry in a pan of fair grease; then cast them in the pot to the pork; then take good broth of mutton or of beef, and cast thereto, and cast thereto powder pepper, canel, cloves, and mace, and let them boil well together; then take fair bread, and vinegar, and steep the bread with the same broth, and strain it on blood, with ale, or else with saunders, and salt, and let them boil enough, and serve it forth.

2 lb pork roast (i.e. about 1½ lb meat)
2 big onions, sliced and fried in lard
5 c beef broth (water plus 5 bouillon cubes, or canned beef broth)
¼ t pepper
1 t cinnamon
¼ t cloves
¼ t mace
¼ c vinegar
¼ loaf of bread = ~ 1 c torn up
small pinch of saunders
½ t at least of salt

Source: "Two Fifteenth Century," p. 8/52 (GOOD) from David Friedman & Elizabeth Cook, "A Miscellany." Online at http://www.daviddfriedman.com/Medieval/miscellany_pdf/Miscellany.htm. Used with permission.

157. Early Explorers of the Americas

982	Eric the Red	off coast of Canada
1000	Leif Ericson	Newfoundland (?)
1492	Christopher Columbus	Carribean Islands
1497	John Cabot	Nova Scotia or Newfoundland
1498	John and Sebastian Cabot	North American coast
1499	Amerigo Vespucci	South America & West Indies
1499	Alonso de Ojeda	South American coast
1500	Vincent y Pinzon	Amazon River
1500	Pedro Alvares Cabral	Brazil
1513	Vasco Nunex de Balboa	Pacific Ocean
1513	Juan Ponce de Leon	Florida
1519	Alonso de Pineda	Mississippi River delta
1519	Hernando Cortés	Mexico
1520	Ferdinand Magellan	Tierra del Fuego, Straits of Magellan

(continued)

157. *(continued)*

1524	Giovanni da Verrazano	North American east coast
1532	Francisco Pizarro	Peru
1534	Jacques Cartier	Canada
1536	Cabeza de Vaca	inland Texas
1539	Francisco do Ulloa	California coast
1539	Hernando de Soto	Mississippi River
1540	Francisco V. de Coronado	U.S. southwest
1540	Hernando Alarcon	Colorado River
1541	Francisco de Orellana	Amazon River
1565	Pedro Menendez de Aviles	St. Augustine
1576	Martin Frobisher	Frobisher's Bay, Canada
1577	Sir Francis Drake	California coast
1585	Sir Walter Raleigh's men	Outer Banks, North Carolina
1598	Juan de Oñate	American southwest
1603	Samuel de Champlain	Lake Champlain, Canada
1607	John Smith	Atlantic coast
1609	Henry Hudson	Hudson Bay, Hudson River
1634	Jean Nicolet	Wisconsin, Lake Michigan
1673	Louis Jolliet, Jacques Marquette	Mississippi River
1679	Louis Hennepin	upper Mississippi River
1682	Sieur de La Salle	Mississippi River
1731	Pierre Gaultier de Varennes	Saskatchewan

158. Foods Eaten by Explorers at Sea

Ever wonder what Christopher Columbus and his crew might have eaten during their long sea voyages? Here are items that would have comprised the typical fare for sea-goers of that era.

salt-cured meats (beef and pork)	peas
raisins	black-eyed peas
rice	goat cheese
salt cod	salted flour
sardines	vinegar
anchovies	honey
sea biscuits (hardtack)	wine
olives	water
olive oil	molasses
dry chickpeas	

Source: Lucio Sorré, *Christopher Columbus: His Gastronomic Persona.* Online at tellobanfi.com/features/story_3.html.

159. Major Indigenous Groups of Latin America

Araucanian
Arawak
Aztec
Carib Chibcha
Gê
Inca
Jivaro
Maya
Olmec
Ona
Tarascan
Toltec
Tupí-Guaraní
Zapotac

160. The Europeans Brought to the Americas . . .

barley
carnation
chicken
Christianity
coffee
cow
crab grass
daffodil
daisy
dandelion

diphtheria
honeybee
horse
lemon
lettuce
malaria
measles
olive
orange

peach
pear
pig
rice
sheep
smallpox
tulip
turnip
wheat

161. The Old World Obtained from the Americas . . .

avocado
bell pepper
cacao (chocolate)
cashew
chili pepper
corn
kidney bean
lima bean
marigold

navy bean
peanut
pecan
pineapple
poinsettia
potato
pumpkin
quinine

squash
sunflower
sweet potato
syphilis
tobacco
tomato
turkey
vanilla

162. The Allies of World War I

Belgium
Brazil
British Empire
China
Costa Rica
Cuba
France
Greece
Guatemala
Haiti
Honduras
Italy
Japan
Liberia
Montenegro
Nicaragua
Panama
Romania
Russia
San Marino
Serbia
Siam
United States

163. The Central Powers of World War I

Austria-Hungary
Bulgaria
Germany
Ottoman Empire

164. Battle Casualties of World War I

Russia	1,700,000
Germany	1,600,000
France	1,385,300
Great Britain	900,000
Austria	800,000
Italy	460,000
Serbia	325,000
Turkey	250,000
Belgium	102,000
Romania	100,000
United States	67,813
Bulgaria	46,000
Greece	7,000
Montenegro	3,000
	2,000

165. Timeline of Aviation History

1783	Frenchman Jean Pilâtre de Rozier made the first human balloon flight.
1797	André-Jacques Garnerin made the first parachute jump.
1894	Otto Lilienthal made glider flights of over 1000 feet.
1903	Orville and Wilber Wright made the first powered flight in a heavier-than-air machine at Kitty Hawk, NC.
1908	Lieutenant Thomas Selfridge became the first passenger fatality in a powered aircraft.
1910	Zeppelin airship begins commercial service.
1914	The first scheduled air service began in Florida on January 1.
1915	Frenchman Roland Garros became the first fighter pilot to shoot down an airplane in air-to-air combat.
1919	Capt. John Alcock and Lt. Arthur Whitten Brown, British World War I fliers, made the first nonstop transatlantic flight.
1927	Charles Lindbergh made the first solo trans-Atlantic non-stop flight.
1930	Frank Whittle patented the jet engine.
1932	Amelia Earhart was the first woman to fly the Atlantic alone.
1937	Fiery crash of the Hindenburg in New Jersey marked the end of the era of the great airships (dirigibles).
1947	Charles E. "Chuck" Yeager flew the X-1 past the sound barrier.
1958	Boeing 707 entered commercial flight, with a capacity of 181 passengers.
1958	First transatlantic jet passenger service offered.
1970	Boeing 747 entered into service.
1976	Concord entered into service.
1991	Stealth Fighter used in the Gulf War.
1998	Over Iraq during Operation Desert Fox, Lt. Kendra Williams became the first U.S. female combat pilot to bomb an enemy target.

Source: Wright Brothers Aeroplane Company and Museum of Pioneer Aviation. Online at http://www.first-to-fly.com/; Lindberg Foundation at http://www.lindberghfoundation.org.

166. The Allies of World War II

Argentina	France	Nicaragua
Australia	Great Britain	Norway
Belgium	Greece	Panama
Bolivia	Guatemala	Paraguay
Brazil	Haiti	Peru
Canada	Honduras	Poland
China	India	Russia
Colombia	Iran	Saudi Arabia
Costa Rica	Iraq	South Africa
Cuba	Lebanon	Syria
Czechoslovakia	Liberia	Turkey
Denmark	Luxembourg	United States
Dominican Republic	Mexico	Uruguay
Ecuador	Mongolian People's	Venezuela
Egypt	Republic	Yugoslavia
El Salvador	Netherlands	
Ethiopia	New Zealand	

167. Allied Military Leaders of World War II

Harold Alexander	Oveta Hobby	Chester Nimitz
Henry Arnold	Ernest King	George S. Patton, Jr.
Omar Bradley	William Leahy	Matthew Ridgeway
Claire Chennault	Curtis LeMay	Joseph Stilwell
Mark Clark	Douglas MacArthur	Maxwell Taylor
Lucius Clay	George C. Marshall	Jonathan Wainwright
James Doolittle	Andrew McNaughton	Archibald Wavell
Dwight D. Eisenhower	Bernard Montgomery	Georgi Zhukov
William Halsey, Jr.	Louis Mountbatten	

168. The Axis Powers of World War II

Albania	Italy
Bulgaria	Japan
Finland	Romania
Germany	Thailand
Hungary	

169. Axis Military Leaders

Karl Doenitz
Hermann Goering
Alfred Jodl
Wilhelm Keitel
Erwin Rommel
Isoruku Yamamoto
Tomobumi Yamashita

170. Authors Whose Books Were Burned by the Nazis

In May of 1933 massive book burnings were conducted throughout Germany by the Nazis. The following authors were among those whose books were burned:

Alfred Adler
Albert Einstein
Sigmund Freud
Maxim Gorki
Heinrich Heine
Ernest Hemingway
Helen Keller
Nikolai Lenin
Jack London
Heinrich Mann
Thomas Mann
Karl Marx

Marcel Proust
Upton Sinclair
Leon Trotsky

171. Weapons of World War II

aerial bombs
aircraft cannons
anti-aircraft guns
assault weapons
atomic bombs
bayonets
bazookas
daggers
depth charges

explosives
field artillery
flamethrowers
hand grenades
incendiary bombs
land mines
machine guns
mortars
naval guns

naval mines
recoilless rifles
rifle grenades
rifles
rockets
semi-automatic pistols
sub-machine guns
V-2 rockets

172. Major Confrontations of World War II

Dunkirk	Kursk
Battle of Britain	Anzio/Cassino
Moscow	Kohima/Imphal
Malta	The Normandy Invasion
Sinking of the *Bismarck*	Arnhem
Midway	Battle of the Bulge
Guadalcanal	Berlin
El Alamein	Okinawa
Stalingrad	

173. Original Members of the United Nations (1945)

Argentina	El Salvador	Panama
Australia	Ethiopia	Paraguay
Belgium	France	Peru
Bolivia	Greece	Philippines
Brazil	Guatemala	Poland
Byelorussian Soviet	Haiti	Saudi Arabia
Socialist Republic	Honduras	South Africa
Canada	India	Syria
Chile	Iran	Turkey
China	Iraq	Ukrainian Soviet
Colombia	Lebanon	Socialist Republic
Costa Rica	Liberia	Union of Soviet
Cuba	Luxembourg	Socialist Republics
Czechoslovakia	Mexico	United Kingdom
Denmark	Netherlands	United States
Dominican Republic	New Zealand	Uruguay
Ecuador	Nicaragua	Venezuela
Egypt	Norway	Yugoslavia

174. Agencies of the United Nations

General Agreement on Tariffs and Trade (GATT)
Food and Agriculture Organization (FAQ)
International Atomic Energy Agency (LAEA)
International Bank for Reconstruction and Development (World Bank)
International Civil Aviation Organization (ICAO)
International Development Association (IDA)
International Finance Corporation (IFC)
International Fund for Agricultural Development (IFAD)
International Labor Organization (ILO)
International Marine Organization (IMO)
International Monetary Fund (IMF)
International Telecommunication Union (ITU)
United Nations Educational, Scientific and Cultural Organization (UNESCO)
United Nations Industrial Development Organization (UNIDO)
Universal Postal Union (UPU)
World Health Organization (WHO)
World Intellectual Property Organization (WIPO)
World Meteorological Organization (WMO)

175. United Nations Secretaries General

Secretary General	Country	Elected
Trygve Lie	Norway	1946
Dag Hammarskjöld	Sweden	1953
U Thant	Burma	1961
Kurt Waldheim	Austria	1972
Javier Perez de Cuellar	Peru	1982
Boutros Boutros-Ghali	Egypt	1992
Kofi Annan	Ghana	1997

176. Greatest Engineering Achievements of the Twentieth Century

1. Electrification
2. Automobile
3. Airplane
4. Water Supply and Distribution
5. Electronics
6. Radio and Television
7. Agricultural Mechanization
8. Computers
9. Telephone
10. Air Conditioning and Refrigeration
11. Highways
12. Spacecraft
13. Internet
14. Imaging
15. Household Appliances
16. Health Technologies
17. Petroleum and Petrochemical Technologies
18. Laser and Fiber Optics
19. Nuclear Technologies
20. High-performance Materials

Source: National Academy of Engineering. Used with permission.

177. Major Allies of the Persian Gulf War

Bangladesh
Britain
Egypt
France
Kuwait
Morocco
Oman
Pakistan
Qatar
Saudi Arabia
Syria
United Arab Emirates
United States

178. Former Republics of the U.S.S.R.

Armenia
Azerbaijan
Byelorussia
Estonia
Georgia
Kazakhstan
Kirghizia
Latvia
Lithuania
Moldavia
Russia
Tadzhikistan
Turkmenistan
Ukraine
Uzbekistan

179. Members of the European Union

Members	*Applicant countries**
Belgium	Bulgaria
Denmark	Cyprus
Germany	Czech Republic
Greece	Estonia
Spain	Hungary
France	Latvia
Ireland	Lithuania
Italy	Malta
Luxembourg	Poland
the Netherlands	Romania
Austria	Slovakia
Portugal	Slovenia
Finland	Turkey
Sweden	
United Kingdom	

*As of March 2002

Source: European Union Web site, March 1, 2002. Online at http://www.eudelindia.org/eu/default.htm.

180. Common Currency (EURO) Participants

Belgium	Italy
Germany	Luxembourg
Greece	The Netherlands
Spain	Austria
France	Portugal
Ireland	Finland

181. Political Assassinations of Modern Times

Victim	Position	Year
Abraham Lincoln	President of the U.S.	1865
Justo Jose de Urquiza	President of Argentina	1870
James Garfield	President of the U.S.	1881
William McKinley	President of the U.S.	1901
Butrus Pasha Ghali	Premier of Egypt	1910
Peter Arkadevich Stolypin	Prime Minister of Russia	1911
Frances Ferdinand	Archduke of Austria	1914
Grigori Rasputin	Advisor to Russian Czar	1916
Nicholas II & family	Czar of Russia	1918
Emiliano Zapata	Mexican revolutionary	1919
Alexander I	King of Yugoslavia	1934
Leon Trotsky	Russian revolutionary	1934
Benito Mussolini	Italian dictator	1945
Mohandas Ghandi	Nationalist of India	1948
Ngo Dinh Dien	President of Vietnam	1963
John F. Kennedy	President of U.S.	1963
Malcolm X	Black spokesman	1965
Robert Kennedy	Attorney General of the U.S.	1968
Martin Luther King	U.S. civil rights leader	1968
Zulfikar Bhutto	Ex–prime minister of Pakistan	1979
Louis Mountbatten	Earl of Burma	1979
Anwar Sadat	President of Egypt	1981
Benigno Aquino, Jr.	Philippine politician	1983
Indira Ghandi	Prime Minister of India	1984
Rajiv Ghandi	Former Prime Minister of India	1991
Yitzhak Rabin	Israeli Prime Minister	1995

HEALTH, WEALTH, AND POPULATION

182. AIDS Statistics

- 19 million have died from AIDS.
- 34.3 million people in the world have AIDS.
- 24.5 million of AIDS victims live in sub-Saharan Africa.
- 3.8 million of them are children under the age of 15.
- 5.4 million new AIDS infections occurred in 1999, 4 million of them in Africa.
- 2.8 million died of AIDS in 1999, 85 percent of them in Africa.
- More than 500,000 babies were infected in 1999 by their mothers, predominantly residents of sub-Saharan Africa.
- 13.2 million children have been orphaned by AIDS; 12.1 million of them in sub-Saharan Africa.
- Approximately one of every four people in Zimbabwe and Botswana have AIDS.

Source: UNAIDS, an umbrella group for five U.N. agencies, the World Bank and the World Health Organization, December 2001.

183. Healthy Life Expectancy Rankings

Based on the World Health Organization's Disability Adjusted Life Expectancy (DALE)

Country	Overall	Males	Females
Japan	74.5	71.9	77.2
Australia	73.2	70.8	75.5
France	73.1	69.3	76.9
Sweden	73.0	71.2	74.9
Spain	72.8	69.8	75.7
Italy	72.7	70.0	75.4
Greece	72.5	70.5	74.6
Switzerland	72.5	69.5	75.5
Canada	72.0	70.0	74.0
United Kingdom	71.7	69.7	73.7
United States	70.0	67.5	72.6

(continued)

183. *(continued)*

Country	Overall	Males	Females
Lowest:			
Ethiopia	33.5	33.5	33.5
Mali	33.1	32.6	33.5
Zimbabwe	32.9	33.4	32.4
Rwanda	32.8	32.9	32.7
Uganda	32.7	32.9	32.5
Botswana	32.3	32.3	32.3
Malawi	29.4	29.3	29.4
Niger	29.1	28.1	30.1
Sierra Leone	25.9	25.8	26.0

Disability Adjusted Life Expectancy (DALE) summarizes the expected number of years to be lived in what might be termed the equivalent of "full health." To calculate DALE, the years of ill health are weighted according to severity and subtracted from the expected overall life expectancy to give the equivalent years of healthy life.

Source: World Health Organization, 2001.

184. Richest Countries

Country	Per Capita GDP*
1. Luxembourg	$34,200
2. United States	33,900
3. Singapore	27,800
4. Switzerland	27,100
5. Monaco	27,000
6. Norway	25,100
7. Belgium	23,900
8. Denmark	23,800
9. Iceland	23,500
10. Austria	23,400

*Gross Domestic Product is the value of the goods and services a country produces.

185. Poorest Countries

	Country	Per Capita GDP*
1.	Sierra Leone	$500
2.	Tanzania	550
3.	Ethiopia	560
4.	Somalia	600
5.	Cambodia	710
6.	Congo	710
7.	Rwanda	720
8.	Comoros	725
9.	Burundi	730
10.	Eritrea	750

*Gross Domestic Product is the value of the goods and services a country produces.

Source: The World Factbook, 2000.

186. Least Developed Countries

Afghanistan
Angola
Bangladesh
Benin
Bhutan
Burkina Faso
Burundi
Cambodia
Cape Verde
Central African Republic
Chad
Comoros
Democratic Republic of the Congo
Djibouti
Equatorial Guinea
Eritrea

Ethiopia
Gambia
Guinea
Guinea-Bissau
Haiti
Kiribati
Lao People's Democratic Republic
Lesotho
Liberia
Madagascar
Malawi
Maldives
Mali
Mauritania
Mozambique
Myanmar

Nepal
Niger
Rwanda
Samoa
Sao Tome and Principe
Sierra Leone
Solomon Islands
Somalia
Sudan
Togo
Tuvalu
Uganda
United Republic of Tanzania
Vanuatu
Yemen
Zambia

Source: World Urbanization Prospects, 1999 Revision. United Nations Population Division.

187. The Work Week Worldwide

Average hours worked per week by full-time employees:

Korea	55.1
Turkey	54.1
Argentina	53.5
China	42.4
United States	42.4
Great Britain	41.9
France	40.3
Japan	36.3
Germany	31.5
Global average	44.6

188. World Population Growth (in billions)

	1950	1975	2000	2030*
World	2.52	4.07	6.06	8.11
More developed regions	0.81	1.05	1.19	1.21
Less developed regions	1.71	3.03	4.87	6.90

*projected

Source: World Urbanization Prospects, 1999 Revision. United Nations Population Division.

189. World Population Milestones

1 billion in 1804
2 billion in 1927
3 billion in 1960
4 billion in 1974
5 billion in 1987
6 billion in 1999
7 billion in 2010 (projected)

Source: United Nations Population Division.

LANGUAGE AND CULTURE

190. Major Languages of the World

Arabic	Japanese	Tamil
Bengali	Javanese	Telugu
Cantonese	Korean	Thai
English	Malay-Indonesian	Turkish
French	Mandarin	Ukranian
German	Portuguese	Urdu
Hindi	Russian	Vietnamese
Italian	Spanish	Wu

191. Major Languages of Europe

Albanian	Frisian	Portuguese
Basque	Gaelic	Provencal
Breton	German	Rhaeto-Romanic
Bulgarian	Greek	Romany
Catalan	Hungarian	Rumanian
Croatian	Icelandic	Russian
Czech	Italian	Serbian
Danish	Lappish	Slovak
Dutch	Latin	Slovenian
English	Latvian	Sorbian
Estonian	Luxembourgian	Spanish
Faroese	Macedonian	Swedish
Finnish	Norwegian	Welsh
Flemish	Polish	Yiddish
French		

192. "Hello" in Other Languages

Czech	pozdroav	**Portuguese**	alô
French	bonjour	**Spanish**	buenos días
German	guten tag	**Svensk**	hallå!
Italian	buon giorno	**Swahili**	maamkio
Polish	halo		

193. "Peace" in Other Languages

Czech	mir, pokoj
French	paix
Gaelic	tosd!
German	der Friede
Italian	pace
Latin	pax
Polish	pokoju, spokój
Portuguese	paz
Spanish	paz
Svensk	frid
Swahili	amani

194. "Love" in Other Languages

Czech	milovati
French	amour
German	die Lieba
Gaelic	gradhaich
Italian	amore
Latin	amor
Portuguese	amor
Spanish	amar
Swahili	upendo

195. Origins of the Names of the Months

January	named after Janus, Roman god of entryways
February	from Februa, the Roman festival of purification celebrated on February 15
March	named for Mars, the Roman god of war
April	from *aperire,* Latin for "to open"
May	derived from *maiores,* Latin for "elders." Romans honored the elderly during this month.
June	either from Juno, the Roman queen of the goddesses, or from *juniores* Latin for "youngsters"
July	named in honor of Julius Caesar
August	named in honor of Roman emperor, Augustus Caesar
September	from *septem,* Latin for seven. This was the seventh month in the Roman calendar.
October	from *octo,* Latin for eight
November	from *novem,* Latin for nine
December	from *decem,* Latin for ten

196. Origins of the Names of the Days of the Week

Sunday	from *Solis Dies,* Latin for "sun's day"
Monday	from *Monan Dæg,* Anglo-Saxon for "moon's day"
Tuesday	from *Tiwes Dæg,* Anglo-Saxon form for Tyr, Norse god of war
Wednesday	from *Wodnes Dæg,* Anglo-Saxon spelling of Odin, the Norse god of war and victory
Thursday	from *Thueres Dæg,* after Thor, the Norse god of thunder
Friday	from *Friges Dæg,* after the Norse goddess of love, Frigg
Saturday	named for the Roman god Saturn

197. Days of the Week in Japan

Nichiyoubi	Sun's Day	Sunday
Getsuyoubi	Moon's Day	Monday
Kayoubi	Fire's Day	Tuesday
Suiyoubi	Water's Day	Wednesday
Mokuyoubi	Wood's Day	Thursday
Kinyoubi	Gold's Day	Friday
Doyoubi	Earth's Day	Saturday

198. Irish Proverbs

It's a dirty bird that won't keep its own nest clean.
A bad workman quarrels with his tools.
Young people don't know what old age is, and old people forget what youth was.
The schoolhouse bell sounds bitter in youth and sweet in old age.
Forgetting a debt doesn't mean it's paid.
Who gossips with you will gossip of you.
Many a sudden change takes place on an unlikely day.
Who keeps his tongue keeps his friends.
A scholar's ink lasts longer than a martyr's blood.
If you lie down with dogs you'll rise with fleas.
A trout in the pot is better than a salmon in the sea.
It is no secret if it is known by three people.

199. Sites of the Modern Olympic Games

	Summer Games	*Winter Games*
1896	Athens, Greece	
1900	Paris, France	
1904	St. Louis, Missouri (U.S.)	
1908	London, England	
1912	Stockholm, Sweden	
1920	Antwerp, Belgium	
1924	Paris, France	Chamonix, France
1928	Amsterdam, Netherlands	St. Moritz, Switzerland
1932	Los Angeles, California (U.S.)	Lake Placid, New York (U.S.)
1936	Berlin, Germany	Garmisch-Partenkirchen, Germany
1948	London, England	St. Moritz, Switzerland
1952	Helsinki, Finland	Oslo, Norway
1956	Melbourne, Australia	Cortina d'Ampezzo, Italy
1960	Rome, Italy	Squaw Valley, California (U.S.)
1964	Tokyo, Japan	Innsbruck, Austria
1968	Mexico City, Mexico	Grenoble, France
1972	Munich, W. Germany	Sapporo, Japan
1976	Montreal, Canada	Innsbruck, Austria
1980	Moscow, USSR	Lake Placid, New York (U.S.)
1984	Los Angeles, California (U.S.)	Sarajevo, Yugoslavia
1988	Seoul, South Korea	Calgary, Alberta, Canada
1992	Barcelona, Spain	Albertville, France

199. *(continued)*

	Summer Games	*Winter Games*
1996	Atlanta, Georgia (U.S.)	Lillehammer, Norway (1994)
2000	Sydney, Australia	Nagano, Japan (1998)
2004	Athens, Greece	Salt Lake City, Utah (U.S.) (2002)
2008	Beijing, China	Turin, Italy (2006)

200. Major World Philosophers

Peter Abelard	(1079–1142)	French
Anaxagoras	(c. 500–428 B.C.)	Greek
St. Anselm	(1033–1109)	Italian
St. Thomas Aquinas	(1225–1274)	Italian
Aristotle	(384–322 B.C.)	Greek
St. Augustine of Hippo	(354–430)	Roman
Sir Francis Bacon	(1561–1626)	English
Jeremy Bentham	(1748–1832)	English
George Berkeley	(1685–1753)	English
Martin Buber	(1878–1965)	German
Auguste Comte	(1798–1857)	French
Democratus	(c. 460–c. 370 B.C.)	Greek
René Descartes	(1596–1650)	French
John Dewey	(1859–1952)	American
Denis Diderot	(1713–1784)	French
Diogenes	(c. 400–325 B.C.)	Greek
Empedocles	(c. 495–435 B.C.)	Greek
Friedrich Engles	(1820–1895)	German
Epictetus	(c. 50–c. 138)	Greek
Epicurus	(341–270 B.C.)	Greek

(continued)

200. *(continued)*

Georg Wilhelm Hegel	(1770–1831)	German
Martin Heidegger	(1889–1976)	German
Thomas Hobbes	(1588–1679)	English
David Hume	(1711–1776)	English
Edmund Husserl	(1859–1938)	German
William James	(1842–1910)	American
Immanuel Kant	(1724–1804)	German
Søren Kierkegaard	(1813–1855)	Danish
Gottfried Wilhelm Leibniz	(1646–1716)	German
John Locke	(1632–1704)	English
Niccolò Machiavelli	(1469–1527)	Italian
Maimonides	(1135–1204)	Spanish
Marcus Aurelius	(121–180)	Roman
Karl Marx	(1818–1883)	German
John Stuart Mill	(1806–1873)	English
George E. Moore	(1873–1958)	English
Sir Thomas More	(1478–1535)	English
Friedrich Wilhelm Nietzche	(1844–1900)	German
Blaise Pascal	(1623–1662)	French
Plato	(c. 428–c. 348 B.C.)	Greek
Pythagoras	(c. 582–c. 507 B.C.)	Greek
Jean Jacques Rousseau	(1712–1778)	Swiss/French
Bertrand Russell	(1872–1970)	English
George Santayana	(1863–1952)	Spanish/American
Jean-Paul Sartre	(1905–1980)	French
Arthur Schopenhauer	(1788–1860)	German
Adam Smith	(1723–1790)	Scottish
Socrates	(464–399 B.C.)	Greek
Benedict Spinoza	(1623–1677)	Dutch
Miguel de Unamuno	(1864–1936)	Spanish
Voltaire	(1694–1778)	French
Alfred North Whitehead	(1889–1951)	English
Zeno the Stoic	(c. 334–c. 262 B.C.)	Greek

MISCELLANEOUS

201. Major Wars

War	*Dates*
Peloponnesian War	431–404 B.C.
Punic Wars	264–146 B.C.
Crusades	1096–1291
Hundred Years War	1337–1453
War of the Roses	1455–1485
Thirty Years' War	1618–1648
French and Indian Wars	1689–1763
Seven Years' Wars	1756–1763
American Revolution	1775–1783
French Revolution	1789–1799
War of 1812	1812–1814
Mexican War	1846–1848
Revolution of 1848	1848
Crimean War	1853–1856
U.S. Civil War	1861–1865
Franco-Prussian War	1870
First Anglo-Boer War	1880–1881
Chinese-Japanese War	1894–1895
Spanish-American War	1898
Second Anglo-Boer War	1904–1905
Russo-Japanese War	1904–1905
Russian Revolution	1905
World War I	1914–1918
Russian Revolution	1917
World War II	1939–1945
Arab-Israeli Wars	1948, 1956, 1967, 1973
Korean War	1950–1953
Vietnam War	1957–1975
Persian Gulf War	1991
Afghanistan War	2001–

202. Nicknames of Various World Leaders

Nickname	*Name*
Almighty Nose	Oliver Cromwell
Badinguet	Napoleon III
Bloody Mary	Queen Mary I of England
Boney	Napoleon Bonaparte
Chairman Mao	Mao Tse-tung
Citizen King	King Louis Philippe
Conqueror, the	William I of England
Desert Fox	Erwin Rommel
Devil's Missionary, the	Voltaire
Divine Madman	Michelangelo
Dizzy	Benjamin Disraeli
El Libertador	Simon Bolivar
Gentleman Johnny	British Gen. John Burgoyne
Goldy	Oliver Goldsmith
Good Queen Bess	Queen Elizabeth I of England
Grand Old Man	William Gladstone
Great Commoner	William Pitt
Great Helmsman	Mao Tse-tung
Last of the Puritans	Samuel Adams
Little Corporal	Napoleon Bonaparte
Iberia's Pilot	Christopher Columbus
Iron Chancellor	Otto von Bismarck
Iron Duke	Duke of Wellington
Iron Lady	Margaret Thatcher
Knight of the Cloak	Sir Walter Raleigh
Lady with a Lamp	Florence Nightingale
Liberator, the	Simon Bolivar
Lenin, Nikolai	Vladimir Ilich Ulyanov
Lion Heart	King Richard I
Old Noll	Oliver Cromwell
Orange Peel	Sir Robert Peel
Peacemaker	King Edward VII
Philosopher, the	Aristotle
Scourge of God	Attila the Hun
Tiger, the	George B. Clemenceau

203. Voter Participation by Country

Country	Turnout* (as percentage of electorate)
Italy	92.5
Iceland	89.5
Indonesia	88.3
New Zealand	86.2
Uzbekistan	86.2
Austria	85.1
Netherlands	84.8
Australia	84.4
Denmark	83.6
Sweden	83.3
Portugal	82.4
Germany	80.6
Greece	80.3
Israel	80.0
Norway	79.5
Finland	79.0
Romania	77.2
United Kingdom	74.9
Venezuela	72.2
Canada	68.4
France	67.3
Bolivia	61.4
Zimbabwe	58.8
Poland	52.3
USA	48.3

*Average participation in all elections, 1945–1998

Source: The International Institute for Democracy and Electoral Assistance. Online at http://www.idea.int/voter_turnout/voter_turnout2.html.

204. Fathers of . . .

America	Samuel Adams, colonial patriot
Comedy	Aristophanes, Greek writer of comedy
The Constitution	James Madison, author of the U.S. Constitution
English Poetry	Geoffrey Chaucer, author of *Canterbury Tales*
The Faithful	Abraham, founder of the Jewish religion
His Country	George Washington, first President of the United States
History	Herodotus, Greek historian
Medicine	Hippocrates, famous Greek physician
English Philosophy	Roger Bacon, English philosopher
Roman Philosophy	Cicero, Roman philosopher and orator
Satire	Archilochus, Greek poet
The Symphony	Joseph Haydn, Austrian composer

Haydn

205. British Positions of Title

King	Queen
Prince of Wales	Princess of Wales
Duke	Duchess
Prince	Princess
Marquess	Marchioness
Earl	Countess
Viscount	Viscountess
Baron	Baroness
Life Baron	Life Baroness
Baronet	Baronetess
Knight	Dame
Lord of the Manor	Lady of the Manor

206. Recent Nobel Peace Prize Laureates

2002	Jimmy Carter
2001	United Nations (U.N.), Kofi Annan
2000	Kim Dae Jung
1999	Médecins Sans Frontières
1998	John Hume and David Trimble
1997	International Campaign to Ban Landmines (ICBL) and Jody Williams
1996	Carlos Filipe Ximenes Belo and José Ramos-Horta
1995	Joseph Rotblat and Pugwash Conferences on Science and World Affairs
1994	Yasser Arafat, Shimon Peres and Yitzhak Rabin
1993	Nelson Mandela and Frederik Willem de Klerk
1992	Rigoberta Menchú Tum
1991	Aung San Suu Kyi
1990	Mikhail Sergeyevich Gorbachev

207. Computer Timeline

1885	William Seward Burroughs filed his first patent for a calculating machine. He is recognized as the inventor of the first practical adding and listing machine.
1881	Engineer Herman Hollerith designed a punched card machine to tabulate the 1890 U.S. census data.
1946	John Presper Eckert and John Mauchly developed the ENIAC I (Electrical Numerical Integrator And Calculator). The military project was designed to calculate artillery-firing tables to improve target accuracy of weapons.
1948	Eckert and Mauchly invented the UNIVAC (Universal Automatic Computer) for the United States Census Bureau.
1948	Scientists at the Bell Telephone Laboratories invented the transistor, replacing vacuum tubes and shepherding the next generation of computers.
1953	As part of the Korean War effort IBM introduced the 701 EDPM, the first commercially successful general-purpose computer.

(continued)

207. *(continued)*

1959	Jack Kilby and Robert Noyce designed the first integrated circuits made of semiconductor material. This permitted computer manufacturers to use chips instead of the individual transistors.
1962	MIT computer programmer Steve Russell created the first computer video game—Spacewar.
1963	BASIC (Beginner's All Purpose Symbolic Instruction Code) was invented by Dartmouth College mathematicians John George Kemeny and Tom Kurtzas as a teaching tool for undergraduates.
1969	Intel developed the first programmable microprocessor chip, the 4004, making the creation of small computers possible.
1969	ARPANET (forerunner to the Internet) connected researchers at four universities in the United States.
1971	Intel introduced the world's first single chip microprocessor, placing all the parts that made a computer think on a single small chip.
1976	Steve Jobs and Steve Wozniak assembled the first Apple-1 computers in a garage.
1979	Duke and University of North Carolina graduate students establish the first USENET newsgroups. Users from all around the globe could join these discussion groups to talk about thousands of subjects.
1980	Bill Gates convinced IBM to let Microsoft keep the rights and to market MS DOS. Gates became a billionaire from the licensing of MS-DOS.
1984	Apple produces the first MacIntosh computers. Price: $2,495.
1991	The World Wide Web is created.
1993	Mosaic, the first graphics-based Web browser, begins operation. Internet traffic mushrooms.
2000	Web size surpasses 1 billion indexable pages.

208. Jurisdictions Most Hospitable to Money Laundering

Cook Islands	Lebanon	Niue
Dominica	The Marshall	The Philippines
Egypt	Islands	Russia
Guatemala	Myanmar	St. Kitts and Nevis
Hungary	Nauru	St. Vincent
Indonesia	Nigeria	The Grenadines
Israel		

Source: Organization for Economic Cooperation and Development (OECD).

209. Online Resources for Teaching World History

Ancient History
http://www.omnibusol.com/ancient.html

Central Intelligence Agency
http://www.cia.gov/cia/

CIA World Factbook
http://www.cia.gov/cia/publications/factbook/index.html

Exploring Ancient World Cultures
http://eawc.evansville.edu/index.htm

Internet Archive of Texts and Documents
History Department of Hanover College
http://history.hanover.edu/texts.htm

Introduction to Medieval History
Paul Halsall/Fordham University
http://www.fordham.edu/halsall/medieval.html

(continued)

209. *(continued)*

National Standards for History
National Center for History in the Schools
http://www.sscnet.ucla.edu/nchs/

RETANET
Resources for Teaching about the Americas
http://ladb.unm.edu/retanet/

Women in the World History Curriculum
http://www.womeninworldhistory.com/

World Civilizations
Washington State University
http://www.wsu.edu:8080/ ~ dee/WORLD.HTM

World History Lesson Plans
AskERIC
http://askeric.org/cgi-bin/lessons.cgi/Social_Studies/World_History

210. Social Studies Activities

Percentage of students reporting doing various activities when they study social studies:

Read from textbook	89
Fill out worksheets	88
Watch television/videos	77
Write reports	77
Discuss current events	75
Memorize reading materials	73
Discuss television/videos	71
Read extra material	60
Debate and discuss	45
Role play, mock trials, etc.	40
Receive visits from leaders	31
Write letters to give their opinion	27

Source: U.S. Dept. of Education, National Center for Educational Statistics, Civic Education Study, 1999.

Lists for
American Government

211. Forms of Government

Aristocracy—government ruled by the wealthy or upper class.

Autocracy—rule by one person who has total control over all others; dictatorship.

Centralism—governmental structure in which administration and power are concentrated in a central institution or group.

Constitutional monarchy—government in which the powers of the monarch are limited by and defined by a constitution.

Democracy—government in which political power is retained by all the people. In a representative democracy, power may be delegated to their elected representatives.

Despotism—autocratic rule; the ruler maintains absolute power. Government in which the dictator or tyrant may possess oppressive power.

Dictatorship—government in which a ruler possesses absolute power.

Fascism—one-party system of government with individuals subjected to the control of the state often by secret police, military police, censorship and government control of finance, industry, and commerce.

Federalism—union of several states under a central government, with individual states retaining specific powers under the central government.

Feudalism—a Medieval system in which vassals received land holdings in exchange for military or other service and homage to their lords.

Matriarchy—society ruled by a woman, with descent and succession being traced through the female's line.

Monarchy—sovereign control of a government by a hereditary ruler, such as a king or queen.

Oligarchy—rule of the government by a few persons.

Patriarchy—rule of a group by the father or male heir.

Republicanism—a representative democracy. Elected officials exercise power vested in them by sovereign citizens.

Theocracy—government in which the clergy rules or in which a god is the civil ruler.

Totalitarianism—system in which a highly centralized government is controlled exclusively by one party and maintained by political suppression. Other political parties are not tolerated or recognized.

212. The Cabinet Positions

Secretary of State
Secretary of the Treasury
Secretary of Defense
Attorney General
Secretary of Agriculture
Secretary of the Interior
Secretary of Housing and Urban
    Development

Secretary of Commerce
Secretary of Labor
Secretary of Transportation
Secretary of Health and Human Services
Secretary of Education
Secretary of Energy
Secretary of Veterans Affairs

213. The Bill of Rights

First Amendment. Forbids the Congress from interfering with freedom of religion, speech or press, or with the right to assemble peaceably, or to petition the government.

Second Amendment. Guarantees the right to bear arms.

Third Amendment. Assures that soldiers can not be arbitrarily lodged in private homes without the consent of the owner.

Fourth Amendment. Forbids unreasonable search or seizure of persons, homes, and effects without a warrant.

Fifth Amendment. Guarantees specific rights when on trial, including no condemnation without trial, no compulsion to be a witness against oneself, and no property taken for public use except with just compensation.

Sixth Amendment. Assures the accused right to a speedy and public trial, right to be represented by an attorney, and right to be faced by accusing witnesses.

Seventh Amendment. In lawsuits of more than $20, a trial by jury may be requested.

Eighth Amendment. Forbids excessive fines and cruel or unusual punishments.

Ninth Amendment. Just because a right is not mentioned in the Constitution does not mean that the people are not entitled to it.

Tenth Amendment. Powers not delegated to the Federal Government are reserved to the States respectively, or to the people.

214. Constitutional Amendments

Amendment XI	(1795)	prohibited citizens of one state from suing the government of another state
Amendment XII	(1804)	established separate ballots for president and vice president in electoral college
Amendment XIII	(1865)	abolished slavery
Amendment XIV	(1868)	made slaves citizens and forebade states from denying civil rights
Amendment XV	(1870)	prohibited states from denying a person the right to vote on account of race
Amendment XVI	(1913)	gave Congress the right to levy an income tax
Amendment XVII	(1913)	provided for direct election of Senators
Amendment XVIII	(1919)	permitted Congress to ban the sale of liquor
Amendment XIX	(1920)	gave women the right to vote
Amendment XX	(1933)	changed the date of the presidential inauguration and set congressional sessions to begin in January
Amendment XXI	(1933)	repealed the 18th amendment
Amendment XXII	(1951)	limited president to two elected terms
Amendment XXIII	(1961)	granted people of the District of Columbia the right to vote for presidential electors
Amendment XXIV	(1964)	prohibited use of the poll tax to deny people voting priviledges
Amendment XXV	(1967)	provided a procedure to fill the vice-presidency in the event of a vacancy
Amendment XXVI	(1971)	lowered the voting age nationally to 18

215. Expansion of the United States

Area	How Obtained	Year
Louisiana	purchased from France	1803
Florida	purchased from Spain	1819
Texas	annexed	1845
Oregon	treaty with Great Britain	1846
Southwestern states	treaty with Mexico	1848
Southern Arizona	bought from Mexico	1853
Alaska	bought from Russia	1867
Hawaii	annexed	1898
Guam	treaty with Spain	1899
Puerto Rico	treaty with Spain	1899
American Samoa	treaty	1900
Virgin Islands	bought from Denmark	1917

216. States in Order of Admission to the Union

1.	Delaware	1787	26.	Michigan	1837
2.	Pennsylvania	1787	27.	Florida	1845
3.	New Jersey	1787	28.	Texas	1845
4.	Georgia	1788	29.	Iowa	1846
5.	Connecticut	1788	30.	Wisconsin	1848
6.	Massachusetts	1788	31.	California	1850
7.	Maryland	1788	32.	Minnesota	1858
8.	South Carolina	1788	33.	Oregon	1859
9.	New Hampshire	1788	34.	Kansas	1861
10.	Virginia	1788	35.	West Virginia	1863
11.	New York	1788	36.	Nevada	1864
12.	North Carolina	1789	37.	Nebraska	1867
13.	Rhode Island	1790	38.	Colorado	1876
14.	Vermont	1791	39.	North Dakota	1889
15.	Kentucky	1792	40.	South Dakota	1889
16.	Tennessee	1796	41.	Montana	1889
17.	Ohio	1803	42.	Washington	1889
18.	Louisiana	1812	43.	Idaho	1890
19.	Indiana	1816	44.	Wyoming	1890
20.	Mississippi	1817	45	Utah	1896
21.	Illinois	1818	46.	Oklahoma	1907
22.	Alabama	1819	47.	New Mexico	1912
23.	Maine	1820	48.	Arizona	1912
24.	Missouri	1821	49.	Alaska	1959
25.	Arkansas	1836	50.	Hawaii	1959

217. Federal Legal Holidays

New Year's Day	January 1
Martin Luther King Day	Third Monday in January
Presidents' Day	Third Monday in February
Memorial Day	Last Monday in May
Independence Day	July 4
Labor Day	First Monday in September
Columbus Day	Second Monday in October
Veterans' Day	November 11
Thanksgiving	Fourth Thursday in November
Christmas Day	December 25

218. Portraits on U.S. Currency

Denomination	*Portrait*
$1	Washington
$2	Jefferson
$5	Lincoln
$10	Hamilton
$20	Jackson
$50	Grant
$100	Franklin
$500	McKinley
$1,000	Cleveland
$5,000	Madison
$10,000	Chase
$100,000	Wilson

Bills larger than $100 are no longer issued and are removed from circulation as they are turned in to the Federal Reserve.

219. U.S. Supreme Court Chief Justices

Chief Justice	Dates
John Jay	1790–1795
John Rutledge	1795*
Oliver Ellsworth	1796–1800
John Marshall	1801–1835
Roger Taney	1836–1864
Salmon P. Chase	1864–1873
Morrison R. Waite	1874–1888
Melville W. Fuller	1888–1910
Edward White	1910–1921
William H. Taft	1921–1930
Charles E. Hughes	1930–1941
Harlan Stone	1941–1946
Frederick Vinson	1946–1953
Earl Warren	1953–1969
Warren Burger	1969–1986
William Rehnquist	1986–

*Was rejected on December 15, 1795

220. Current Supreme Court Members

(In order of seniority)

William H. Rehnquist (chief justice)
John Paul Stevens
Sandra Day O'Connor
Antonin Scalia
Anthony M. Kennedy
David H. Souter
Clarence Thomas
Ruth Bader Ginsburg
Stephen G. Breyer

221. Landmark Supreme Court Personal Rights Cases

Dred Scott vs. Sandford, 1856	Blacks are not citizens, Congress cannot ban slavery
Plessy vs. Ferguson, 1896	Allowed "separate but equal" segregation policies
Korematsu vs. United States, 1941	Allowed internment of U.S. Japanese during World War II
Brown vs. Topeka Board of Education, 1954	"Separate but equal" educational facilities are unconstitutional
Engel vs. Vitale, 1962	School prayers may not be required
Gideon vs. Wainwright, 1963	Right to paid defense lawyer
Miranda vs. Arizona, 1966	Accused must be informed of rights, including right to remain silent
Alexander vs. Holmes Co. Board of Ed., 1969	Demanded immediate desegregation of all public schools
Roe vs. Wade, 1973	States may not prevent women (under specified conditions) from having an abortion during first 6 months of pregnancy
United Steelworkers of America vs. Weber, 1979	Affirmative action hiring programs are permitted

222. Miranda Rights

You have the right to remain silent.

If you choose to speak, anything you say may be used in a court of law against you.

You have the right to speak with an attorney before talking to the police and to have a lawyer present when you are talking to the police.

If you do not have a lawyer, you have the right to remain silent until you have contacted one.

If you cannot afford a lawyer, the court will appoint one for you.

223. Federal Reserve Banks

District	Bank
District	*Bank*
First	Boston
Second	New York
Third	Philadelphia
Fourth	Cleveland
Fifth	Richmond
Sixth	Atlanta
Seventh	Chicago
Eighth	St. Louis
Ninth	Minneapolis
Tenth	Kansas City, MO
Eleventh	Dallas
Twelfth	San Francisco

224. Standing Congressional Committees

House of Representatives	Senate
Agriculture	Agriculture, Nutrition, and Forestry
Appropriations	Appropriations
Armed Services	Armed Services
Budget	Banking, Housing, and Urban Affairs
Education and the Workforce	Budget
Energy and Commerce	Commerce, Science, and Transportation
Financial Services	Energy and Natural Resources
Foreign Affairs	Environment and Public Works
Government Reform	Finance
House Administration	Foreign Relations
International Relations	Governmental Affairs
Judiciary	Health, Education, Labor, and Pensions
Resources	Indian Affairs
Rules	Judiciary
Science	Rules and Administration
Small Business	Small Business and Entrepreneurship
Standards of Official Conduct	Veterans' Affairs
Transportation and Infrastructure	
Veterans' Affairs	
Ways and Means	

225. Social Security Programs

Retirement payments
Disability payments
Survivors' payments
Medicare
Unemployment benefits
Workers' compensation

226. Kinds of Taxes

capital gains
excess profits
excise
franchise
gasoline
income
inheritance
license
poll
property
sales
tariff
value-added

227. Military Ranks: Officers

Army, Marine, Air Force	*Navy*
General	Fleet Admiral
Lieutenant General	Vice Admiral
Major General	Rear Admiral, Upper Half
Brigadier General	Rear Admiral, Lower Half
Colonel	Captain
Lieutenant Colonel	Commander
Major	Lieutenant Commander
Captain	Lieutenant
First Lieutenant	Lieutenant, Junior Grade
Second Lieutenant	Ensign
Chief Warrant Officer	Chief Warrant Officer
Warrant Officer	Warrant Officer

228. Order of Succession to the Presidency

Vice President
Speaker of the House of
  Representatives
President Pro Tempore of the
  Senate
Secretary of State
Secretary of Treasury
Secretary of Defense
Attorney General
Secretary of Interior

Secretary of Agriculture
Secretary of Commerce
Secretary of Labor
Secretary of Health and Human
  Services
Secretary of Housing and Urban
  Development
Secretary of Transportation
Secretary of Energy
Secretary of Education

229. Presidents of the United States

President	Served	President	Served
George Washington	1789–1797	Benjamin Harrison	1889–1893
John Adams	1797–1801	Grover Cleveland	1893–1897
Thomas Jefferson	1801–1809	William McKinley	1897–1901
James Madison	1809–1817	Theodore Roosevelt	1901–1909
James Monroe	1817–1825	William H. Taft	1909–1913
John Quincy Adams	1825–1829	Woodrow Wilson	1913–1921
Andrew Jackson	1829–1837	Warren G. Harding	1921–1923
Martin Van Buren	1837–1841	Calvin Coolidge	1925–1929
William Henry Harrison	1841–1841	Herbert Hoover	1929–1933
John Tyler	1841–1845	Franklin D. Roosevelt	1933–1945
James K. Polk	1845–1849	Harry S. Truman	1945–1953
Zachary Taylor	1849–1850	Dwight D. Eisenhower	1953–1961
Millard Fillmore	1850–1853	John F. Kennedy	1961–1963
Franklin Pierce	1853–1857	Lyndon B. Johnson	1963–1969
James Buchanan	1857–1861	Richard M. Nixon	1969–1974
Abraham Lincoln	1861–1865	Gerald R. Ford	1974–1977
Andrew Johnson	1865–1869	James E. Carter, Jr.	1977–1981
Ulysses S. Grant	1869–1877	Ronald Reagan	1981–1989
Rutherford B. Hayes	1877–1881	George Bush	1989–1993
James A. Garfield	1881–1881	William Jefferson Clinton	1993–2001
Chester A. Arthur	1881–1885	George Walker Bush	2001–
Grover Cleveland	1885–1889		

230. Presidents Who Were Not Lawyers

President	*Occupation*
George Washington	planter, solider
William Henry Harrison	soldier, farmer
Zachary Taylor	soldier
Andrew Johnson	tailor
Ulysses S. Grant	soldier
Theodore Roosevelt	author, public official
Woodrow Wilson	educator
Warren G. Harding	newspaper editor
Herbert Hoover	engineer
Harry S Truman	businessman
Dwight D. Eisenhower	soldier
John F. Kennedy	author, public official
Lyndon B. Johnson	teacher, public official
James E. Carter, Jr.	businessman
Ronald Reagan	actor
George W. Bush	businessman

231. Vice Presidents of the United States

John Adams**	1789–1797		Garrett Hobart	1897–1899
Thomas Jefferson**	1797–1801		Theodore Roosevelt*	1901
Aaron Burr	1801–1805		Charles Fairbanks	1905–1909
George Clinton	1805–1812		James Sherman	1909–1912
Elbrige Gerry	1813–1814		Thomas Marshall	1913–1921
Daniel Tompkins	1817–1825		Calvin Coolidge*	1921–1923
John C. Calhoun	1825–1832		Charles Dawes	1925–1929
Martin Van Buren**	1833–1837		Charles Curtis	1929–1933
Richard Johnson	1837–1841		John N. Garner	1933–1941
John Tyler*	1841		Henry Wallace	1941–1945
George Dallas	1845–1849		Harry S Truman*	1945
Millard Fillmore*	1849–1850		Alben Barkley	1949–1953
William King	1853		Richard Nixon**	1953–1961
John C. Breckinridge	1857–1861		Lyndon B. Johnson*	1961–1963
Hannibal Hamlin	1861–1865		Hubert Humphrey	1965–1969
Andrew Johnson*	1865		Spiro Agnew	1969–1973
Schuyler Colfax	1869–1873		Gerald Ford*	1973–1974
Henry Wilson	1873–1875		Nelson Rockefeller	1974–1977
William Wheeler	1877–1881		Walter Mondale	1977–1981
Chester A. Arthur*	1881		George Bush**	1981–1989
Thomas Hendricks	1885		Dan Quayle	1989–1993
Levi Morton	1889–1893		Al Gore	1993–2001
Adlai E. Stevenson	1893–1897		Dick Cheney	2001–

*Became president after death or resignation of president

**Later elected president

232. Federalist Candidates for President

1788	George Washington*
1792	George Washington*
1796	John Adams*
1800	John Adams
1804	Charles Pinckney
1808	Charles Pinckney
1812	DeWitt Clinton
1816	Rufus King

Adams

*Winner of election

233. Whig Candidates for President

1832	Henry Clay
1836	William H. Harrison
1840	William H. Harrison*
1844	Henry Clay
1848	Zachary Taylor*
1852	Winfield Scott
1856	Millard Fillmore

Fillmore

*Winner of election

234. Republican Candidates for President

1856	John C. Fremont		1932	Herbert Hoover
1860	Abraham Lincoln*		1936	Alf Landon
1864	Abraham Lincoln*		1940	Wendell Wilkie
1868	Ulysses S. Grant*		1944	Thomas Dewey
1872	Ulysses S. Grant*		1948	Thomas Dewey
1876	Rutherford B. Hayes*		1952	Dwight D. Eisenhower*
1880	James Garfield*		1956	Dwight D. Eisenhower*
1884	James G. Blaine		1960	Richard Nixon
1888	Benjamin Harrison*		1964	Barry Goldwater
1892	Benjamin Harrison		1968	Richard Nixon*
1896	William McKinley*		1972	Richard Nixon*
1900	William McKinley*		1976	Gerald Ford
1904	Theodore Roosevelt*		1980	Ronald Reagan*
1908	William H. Taft*		1984	Ronald Reagan*
1912	William H. Taft		1988	George Bush*
1916	Charles E. Hughes		1992	George Bush
1920	Warren G. Harding*		1996	Bob Dole
1924	Calvin Coolidge*		2000	George W. Bush*
1928	Herbert Hoover*			

*Winner of election

235. Democratic Candidates for President

1796	Thomas Jefferson*	1900	William J. Bryan
1800	Thomas Jefferson**	1904	Alton B. Parker
1804	Thomas Jefferson**	1908	William J. Bryan
1808	James Madison**	1912	Woodrow Wilson**
1812	James Madison**	1916	Woodrow Wilson**
1816	James Monroe**	1920	James Cox
1820	James Monroe**	1924	John W. Davis
1824	John Quincy Adams**	1928	Alfred E. Smith
1828	Andrew Jackson**	1932	Franklin D. Roosevelt**
1832	Andrew Jackson**	1936	Franklin D. Roosevelt**
1836	Martin Van Buren**	1940	Franklin D. Roosevelt**
1840	Martin Van Buren	1944	Franklin D. Roosevelt**
1844	James K. Polk**	1948	Harry Truman**
1848	Lewis Cass	1952	Adlai E. Stevenson
1852	Franklin Pierce**	1956	Adlai E. Stevenson
1856	James Buchanan**	1960	John F. Kennedy**
1860	Stephen Douglas	1964	Lyndon B. Johnson**
1864	George McClellan	1968	Hubert H. Humphrey
1868	Horatio Seymour	1972	George McGovern
1872	Horace Greeley	1976	James E. Carter, Jr.**
1876	Samuel Tilden	1980	James E. Carter, Jr.
1880	Winfield Hancock	1984	Walter Mondale
1884	Grover Cleveland**	1988	Michael Dukakis
1888	Grover Cleveland	1992	William Clinton**
1892	Grover Cleveland**	1996	William Clinton**
1896	William J. Bryan	2000	Al Gore

*Indudes the Democratic-Republicans, predecessors to the Democratic Party

**Winner of election

236. Presidents with Most Vetoes

Franklin D. Roosevelt	635
Grover Cleveland	584
Harry Truman	258
Dwight Eisenhower	188
Ulysses S. Grant	93
Theodore Roosevelt	82

237. Presidents Who Died in Office

William H. Harrison, 1841
Zackary Taylor, 1850
Abraham Lincoln, 1865*
James Garfield, 1881*
William McKinley, 1901*
Warren G. Harding, 1923
Franklin D. Roosevelt, 1945
John F. Kennedy, 1963*

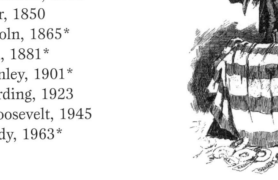

*Assassinated

238. Presidential Firsts

First President . . .

to accept no salary as President	George Washington
to appear on a U.S. postage stamp	George Washington
to reside in Washington, D.C.	John Adams
whose son became President	John Adams
to be inaugurated in Washington, D.C.	Thomas Jefferson
to be a widower when elected	Thomas Jefferson
to have been a Congressman	James Madison
to be a Senator	James Monroe
to have a billiard table in the White House	John Q. Adams
Phi Beta Kappa member	John Q. Adams
born in a log cabin	Andrew Jackson
to ride on a railroad	Andrew Jackson
to pay off the national debt	Andrew Jackson
to marry a divorcee	Andrew Jackson
to receive an assassination attempt	Andrew Jackson
nominated at a national convention	Andrew Jackson

(continued)

238. *(continued)*

First President . . .

to have fought a duel	Andrew Jackson
born a citizen of the United States	Martin Van Buren
to die in office	William H. Harrison
married during his term in office	John Tyler
to be burned in effigy on the White House lawn	John Tyler
to have served as Speaker of the House	James K. Polk
to install a bathtub in the White House	Millard Fillmore
to be a bachelor	James Buchanan
assassinated	Abraham Lincoln
to wear a beard	Abraham Lincoln
depicted on a U.S. coin	Abraham Lincoln
to receive a patent	Abraham Lincoln
to have served as a preacher	Andrew Johnson
to be a graduate of West Point	Ulyssess S. Grant
to use a telephone	James Garfield
who was also a preacher	James Garfield
whose mother saw him inaugurated	James Garfield
married in the White House	Grover Cleveland
to ride in an automobile	Theodore Roosevelt
to receive a Nobel Peace prize	Theodore Roosevelt
to fly in an airplane	Theodore Roosevelt
to ride in a submarine	Theodore Roosevelt
to become Chief Justice of the Supreme Court	William Howard Taft
buried in Arlington National Cemetery	William Howard Taft
to throw out a baseball to open the season	William Howard Taft
to visit Europe while in office	Woodrow Wilson
to earn a doctorate	Woodrow Wilson
to use loud speakers at his inauguration	Warren G. Harding
to speak over radio	Warren G. Harding
to ride an auto at his inaugural	Warren G. Harding
see talking pictures in the White House	Calvin Coolidge
born west of the Mississippi	Herbert Hoover
to have a phone on his desk	Herbert Hoover
to be a millionaire	Herbert Hoover
inaugurated on January 20	Franklin D. Roosevelt
to fly in an airplane while in office	Franklin D. Roosevelt
to have air conditioning in the White House	Franklin D. Roosevelt
to be elected more than two terms	Franklin D. Roosevelt
to ride a diesel train	Franklin D. Roosevelt
to appear on television	Franklin D. Roosevelt
to fly in a helicopter	Dwight D. Eisenhower

238. (continued)

First President . . .

to earn an airplane pilot's license	Dwight D. Eisenhower
to appear on color television	Dwight D. Eisenhower
who was a Catholic	John F. Kennedy
to appoint his brother to the cabinet	John F. Kennedy
to resign from office	Richard Nixon
whose parents were divorced	Gerald Ford
born in a hospital	Jimmy Carter
to have been divorced	Ronald Reagan
to appoint a woman to the Supreme Court	Ronald Reagan
to appoint a female Secretary of State	Bill Clinton
to have wife elected to U.S. Senate	Bill Clinton

239. Nicknames of the Presidents

George Washington	Father of His Country, The Sage of Mt. Vernon
John Adams	The Atlas of Independence, Bonny Johnny, His Rotundity
Thomas Jefferson	Apostle of Democracy, The Pen of the Revolution
James Madison	Father of the Constitution, Sage of Montpelier
James Monroe	The Last of the Cocked Hats
John Quincy Adams	Old Man Eloquent, Publicola
Andrew Jackson	Old Hickory, The Old Hero, King Andrew the First
Martin Van Buren	The Red Fox of Kinderbrook, The Little Magician
William Henry Harrison	Old Tippecanoe, The Cincinnatus of the West
John Tyler	His Accidency, Young Hickory
James K. Polk	Polk the Purposeful, Napoleon of the Stump
Zachary Taylor	Old Rough and Ready, Old Zack
Millard Fillmore	The Accidental President, The Wool Carder President
Franklin Pierce	Handsome Frank, Purse
James Buchanan	Old Buck, The Do-Nothing President
Abraham Lincoln	The Great Emancipator, Honest Abe, The Rail Splitter

(continued)

239. *(continued)*

Andrew Johnson	The Tailor, Sir Veto, Father of the Homestead Act
Ulysses S. Grant	American Caesar, The Galena Tanner, Useless Grant
Rutherford B. Hayes	His Fraudulency, Old 8 to 7
James A. Garfield	The Canal Boy, The Preacher President
Chester A. Arthur	
Grover Cleveland	Grover the Good, Old Grover
Benjamin Harrison	Young Tippecanoe, Little Ben, The Centennial President
William McKinley	Liberator of Cuba, The Idol of Ohio, Wobbly Willie
Theodore Roosevelt	The Rough Rider, The Cowboy President, T.R.
William H. Taft	
Woodrow Wilson	The Professor, The Phrasemaker
William G. Harding	W.G.
Calvin Coolidge	Silent Cal
Herbert Hoover	Chief, Grand Old Man
Franklin D. Roosevelt	FDR, The Boss, King Franklin
Harry S Truman	Give 'em Hell Harry, Haberdasher Harry
Dwight D. Eisenhower	General Ike, Kansas Cyclone, Duckpin
John F. Kennedy	JFK
Lyndon B. Johnson	LBJ
Richard M. Nixon	Tricky Dick, Richard the Chicken-Hearted
Gerald Ford	Jerry
Jimmy Carter	The Peanut Farmer, Cousin Hot
Ronald Reagan	The Great Communicator, The Teflon President
George Bush	Poppy
Bill Clinton	Slick Willie
George W. Bush	Dubya

240. States Claiming the Most Presidents

Virginia	*Ohio*
George Washington	Ulysses S. Grant
Thomas Jefferson	Rutherford B. Hayes
James Madison	James A. Garfield
James Monroe	Benjamin Harrison
William Henry Harrison	William McKinley
John Tyler	William Howard Taft
Zachary Tyler	Warren G. Harding
Woodrow Wilson	

241. Unsuccessful Presidential Assassinations

Theodore Roosevelt	1912
Franklin D. Roosevelt	1933
Harry S Truman	1950
Gerald Ford	1975
Ronald Reagan	1981

242. Presidential Trivia Quiz

1. Who was the only president to win an Emmy award?
2. Who was the only president elected by a unanimous electoral vote?
3. Name three of the five presidents who became president, but were never elected to that office.
4. Who are the two presidents who were impeached?
5. Which two presidents graduated from West Point Military Academy?
6. Who hanged two men?
7. What president donated his entire presidential salary to charity?
8. Which presidents served as president of Princeton College before?
9. Which presidents have state capitals named after them?
10. Who was the first Roman Catholic president?
11. Who invited Booker T. Washington to dine with him at the White House?
12. Which president ended segregation in the military?
13. Who was the only president who did not belong to a political party?
14. Who was the first president in office to have his photograph taken?

(continued)

242. *(continued)*

15. Who was the first president to name a black person to his Cabinet?

16. Which president starred in the movie *Bedtime for Bonzo*?

17. Who was the first president to ride in an automobile, fly in an airplane or go underwater in a submarine?

18. What 13-year old future president was taken prisoner by the British during the American Revolution?

19. What was the annual salary paid all presidents from George Washington through the first term of Ulysses S. Grant?

20. A *Chicago Times* review of one presidential speech read: "The cheek of every American must tingle with shame as he reads the silly, flat and dish-watery utterances of the man who has been pointed out to intelligent foreigners as the president of the United States." Which president and what speech was being described?

21. Which president said of his young daughter, "I can do one of two things. I can be president of the United States, or I can control Alice. I cannot possibly do both."?

22. Who was the only president to order dropping a nuclear bomb on an enemy?

23. What president's campaign slogan was, "Not Just Peanuts?"

24. Who ordered his press secretary to go out and purchase almost 1,200 of the president's favorite brand of Cuban cigars before the president signed the embargo on importing goods from Cuba?

25. What president, a classmate of Nathaniel Hawthorne and Henry Wadsworth Longfellow, had the lowest grades in his class during his second year at Bowdoin College? After reforming his study habits, he graduated third in his class.

242. *(continued)*

Answers:

1. Richard Nixon received the Best Spoken Word award for his television interview with David Frost
2. George Washington
3. Chester A. Arthur, John Tyler, Millard Fillmore, Andrew Johnson, Gerald Ford
4. Andrew Johnson and Bill Clinton
5. Ulysses S. Grant (1843) and Dwight D. Eisenhower (1915)
6. Grover Cleveland while serving as a sheriff
7. Herbert Hoover
8. Woodrow Wilson
9. James Madison (WI), Thomas Jefferson (MO), Andrew Jackson (MS), Abraham Lincoln (NE)
10. John F. Kennedy
11. Theodore Roosevelt
12. Harry Truman, during the Korean War
13. George Washington
14. James K. Polk
15. Lyndon Johnson
16. Ronald Reagan
17. Theodore Roosevelt
18. Andrew Jackson. He was nicked by the saber of a British soldier when he refused to shine his captor's shoes.
19. $25,000
20. Abraham Lincoln and the Gettysburg Address
21. Theodore Roosevelt
22. Harry Truman
23. Jimmy Carter, owner of a Georgia peanut farm
24. John F. Kennedy
25. Franklin Pierce

243. Debate Topics

The military draft should be reinstated.

Compulsory education should be abolished.

Corporal punishment should be banned from all schools.

The electoral college should be abolished.

Affirmative action programs are no longer needed.

Communism is dead.

All students should be required to learn a foreign language.

The presidential term should be lengthened to six years.

Representatives and senators should have a limited number of terms.

The health care system should be socialized to guarantee medical care to all.

A national competency examination for high school graduation should be
enacted.

Foreign ownership of American property should be restricted.

The presidential primary election should be abolished.

Television advertising for beer should be banned.

Puerto Rico should be granted statehood.

The death penalty should be abolished.

The world is a better place to live today than 100 years ago.

Democracy is the best form of government for all peoples of the world.

The U.S. Government must finance a national high speed rail system.

The United States must maintain a role as the "world's policeman."

All advertisements for cigarettes should be prohibited.

The inheritance tax should be abolished.

All students are entitled to a college education, even if they can not afford to
pay for it themselves.

Gambling should be legalized.

The use of all mind-altering drugs should be legalized.

Mandatory drug testing on the job should not be permitted.

The motto "In God we trust" should be removed from U.S. money.

Local schools should be free to determine whether or not to teach the theory
of evolution.

The U.S. Government must finance the search for an alternative fuel to oil.

Women should be used in combat roles.

A Department of Peace should be added to the presidential cabinet.

Governments should censor material on the World Wide Web.

We should ban the keeping of animals in zoos.

Cloning of human beings should be banned.

244. Significant Third Parties

Party	Presidential Election	% Popular Vote	Electoral Votes
Anti-Masonic	1832	7.8	7
Free-Soil	1848	10.1	0
American ("Know Nothing")	1856	21.5	8
Southern Democrats	1860	18.1	72
Constitutional Union	1860	12.6	39
Populist	1892	8.5	22
Progressive ("Bull Moose")	1912	6.0	0
Progressive	1924	16.6	13
State's Rights Democrat	1948	2.4	39
American Independent	1968	13.5	46
John B. Anderson (Independent)	1980	7.1	0
H. Ross Perot (Independent)	1992	18.9	0
Reform Party	1996	8.4	0
Green Party	2000	2.7	0

245. Historic Sites in Washington, D.C.

Arlington National Cemetery
Blair House
Ford's Theatre
Government Printing Office
J. Edgar Hoover Building (FBI)
Jefferson Memorial
Library of Congress
Lincoln Memorial
National Archives

Pentagon
Smithsonian Museums
Supreme Court Building
Tomb of the Unknown Soldier
United States Capitol Building
Vietnam Memorial
Washington Monument
Watergate Hotel
White House

246. Civil Rights Organizations

American Arab Anti-Discrimination Committee, 1980
American Civil Liberties Union, 1895
Americans for Democratic Action, 1947
Anti-Defamation League of B'nai B'rith, 1913
Congress of Racial Equality, 1942
National Association for the Advancement of Colored People, 1909
National Urban League, 1919
Operation PUSH (People United to Save Humanity), 1976
Southern Christian Leadership Conference, 1957
Student Non-violent Coordinating Committee, 1960

247. Early Black Civil Rights Leaders

Richard Allen	1760–1831
Mary McLeod Bethune	1875–1955
Frederick Douglas	1817–1895
W. E. B. DuBois	1868–1963
Henry H. Garnet	1815–1882
Marcus Garvey	1887–1940
Lester Granger	1896–1976
Eugene Jones	1884–1951
Martin Luther King, Jr.	1929–1968
Malcolm X	1925–1965
Kelly Miller	1863–1939
Mary Church Terrell	1863–1954
Harriet Ross Tubman	1820–1913
Roy Wilkins	1910–1981
Whitney Young, Jr.	1922–1971

King

248. The U.S. Senate: Facts and Milestones

First Meetings
- Session: New York City, March 4, 1789
- Meeting in Philadelphia: December 6, 1790
- Meeting in Washington, DC: November 17, 1800
- Meeting in current chamber: January 4, 1859

Firsts Among Members
1. First senators elected: Robert Morris (PA) and William Maclay (PA), September 30, 1788.
2. First former senator to be elected president: James Monroe (VA), November 1816.
3. First incumbent senator to be elected president: Warren Harding (OH), November 2, 1920.
4. First former president to be elected senator: Andrew Johnson (TN), March 4, 1875.
5. First female senator: Rebecca Felton (D-GA) was appointed to the Senate, and took the oath of office on November 21, 1922.
6. First woman elected: Hattie Caraway (D-AR), January 12, 1932.
7. First African American: Hiram R. Revels (R-MS), took the oath of office on February 25, 1870.
8. First African American female senator: Carol Moseley-Braun (D-IL) took the oath of office on January 5, 1993.

First Events
1. First radio broadcast from chamber: March 4, 1929.
2. First television broadcast from chamber: December 19, 1974 (Vice President Nelson Rockefeller takes oath of office).
3. First regular television broadcast from chamber: C-Span began Senate coverage on June 2, 1986.

Record Holders
1. Longest-serving: Strom Thurmond (R-SC), 46 years and 6 months (as of February 2002).
2. Oldest: Strom Thurmond (R-SC), 99 years (as of December 2001).
3. Youngest: John H. Eaton (TN), 28 years, 5 months (contrary to the Constitution's minimum age requirement of 30 years, he was sworn in on November 16, 1818).
4. Longest speech since 1900: Senator Strom Thurmond (D-SC), filibustering the 1957 Civil Rights Act, spoke for 24 hours, 18 minutes.

Source: U.S. Senate web site at http://www.senate.gov/learning/brief_1.html.

249. Salaries of U.S. Government Leaders

President	$400,000*
Vice President	186,300
Senator	145,100
Representative	145,100
Majority and Minority Leaders	161,200
Speaker of the House	186,300
Chief Justice, U.S. Supreme Court	186,300
Assoc. Justice, U.S. Supreme Court	178,300

*Not counting travel and expense allowances

Source: Office of Personnel Management. Online at www.opm.gov.

250. U.S. Voter Registration and Turnout by Age (in 1996 national election)

Age	% Registered	% Voted
18–20	46	31
21–24	51	33
25–44	62	49
45–64	74	64
65 +	77	67
Total	66	54

Source: Federal Election Commission (1996 data), online at http://www.fec.gov/pages/agedemog.htm.

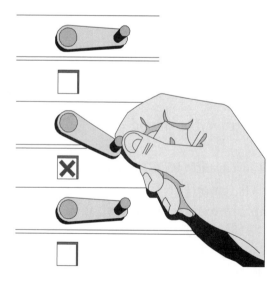

251. Top 10 Lobbyists' Expenditures in Washington, D.C.

Chamber of Commerce of the U.S.	$18,760,000
American Medical Association	$18,180,000
Philip Morris	$14,820,000
American Hospital Association	$12,480,000
Exxon Mobil Corp	$11,695,800
Edison Electric Institute	$11,580,000
Blue Cross/Blue Shield	$11,162,354
SBC Communications	$9,500,000
Schering-Plough Corp	$9,231,000
AT&T	$8,560,000

Source: Influence, Inc.: Lobbyists Spending in Washington (2000 edition). Online at http://www.opensecrets.org/pubs/lobby00/index.asp.

252. Government's Greatest Endeavors of the Second Half of the Twentieth Century*

1. Rebuild Europe after World War II.
2. Expand the Right to Vote.
3. Promote equal access to public accommodations.
4. Reduce disease.
5. Reduce workplace discrimination.
6. Ensure safe food and drinking water.
7. Strengthen the nation's highway system.
8. Increase access to health care for older Americans.
9. Reduce the federal budget deficit.
10. Promote financial security in retirement.

*As selected by 450 professors belonging to the American Historical Association and the American Political Science Association

Source: The Brookings Institution Center for Public Service at http://www.brook.edu. Used with permission.

253. Most Frequently Challenged Books of 1990–2000

1. *Scary Stories* (Series) by Alvin Schwartz
2. *Daddy's Roommate* by Michael Willhoite
3. *I Know Why the Caged Bird Sings* by Maya Angelou
4. *The Chocolate War* by Robert Cormier
5. *The Adventures of Huckleberry Finn* by Mark Twain
6. *Of Mice and Men* by John Steinbeck
7. *Harry Potter* (Series) by J. K. Rowling
8. *Forever* by Judy Blume
9. *Bridge to Terabithia* by Katherine Paterson
10. *Alice* (Series) by Phyllis Reynolds Naylor
11. *Heather Has Two Mommies* by Leslea Newman
12. *My Brother Sam is Dead* by James Lincoln Collier and Christopher Collier
13. *The Catcher in the Rye* by J. D. Salinger
14. *The Giver* by Lois Lowry
15. *It's Perfectly Normal* by Robie Harris
16. *Goosebumps* (Series) by R. L. Stine
17. *A Day No Pigs Would Die* by Robert Newton Peck
18. *The Color Purple* by Alice Walker
19. *Sex* by Madonna
20. *Earth's Children* (Series) by Jean M. Auel

Source: American Library Association.

254. Capital Punishment Statistics

- In 2000, 85 persons in 14 States were executed—40 in Texas; 11 in Oklahoma, 8 in Virginia, 6 in Florida, 5 in Missouri, 4 in Alabama, 3 in Arizona, 2 in Arkansas, and 1 each in Delaware, Louisiana, North Carolina, South Carolina, Tennessee, and California.

- Of persons executed in 2000:
  49 were white
  35 were black
  1 was American Indian

- Of those executed in 2000:
  83 were men
  2 were women

- Eighty of the executions in 2000 were carried out by lethal injection and 5 by electrocution.

- Thirty-eight states and the federal government in 2000 had capital statutes.

- As of May 2001, there are 3,726 people on death row.

- Among inmates under sentence of death and with available criminal histories:
  nearly 2 in 3 had a prior felony conviction
  about 1 in 12 had a prior homicide conviction

- Among persons for whom arrest information was available, the average age at time of arrest was 28; 2% of inmates were age 17 or younger.

- At year end, the youngest inmate under sentence of death was 18; the oldest was 85.

- More than 4,500 people have been executed in the United States since 1930.

- Homicide is the second leading cause of death for persons 15 to 24 years of age and is the leading cause of death for African American and Hispanic youth.

Source: U.S. Department of Justice, Bureau of Justice Statistics. Online at http://www.ojp.usdoj.gov/bjs/cp.htm.

255. Firearm-Related Deaths

	Rate per 100,000
TOTAL	11.3
Gender	
Female	3.3
Male	20.1
Race and ethnicity	
American Indian or Alaska Native	11.3
Asian or Pacific Islander	4.2
Black or African American	20.3
White	10.0
Hispanic or Latino	9.7
Education level (aged 25 to 64 years)	
Less than high school	21.4
High school graduate	17.7
At least some college	7.0
Select firearm-related deaths	
Homicides	4.3
Suicides	6.5
Unintentional deaths	0.5

Source: Youth Violence: A Report of the Surgeon General, January 2001. Online at www.surgeongeneral.gov.

256. Minimum Wage Changes, 1938–1997

(non-farm laborers)

1938	$0.25	**1976**	$2.20
1939	$0.30	**1977**	$2.30
1945	$0.40	**1978**	$2.65
1950	$0.75	**1979**	$2.90
1956	$1.00	**1980**	$3.10
1961	$1.15	**1981**	$3.35
1963	$1.25	**1990**	$3.80
1967	$1.40	**1991**	$4.25
1968	$1.60	**1996**	$4.75
1974	$1.90	**1997**	$5.15
1975	$2.00		

Source: U.S. Department of Labor at http://www.dol.gov.

257. American Nobel Peace Prize Winners, 1906–2002

1906	Theodore Roosevelt, negotiated peace of Russo-Japanese War.
1912	Elihu Root, organized Central American Peace Conference.
1919	Woodrow Wilson, promoted the League of Nations.
1925	G. Dawes, designed plan of payment for German reparations.
1929	Frank Billings Kellogg, negotiated Kellogg-Briand Peace Pact.
1931	Jane Addams, organized Women's International League for Peace and Freedom, and Nicholas M. Butler, for work with Carnegie Endowment for International Peace.
1945	Cordell Hull, worked for peace as Secretary of State.
1946	John R. Mott, for YMCA and refugee work, and Emily Greene Black, who worked with Women's International League for Peace and Freedom.
1950	Ralph J. Bunche, mediated for UN in Palestine.
1953	George C. Marshall, pioneered European Recovery Program.
1962	Linus Pauling, promoted ban on nuclear weapons tests.
1970	Norman E. Borlaug, developed high-yield cereals for Third World countries.
1973	Henry Kissinger, negotiated cease-fire in Vietnam.
1986	Elie Wiesel, worked on behalf of the victims of racism.
2002	Jimmy Carter, worked to mediate international conflicts.

258. Canons of Conduct by Thomas Jefferson

Never put off to tomorrow what you can do today.

Never trouble another with what you can do yourself.

Never spend your money before you have it.

Never buy a thing you do not want because it is cheap, it will be dear to you.

Take care of your cents. Dollars will take care of themselves.

Pride costs more than hunger, thirst or cold.

We never repent of eating too little.

Nothing is troublesome that one does willingly.

Take things always by the smooth handle.

Think so as to please, and so let others if you will have no disputes.

When angry, count to 10 before you speak, if very angry, count to 100.

259. Quotations on Freedom

They that can give up essential liberty to obtain temporary safety deserve neither liberty nor safety.
—BENJAMIN FRANKLIN

Freedom lies in being bold.
—ROBERT FROST

Conformity is the jailer of freedom and the enemy of growth.
—JOHN F. KENNEDY

If there is no struggle, there is no progress. Those who profess to favor freedom, and deprecate agitation, are men who want crops without plowing up the ground, they want rain without thunder and lightning.
—FREDERICK DOUGLASS

Freedom is not worth having if it does not connote freedom to err.
—MOHANDAS GANDHI

Freedom is nothing but a chance to be better.
—ALBERT CAMUS

When freedom does not have a purpose, when it does not wish to know anything about the rule of law engraved in the hearts of men and women, when it does not listen to the voice of conscience, it turns against humanity and society.
—POPE JOHN PAUL II

260. Journals Related to Government

Administration and Society
American Journal of Political Science
American Politics Quarterly
Bureaucrat, The
Columbia Journal of Law and Social Problems
Comparative Political Studies
Congressional Quarterly
Contemporary Policy Issues
Critical Review
Employee Relations Law Journal
Global Affairs
Harvard Law Review
Human Rights Quarterly
International Journal of Public Administration
Journal of Church and State
Journal of Conflict Resolution
Journal of International Affairs
Journal of Law and Society
Journal of Political and Military Sociology
Journal of Public Policy
Law and Policy
Law and Social Inquiry
Law and Society Review
Legislative Studies Quarterly
New Left Review

New Statesman and Society
Northwest University Law Review
Peace and Change
Philosophy and Public Affairs
Policy Sciences
Policy Studies Journal
Political Science Quarterly
Political Studies
Political Theory
Politics
Popular Government
Population Bulletin
Presidential Studies Quarterly
Public Administration
Public Administration Quarterly
Public Administration Review
Public Choice
Publius: The Journal of Federalism
Reason
Society
Southern California Law Review
Texas Law Review
Theory and Decision
Vietnam Generation
Western Political Quarterly
Without Prejudice
World Policy Journal

261. Online Resources for Teaching American Government

American Civil Liberties Union
http://www.aclu.org

American Political Science Association
http://www.apsanet.org

Center for Information and Research on Civic Learning and Engagement (CIRCLE)
http://www.civicyouth.org

(continued)

261. *(continued)*

Civics Online
http://civics-online.org

Democratic National Committee
http://www.democrats.org

FedLaw
http://fedlaw.gsa.gov

National Archives and Records Administration
http://www.nara.gov

Political Resources on the Net
http://www.politicalresources.net/
http://politicalresources.com

Republican National Committee Official Party Site
http://www.rnc.org

Social Studies Government Lessons
http://www.edhelper.com/cat273.htm

State Net
http://www.statenet.com

Thomas: U.S. Congress
http://thomas.loc.gov/home/thomas2.html

U.S. Government Lesson Plans
AskERIC
http://askeric.org/cgi-bin/lessons.cgi/Social_Studies/US_Government

U.S. House of Representatives
http://www.house.gov

U.S. Senate
http://www.senate.gov

U.S. Supreme Court
http://www.supremecourtus.gov

White House
http://www.whitehouse.gov

Lists for
Consumer Economics

262. Primary Federal Consumer Protection Agencies

Consumer Product Safety Commission
Environmental Protection Agency
Federal Reserve System
Federal Trade Commission
Food and Drug Administration
Food Safety and Quality Service
National Highway Safety Administration
United States Postal Inspection Service
United States Attorney General's Office

263. Areas Needing Consumer Protection

False or misleading advertising
Excessive interest rates
Pollution of the environment
Against the power of monopolies
Unfair selling practices
Selling harmful products
Deceptive labeling

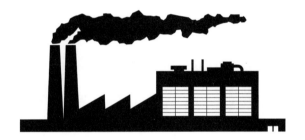

264. How to Complain Effectively

Save and submit any receipts or warranties.
Get your facts first.
Allow a reasonable time for action.
Be specific about what you want.
Avoid personal attacks; use objective language.
Contact the Better Business Bureau for advice on options.
Learn how to use the small claims court.
Check out relevant trade associations.
Be persistent.

265. Life Expectancy of Household Appliances (in years)

Compactors	10
Dishwashers	10
Dryers	14
Disposal	10
Freezers, compact	12
Freezers, standard	16
Microwave ovens	11
Electric ranges	17
Gas ranges	19
Gas ovens	14
Refrigerators	17
Washers, automatic	13

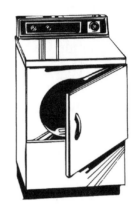

Source: Appliance Statistical Review, April 1990.

266. Appliances in U.S. Households

Clothes washer	77.5%
Clothes dryer	71.2%
Dishwasher	50.2%
Microwave oven	83.0%
Range	99.2%
Refrigerator	99.8%
Stereo equipment	68.8%
TV, color	98.7%

Source: 2001 Statistical Abstract of the United States.

267. Metric Conversion

Length		Length	
U.S. unit	*Metric equivalent*	*Metric*	*U.S. equivalent*
inch	2.54 centimeters	millimeter	.039 inches
foot	30.48 centimeters	centimeter	.394 inches
yard	.914 meters	decimeter	3.937 inches
rod	5.029 meters	meter	39.37 inches
mile	1.609 kilometers	kilometer	.621 mile

Capacity		Capacity	
pint	.473 liters	milliliter	0.34 fluid ounces
quart	.946 liters	liter	1.057 liquid quarts
gallon	3.79 liters	kililiter	264.18 gallons

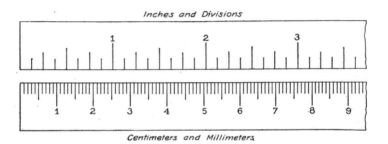

Inches and Divisions

Centimeters and Millimeters

268. Liquid Measures

4 gills = 1 pint
2 pints = 1 quart
4 quarts = 1 gallon
31½ gallons = 1 barrel
2 barrels = 1 hogshead

269. Length Measurements

12 inches = 1 foot
3 feet = 1 yard
5½ yards = 1 rod or pole
40 rods = 1 furlong
8 furlongs = 1 statute mile (5,280 feet)

270. Nautical Measurements

6 feet = 1 fathom
120 fathoms = 1 cable length
6,082 feet = 1 nautical mile

271. Area Measurements

144 sq. inches = 1 sq. foot
9 sq. feet = 1 sq. yard
30 sq. yards = 1 sq. rod
160 sq. rods = 1 acre
640 sq. rods = 1 sq. mile
6 sq. miles = 1 township

272. Household Measures

Unit	Equivalent
teaspoon	⅙ fluid ounce
tablespoon	3 teaspoons
cup	16 tablespoons
pint	2 cups
quart	2 pints
gallon	4 quarts
peck	8 quarts
bushel	4 pecks

273. Weight Measures

1 carat = 200 milligrams = 3.086 grains
1 gram = .001 kilograms = .035 ounces
1 milligram = .001 grams
1 ounce = 28 grams
1 pound = 16 ounces = 453.6 grams
1 kilogram = 1,000 grams = 2.21 pounds
1 short ton = 2,000 pounds
1 long ton = 2,240 pounds

274. Dry Measures

2 pints = 1 quart
8 quarts = 1 peck
4 pecks = 1 bushel
3.28 bushels = 1 barrel

Pint   **Quart**   **Peck**   **Half-Bushel**   **Bushel**

275. Hottest Job Prospects, 2000–2010

Computer software engineers
Computer support specialists
Network and computer systems administrators
Network systems and data communications analysts
Desktop publishers
Database administrators
Personal and home care aides
Computer systems analysts
Medical assistants
Social and human service assistants
Physician assistants
Medical records and health information technicians
Computer and information systems managers
Home health aides
Physical therapist aides
Occupational therapist aides
Audiologists
Fitness trainers and aerobics instructors
Veterinary assistants and laboratory animal caretakers

Source: U.S. Department of Labor. Online at http://www.bls.gov/emp/emptab3.htm.

276. Occupations Losing the Most Jobs, 2000–2010

Occupation	Thousands
Farmers and ranchers	–328,000
Order clerks	–71,000
Tellers	–59,000
Insurance claims and policy processing clerks	–58,000
Word processors and typists	–57,000
Sewing machine operators	–51,000
Dishwashers	–42,000
Switchboard operators, including answering service	–41,000
Loan interviewers and clerks	–38,000
Computer operators	–33,000

Source: Bureau of Labor Statistics Employment Projections, January 2002.

277. Leading Occupations of Employed Women

	Total Employed Women* (1,000s)	Percent Women	Ratio of Women's Earnings to Men's Earnings
Sales workers, retail and personal services	4,306	63.5	55.8
Secretaries	2,594	98.9	NA
Managers and administrators	2,418	31.0	66.3
Cashiers	2,277	77.5	88.2
Sales supervisors and proprietors	1,989	40.3	69.8
Registered nurses	1,959	97.8	87.9
Elementary school teachers	1,814	83.3	81.5
Nursing aides, orderlies, and attendants	1,784	90.0	88.1
Bookkeepers, accounting & auditing clerks	1,584	92.1	88.7
Receptionists	984	96.8	NA
Sales workers, other commodities	949	66.5	69.3
Accountants and auditors	903	56.7	72.4
Cooks	899	43.3	89.5
Investigators and adjusters, exclud. insurance	833	75.9	82.6
Janitors and cleaners	811	36.3	83.1
Secondary school teachers	764	57.9	88.6
Hairdressers and cosmetologists	748	91.2	NA
General office clerks	722	83.6	91.3
Mgrs, food serving and lodging establishments	677	46.8	73.0
Teachers' aides	646	91.0	NA

*2000 annual averages for full-time workers

Source: Women's Bureau, U.S. Dept. of Labor at www.dol.gov/dol.

278. Effects of Mandatory Overtime

Decreased attention

Less sleep

Higher number of accidents

Increased fatigue

Increased levels of depression

Greater risk of injury and illness

Higher job stress levels

Eventual job burnout

Less community volunteering

Elimination of after-work classes

More likely to drive while feeling drowsy

Source: Lonnie Golden & Helene Jorgensen. Time after time: Mandatory overtime in the U.S. economy. Economic Policy Institute at http://www.epinet.org/.

279. Most Dangerous Jobs in America

Fatality rate per 100,000 employees

Timber cutters	122.1
Airplane pilots	100.8
Construction laborers	28.3
Truck drivers	27.6
Farming occupations	25.1
Groundskeepers	14.9
Laborers (non-const.)	13.2
Police & detectives	12.1
Fatality rate for all occupations:	4.3

Source: Bureau of Labor Statistics, 2000.

280. Nontraditional Occupations for Women

	Percent Female
Crane and tower operators	1.4
Construction trades	2.3
Tool and die makers	2.7
Excavating and loading machine operators	3.1
Firefighting and fire-prevention occupations	3.6
Construction laborers	3.7
Garbage collectors	3.7
Airplane pilots and navigators	3.9
Rail transportation occupations	3.9
Truck drivers	4.7
Welders and cutters	4.9
Mechanics and repairers	4.9
Grading, dozer, and scraper operators	5.5
Machinists	6.3
Forestry and logging occupations	8.3

Source: Women's Bureau (March 2001). U.S. Dept. of Labor.

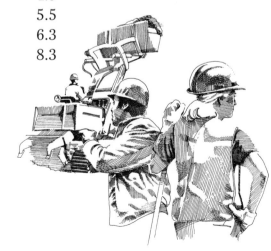

281. Career Opportunities in Economics

account executive
bank manager
claims adjuster
consumer advocate
credit manager
economic development planner
economic forecaster
econometrician
economist
environmental economist
financial analyst
fund raiser
internal auditor
investment counselor
labor specialist
loan counselor

lobbyist
market researcher
marketing representative
mortgage loan officer
portfolio administrator
rate analyst
real estate broker
rent control administrator
revenue officer
risk analyst
securities analyst
stock broker
tax auditor
teacher
underwriter
urban planner

282. Investment Opportunities

art and collectibles
bonds
certificates of deposit
common stocks
GNMA's
gold and precious metals
limited partnerships
money market accounts
municipal bonds
mutual funds, bond

mutual funds, stock
NOW accounts
passbook savings accounts
preferred stocks
real estate unit trusts
U.S. notes and bonds
U.S. savings bonds
U.S. treasury bills
zero coupon bonds

283. Types of Mortgages

adjustable rate mortgage
assumable mortgage
balloon mortgage
fixed rate mortgage
graduated payment adjustable rate
  mortgage
graduated payment mortgage
growing equity mortgage
home equity mortgage

installment contract interest rate
  buydowns
lease with option to buy
seller mortgage
shared appreciation mortgage
shared equity mortgage
wrap-around mortgage
zero interest mortgage

284. Best Time to Buy

January	appliances
	books
	carpeting
	china
	furniture
	furs
	houses
	linen, white goods
	shoes
	tools
	towels
February	housewares
	electronic appliances
	men's clothing
	sports equipment
	toys
	used cars
March	children's shoes
	garden supplies
	ice skates
	luggage
	ski equipment
April	paint supplies
	women's shoes
May	lawn furniture
	purses
	shoes

June	women's shoes
July	appliances
	luggage
	summer clothes
	summer sports gear
	swimming suits
August	coats
	furniture
	linen, white goods
	school clothes
	tires
September	cars
	bicycles
	fall clothing
	gardening supplies
October	cars
	china
	coats
	school supplies
	winter clothing
November	blankets
	large appliances
	men's suits
	shoes
December	after-Christmas sales
	hats
	used cars

285. Personal Budget Expenses

rent or mortgage payments
property taxes
electricity, gas, oil
water & sewer
home maintenance
property insurance
telephone
car payments
auto insurance
auto maintenance & repairs
taxes, auto tags, fees
parking
gas & oil
groceries
meals away from home
clothing
laundry, dry cleaning

doctors, dentists
medical supplies
health insurance
life insurance
personal care
education
vacations
recreation, movies
subscriptions & books
hobbies
dues to clubs and organizations
church donations
donations to charities
gifts
savings
interest on credit cards
miscellaneous expenses

286. Parts of a Check

account number
American Bankers Association routing number
amount in numbers
amount in words
check issue date
check number
check writer's signature
memo
payee
pay to the order of
routing information
writer's name and address
endorsement line (on back)

287. Sources of Loans

state or federal guaranteed student loans
personal loans from banks
pawnshops
friends, relatives
against cash value of insurance
bank charge cards
savings and loan institutions
banks
credit unions
co-signed loans from banks
second mortgage bank loans
seller financed mortgages
unsecured personal loans

288. Personal Assets

equity in home
automobile
retirement fund
household items, furniture
savings account
checking account
stocks
bonds
mutual funds
other investments, collections
insurance
cash value
money owed to you (cash)

289. U.S. Household Income and Benefits

Total households	$104,733,569*
Less than $10,000	$10,022,803
$10,000 to $14,999	6,995,026
$15,000 to $24,999	13,994,472
$25,000 to $34,999	13,491,042
$35,000 to $49,999	17,032,000
$50,000 to $74,999	20,017,509
$75,000 to $99,999	10,479,853
$100,000 to $149,999	8,125,132
$150,000 to $199,999	2,336,503
$200,000 or more	2,239,229
Median household income	$41,349
Mean household income	$55,263

*In 2000 inflation-adjusted dollars

Source: 2000 U.S. Census.

290. Credit Rules

- Credit cards are just like a loan; you have to pay what you owe.
- Keep track of how much you spend. Remember that incidental and impulse purchases add up fast.
- Save your receipts. Compare them with your monthly bill. Promptly report problems to the company that issued the card.
- Never lend your card to anyone.
- Owing more than you can repay can damage your credit rating. That can make it hard to finance a car, rent an apartment, get insurance—even get a job.
- Pay your bill on time, and in full when possible. If you don't, you'll have to pay finance charges on the unpaid balance—and it takes forever to get caught up if you just pay the minimum.
- Federal law limits your liability for unauthorized charges to $50 per card.

Source: Federal Trade Commission (FTC). http://www.ftc.gov.

291. Preventing Credit and Debit/Check Card Fraud

- Sign cards when they arrive, so no one can forge your signature on the cards and use them.
- Keep a record of your card numbers and expiration dates and the phone number of the card issuer in a safe place. If your card is stolen or missing, notify the card company immediately.
- Don't give your credit card number over the phone to unfamiliar companies or to people who say they need it to "verify" your identity in order to give you a prize.
- Destroy carbons and incorrect charge slips.
- Draw a line through blank spaces on charge slips. Do not sign a blank charge slip.
- Keep copies of all sales slips. Open credit card bills promptly and compare the sales slips with the charges on your bill.
- Report billing errors and unauthorized charges to your credit card company right away.

Source: The Consumer Action Handbook, 2002 edition. Federal Consumer Information Center.

292. A Summary of Your Rights Under the Fair Credit Reporting Act

The federal Fair Credit Reporting Act (FCRA) is designed to promote accuracy, fairness, and privacy of information in the files of every "consumer reporting agency" (CRA). The FCRA gives you specific rights, as outlined below. You may have additional rights under state law. You may contact a state or local consumer protection agency or a state attorney general to learn those rights.

- You must be told if information in your file has been used against you.
- You can find out what is in your file. At your request, a CRA must give you the information in your file, and a list of everyone who has requested it recently.
- You can dispute inaccurate information with the CRA. If you tell a CRA that your file contains inaccurate information, the CRA must investigate the items (usually within 30 days) by presenting to its information source all relevant evidence you submit, unless your dispute is frivolous.
- Inaccurate information must be corrected or deleted. A CRA must remove or correct inaccurate or unverified information from its files, usually within 30 days after you dispute it.

(continued)

292. *(continued)*

- You can dispute inaccurate items with the source of the information. If you tell anyone—such as a creditor who reports to a CRA—that you dispute an item, they may not then report the information to a CRA without including a notice of your dispute.

- Outdated information may not be reported. In most cases, a CRA may not report negative information that is more than seven years old; ten years for bankruptcies.

- Access to your file is limited. A CRA may provide information about you only to people with a need recognized by the FCRA—usually to consider an application with a creditor, insurer, employer, landlord, or other business.

- Your consent is required for reports that are provided to employers, or reports that contain medical information.

- You may choose to exclude your name from CRA lists for unsolicited credit and insurance offers.

- You may seek damages from violators. If a CRA, a user or (in some cases) a provider of CRA data, violates the FCRA, you may sue them in state or federal court.

Source: Federal Trade Commission. Online at www.ftc.gov.

293. Top Consumer Complaints

Health care	2%
Office supplies and services	4%
Travel, vacation & timeshare	5%
Business opportunities and work-at-home plans	5%
Telephone: Pay-per call/info services	6%
Magazines and buyers clubs	6%
Advance-fee loans and credit protection/repair	8%
Internet auctions	9%
Internet services and computer complaints	10%
Prizes/sweepstakes and lotteries	11%
Identity theft	23%
Other	11%

Source: Federal Trade Commission, 2001.

294. Tips for Shopping Smart and Avoiding Fraud

The most common problems you might encounter when shopping on the phone, online or by mail order are delayed delivery, out of stock items, incorrect items shipped, damaged items received and price changes. To avoid these problems:

- Know whom you are dealing with. If the company isn't familiar to you, check it out with your local or state consumer protection
- Keep track of your order. If it's late, it is your choice whether to wait longer or cancel. If you cancel, your money must be refunded within 7 days (or your account must be credited within one billing cycle if you charged the order). The company can't substitute a merchandise credit for a refund.
- When you use a credit card to pay for products or services, you have a right to dispute the charges if the items were not delivered or were misrepresented.
- Never send cash—you won't have any proof of payment.
- Don't act immediately. High pressure sales tactics are a danger sign of fraud. Get all the information and consider it carefully.
- Don't believe promises of easy money. No one can legitimately claim you'll make big earnings from business opportunities, promise high returns on investments, or guarantee that you will win a lottery or sweepstakes.
- Be careful what information you provide. Give your credit card, debit card, or bank account number only if you're paying for a purchase using that account—never to verify your identity. Don't provide your social security number unless you're applying for credit or employment. Using your personal information, crooks can steal from you and impersonate you to steal from others.
- Do not be taken in by lotteries, pyramid schemes, multi-level marketing schemes, or companies that ask for payment in advance, especially for employment referrals, credit repair, or providing a loan or credit card.
- Walk away or hang up when you hear the following: "Sign now or the price will increase"; "You have been specially selected . . . "; "You have won . . ."; "All we need is your credit card (or bank account) number—for identification only"; "All you pay for is postage, handling, taxes . . ."; "Make money in your spare time—guaranteed income . . ."; "We really need you to buy magazines (a water purifier, a vacation package, office products) from us because we can earn 15 extra credits . . ."; "I just happen to have some leftover material . . ."
- Sweepstakes: Don't pay if it's free or you have won. It's another danger sign of fraud if you are asked to pay a fee to get something free, claim a prize, or win a vacation.

Source: The Consumer Action Handbook, 2002 edition.

295. Home Ownership in the United States

Approximately two-thirds of U.S. householders (69.8 million or 66.2 percent) owned their homes, according to 2000 census data.

Between 1890 and 1940, less than half of U.S. households owned their homes.

The number of housing units in the United States exceeded 115.9 million in 2000.

The Great Depression drove ownership rates to their lowest level of the century in 1940 (43.6 percent).

Since the 1950 census, when homeowners represented 55 percent of all householders, the rate of homeownership has increased steadily.

By 1960, because of the post-World War II economic boom, favorable tax laws and easier mortgage financing, homeownership topped 60 percent.

Approximately 4 out of 5 married-couple families owned their homes in 2000.

Women who lived alone were more likely than lone male householders to be owners (56 percent versus 47 percent).

Only about 18 percent of young householders under 25 were homeowners, but the percentage climbed to 81 percent for householders 65 to 74 years old.

Source: Housing Characteristics: 2000, U.S. Census Bureau.

296. U.S. Inflation: 1900–2000

How much an item costing $100 in 1900 would cost each decade later:

1900	$100.00
1910	$107.92
1920	$206.98
1930	$205.06
1940	$166.49
1950	$285.81
1960	$349.64
1970	$439.78
1980	$872.39
1990	$1489.61
2000	$1995.03

297. Ways to Improve Gas Mileage

- steady acceleration, avoid jackrabbit starts
- minimize short trips, combine shorter errands
- change oil and filters as specified by auto manufacturer
- keep carburetor and ignition system tuned
- slow down; mileage decreases above 55 mph
- avoid heavy loads when possible
- rough roads will decrease mileage
- use air conditioning only when necessary
- driving into headwinds cuts fuel economy
- cold weather will yield lower mileage

298. Household Safety Checklist

storage rack for knives
ladders properly maintained
secure handrails on all stairs
know how to turn off gas main
nightlights used
medicines out of reach of children
non-skid mat in shower or tub
no electric appliances near sink
proper stair treads

appliances properly grounded
door off any unused refrigerator
emergency numbers readily available
proper guards on any power tools
use of goggles with power tools
power tools grounded
appropriate lighting in work areas
safety glass installed in all doors
dead limbs trimmed from trees

299. Home Fire Safety Checklist

smoke detectors throughout home
working batteries in all smoke detectors
workable fire extinguishers available
sleep with bedroom doors
closed fireproof wastebaskets
proper containers and storage for flammable
   liquids
sufficient wall outlets
screen in front of fireplace
oil rags properly disposed or stored
fire-retardant curtains
use proper size fuses
door and windows can be opened from inside
wastebaskets emptied regularly
annual inspection of chimney
periodically check all fire extinguishers
space heaters away from curtains
appropriate electric cords
properly serviced furnace
no piles of rubbish near house
fire escape plan rehearsed
matches and lighters stored away from children

300. Labor Unions

Amalgamated Clothing and Textile Workers Union (ACTWU)
American Federation of Labor & Congress of Industrial Organizations
   (AFLCIO)
American Federation of Musicians of the United States and Canada (AF of M)
American Federation of State, County and Municipal Employees
Actors Equity Association
Airline Pilots Association
Allied Industrial Workers of America (AIW)
Aluminum Brick & Glass Workers International Union (ABG-WIU)
American Association of University Professors (AAUP)
American Federation of Government Employees (AFGE)
American Federation of Teachers (AFT)
American Postal Workers Union (APWU)
Bakery, Confectionary & Tobacco Workers International Union (BC&T)
Brotherhood of Painters and Allied Trades (IBPAT)

300. *(continued)*

Brotherhood of Railway, Airline and Steamship Clerks, Freight Handlers, Express and Station Employees (BRAC)

Brotherhood of Teamsters, Chauffeurs, Warehousemen and Helpers of America (IBT)

Carpenters and Joiners of America

Chemical Workers Union

Communication Workers of America

Farm Workers of America (UFW)

Food and Commercial Workers International Union (UFCW)

Fraternal Order of Police

Glass, Pottery, Plastics & Allied Workers International Union (GPPAW)

Graphic Communications International Union (GCIU)

Hotel Employees and Restaurant Employees International Union

International Association of Bridge, Structural and Ornamental Iron Workers

International Association of Firefighters

International Brotherhood of Electrical Workers (IBEW)

International Ladies Garment Workers Union

International Ladies Garment Workers Union Longshoremen's Association

Laborers' International Union of North America

Machinists and Aerospace Workers

National Association of Letter Carriers (NALC)

National Education Association (NEA)

Oil, Chemical, and Atomic Workers International Union (OCAW)

Retail, Wholesale and Department Store Union

Service Employees International Union (SEIU)

Sheet Metal Workers' International Association (SMWIA)

Union of Operating Engineers (UOE)

United Garment Workers of America (UGWA)

United Mines Workers of America (UMWA)

United Paperhangers International Union (UPIU)

United Steelworkers of America (USWA)

United Transportation Union (UTU)

301. Factors to Consider in Selecting a Car

braking ability
cargo room
color
comfort
convenience of controls
convenience of displays
cost
dealer's reputation
gas mileage (mpg)
head room
leg room
maneuverability
noise, riding

options available
power
reliability
repair record
safety rating
service availability
smoothness of ride
style
transmission, smooth
  shifting
trunk space
warranty

302. Factors Affecting the Cost of a Diamond

color
clarity
cut
carat weight

303. Factors to Consider in Selecting a College

admission standards
advising services
attractiveness of campus
campus safety record
climate
cost
distance from home
employment placement services
extracurriculuar activities
financial aid
majors available
male–female ratio
number of students
reputation of faculty
student–faculty ratio
student–faculty relationships
student services

304. Abbreviations of Academic Degrees

B.A.	Bachelor of Arts		**D.O.**	Doctor of Osteopathy
B.B.A.	Bachelor of Business Administration		**D.S.**	Doctor of Science
B.D.	Bachelor of Divinity		**D.V.M.**	Doctor of Veterinary Medicine
B.E.	Bachelor of Education		**Ed.B.**	Bachelor of Education
B.E.E.	Bachelor of Electrical Engineering		**Ed.D.**	Doctor of Education
B.F.A.	Bachelor of Fine Arts		**Ed.M.**	Master of Education
B.L.S.	Bachelor of Library Science		**E.E.**	Electrical Engineer
B.S.	Bachelor of Science		**J.D.**	Doctor of Jurisprudence
B.T.	Bachelor of Theology		**L.B.**	Bachelor of Letters
C.E.	Civil Engineer		**L.H.D.**	Doctor of Humanities
Ch.D.	Doctor of Chemistry		**LL.D.**	Doctor of Laws
Ch.E.	Chemical Engineer		**M.A.**	Master of Arts
D.C.	Doctor of Chiropractic		**M.Agr.**	Master of Agriculture
D.D.	Doctor of Divinity		**M.B.A.**	Master of Business Administration
D.D.S.	Doctor of Dental Surgery		**M.D.**	Doctor of Medicine
D.F.A.	Doctor of Fine Arts		**M.S.W.**	Masters of Social Work
D.L.S.	Doctor of Library Science		**Ph.D.**	Doctor of Philosophy
			Psy.D.	Doctor of Psychology

305. American Architectural Styles

Art Deco	Prairie
Art Moderne	Pueblo
Bungalow	Queen Anne
Cape Cod	Ranch
Chateau	Renaissance Revival
Colonial Revival	Roman Classicism
Dutch Colonial	Romanesque
Egyptian Revival	Revival
Georgian	Saltbox
Gothic Revival	Second Empire
Greek Revival	Second Renaissance Revival
Federal	Shingle
French Colonial	Southern Colonial
International	Spanish Colonial
Italian Villa	Split-Level
Italianate	Sullivanesque
Mission	Victorian Gothic
Octagon	Victorian Romanesque

306. Recording Industry Consumer Profile, 1991–2000

Age	Percent of Total Recording Industry Sales									
	1991	1992	1993	1994	1995	1996	1997	1998	1999	2000
10–14 yrs.	8.2	8.6	8.6	7.9	8.0	7.9	8.9	9.1	8.5	8.9
15–19 yrs.	18.1	18.2	16.7	16.8	17.1	17.2	16.8	15.8	12.6	12.9
20–24 yrs.	17.9	16.1	15.1	15.4	15.3	15.0	13.8	12.2	12.6	12.5
25–29 yrs.	14.5	13.8	13.2	12.6	12.3	12.5	11.7	11.4	10.5	10.6
30–34 yrs.	12.5	12.2	11.9	11.8	12.1	11.4	11.0	11.4	10.1	9.8
35–39 yrs.	9.8	10.9	11.1	11.5	10.8	11.1	11.6	12.6	10.4	10.6
40–44 yrs.	6.7	7.4	8.5	7.9	7.5	9.1	8.8	8.3	9.3	9.6
45 + yrs.	11.8	12.2	14.1	15.4	16.1	15.1	16.5	18.1	24.7	23.8

Source: Recording Industry Association of America.

Graph analysis activity

1. What percent of the 1994 recording industry sales were made by people 20 to 24 years old?

2. Youth under 20 years of age accounted for what percentage of the recording industry sales in 2000?

3. Which age group showed the greatest growth in its proportion of recording industry purchases from 1991 to 2000?

4. What factors might account for the dramatic growth in the proportion of purchases made by the group in the previous question?

Answers: 1. 15.4% 2. 21.8 3. 45 + 4. Increased cost of CD's; rise of Internet resources such as Napster; new formats, such as MP3; aging Baby Boomers swelled the number of folks over 45.

307. Recording Industry Sales, 1991–2000

	Percent of Year's Sales									
Medium	1991	1992	1993	1994	1995	1996	1997	1998	1999	2000
Full-length CD	38.9	46.5	51.1	58.4	65.0	68.4	70.2	74.8	83.2	89.3
Full-length Cassette	49.8	43.6	38.0	32.1	25.1	19.3	18.2	14.8	8.0	4.9
Single (all types)	8.8	7.5	9.2	7.4	7.5	9.3	9.3	6.8	5.4	2.5
Music Video	0.4	1.0	1.3	0.8	0.9	1.0	0.6	1.0	0.9	0.8
Vinyl LP	1.7	1.3	0.3	0.8	0.5	0.6	0.7	0.7	0.5	0.5
	100%	100%	100%	100%	100%	100%	100%	100%	100%	100%

Source: Recording Industry Association of America.

308. Amusement Ride Injuries

	Non-Occupational Amusement Ride Injuries		
Year	Fixed Site	Mobile Site	Total
1993	4,195	2,990	7,185
1994	3,766	2,949	6,715
1995	3,969	3,251	7,220
1996	3,419	2,963	6,383
1998	6,523	2,751	9,274
1999	7,629	2,788	10,417
2000	6,594	3,985	10,580

Source: U.S. Consumer Product Safety Commission.

309. Biggest Companies in the U.S.

	2001 revenues in billions
Wal-mart Stores	$220.4
Exxon Mobil	$212.9
General Motors	$177.3
Ford Motor	$162.4
General Electric	$126.0

Source: The Associated Press.

310. Busiest U.S. Airports

(ranked by number of passengers boarding major carriers)

1. Atlanta (Hartfield Intl.)
2. Chicago (O'Hare)
3. Dallas/Ft. Worth
4. Los Angeles
5. Denver
6. Detroit (Wayne County)
7. San Francisco
8. Phoenix (Sky Harbor Intl.)
9. Las Vegas (McCarran Intl.)
10. Minneapolis (Minneapolis/St. Paul Intl.)

Source: U.S. Bureau of Transportation Statistics, 2000. Online at http://www.bts.gov/.

311. Candy Consumption in the U.S.

In the year 2000:

- Total candy consumption: 7.1 billion pounds
- Total chocolate consumption: 3.3 billion pounds

Estimated retail sales:

- Total—$23.8 billion
- Chocolate—$13 billion
- Non-chocolate—$7.5 billion
- Gum—$2 billion—.5 billion pounds

Halloween is the top candy holiday (almost $2 billion in sales), followed by Easter ($1.9 billion), Valentine's Day ($1.6 billion), and winter holidays ($1.4 billion).

Americans will purchase an estimated 20 million pounds of candy corn for Halloween, and 93 percent of children will go trick-or-treating.

Source: Candy USA at http://www.candyusa.org/. Used with permission.

312. Eight Rungs of the Giving Ladder

Maimonides, a 12th-century Jewish scholar, invented the following ladder of giving. Each rung up represents a higher degree of virtue:

1. The lowest: Giving begrudgingly and making the recipient feel disgraced or embarrassed.
2. Giving cheerfully but giving too little.
3. Giving cheerfully and adequately but only after being asked.
4. Giving before being asked.
5. Giving when you do not know who is the individual benefiting, but the recipient knows your identity.
6. Giving when you know who is the individual benefiting, but the recipient does not knows your identity.
7. Giving when neither the donor nor the recipient is aware of the other's identity.
8. The Highest: Giving money, a loan, your time or whatever else it takes to enable an individual to be self-reliant.

Source: American Institute of Philanthropy. Online at www.charitywatch.org/articles/eightrungs.html.

313. Home Computer Use and the Internet

Facts from 2000 Census Data

A ratio of 9 in 10 school-aged children (6 to 17 years old) had access to a computer in 2000, with 4 in 5 using a computer at school and 2 in 3 with one at home, according to census data.

Approximately 54 million households, or 51 percent, had one or more computers in the home in August 2000, up from 42 percent in December 1998.

Of the total U.S. population, about 1 in 3 adults used E-mail from home in 2000.

Nearly 9 in 10 family households with annual incomes of $75,000 or more had at least one computer and about 8 in 10 had at least one household member who used the Internet at home.

Among family households with incomes below $25,000, nearly 3 in 10 had a computer and about 2 in 10 had Internet access.

Two-thirds of households with a school-age child had a computer, and 53 percent had Internet access.

E-mail is the most common Internet application at home, used by 88 percent of adults and 73 percent of children who are online.

Ninety-four million people used the Internet at home in 2000, up from 57 million in 1998.

Source: Home Computers and Internet Use in the United States, U.S. Census Bureau. August 2000.

314. Internet Usage Statistics

(Data for January 2002)

- An estimated 37 million Web sites were online.

- The global online population exceeded 529 million; projected to grow to 741 million by the end of 2002.

- Only 43% of the world's Internet users were native English speakers.

- 143 million people, or 54% of the total U.S. population, were online.

- U.S. Internet users go online 9.8 hours per week.

- 48.9% of U.S. Internet users made online purchases in 2001.

- Television viewing diminished as Internet usage increased. In 2001 Internet users watched 4.5 hours per week less television than non-users.

- Internet users make an estimated 275,000,000 searches each day.

- Males constitute 59% of the online population.

- U.S. users generated an estimated 2.6 trillion electronic mail messages in 2001.

Sources: U.S. Department of Commerce; NUA Internet Surveys at nua.com; Electronic Messaging Association.

315. Internet Activities

About 106 million Americans have gone online. Here are the kinds of things they do:

	Percent of those with Internet access
Send E-mail	93
Do an Internet search to answer a question	80
Look for info on a hobby	79
Research a product or service before buying it	73
Get travel information	68
Surf the Web for fun	68
Surf for info about movies, books, other leisure activities	65
Check the weather	64
Get news	63
Look for health/medical information	57
Research for school or training	53
Buy a product	52
Do any type of research for your job	52
Visit a government Web site	51

(continued)

315. *(continued)*

	Percent of those with Internet access
Watch a video clip or listen to an audio clip	50
Look for political news/information	48
Get financial information	45
Send an instant message	44
Buy or make a reservation for travel	38
Check sports scores	38
Look for information about a job	37
Listen to music online	37
Visit an online support group	36
Play a game	34
Chat in a chat room or in an online discussion	26
Download music files	25
Look for information about a place to live	22
Look for religious/spiritual information	19
Bank online	18
Participate in an online auction	15
Buy or sell stocks, bonds, or mutual funds	14
Make a phone call	10
Go to a dating Web site	9
Buy groceries	8
Gamble	5

Source: Pew Internet & American Life Project Survey, Nov.–Dec. 2001. Online at http://www.pewinternet.org. Used with permission.

316. Identity Theft

Over 86,000 identity thefts were reported in 2001. The average amount of out-of-pocket expenses per victim was $1,173.

How Victims' Information Was Used	*Percent of All Victims**
Credit card fraud	42
Phone or utilities fraud	20
Bank fraud	13
Employment-related fraud	9
Loan fraud	7
Government documents/benefits fraud	6
Other identity theft fraud	19

*Approximately 20% of all victims experienced more than one type of identity theft.

Source: Identity Theft Data Clearinghouse, Federal Trade Commission, 2002.

317. Tips for Wise Online Shopping

- Know whom you are dealing with.
- Protect your privacy.
- Order only on a secure online server.
- Guard your online password.
- Pay the safest way.

- Check the return/refund policy.
- Always read the fine print.
- Check the delivery dates.
- Review warranties.
- Compare prices.
- Check handling and shipping fees.

Source: Federal Trade Commission (FTC). Online at http://www.ftc.gov/bcp/menu-internet.htm.

318. Economics Related Journals

The Action Faction
The American Economic Review
The American Economist
American Journal of Economies and Sociology
Business Economies
Canadian Consumer
Challenge
Changing Times
Consumer Bulletin
Consumer Life
Consumer Reports
Consumer's Digest Magazine
Dollars and Sense
Economic Development and Cultural Change
Economic Facts
Economic Geography
Economic Inquiry
The Energy Journal
Explorations in Economic History
FDA Consumer
The Financial Review
Fortune
Growth and Change

Harvard Business Review
Inquiry
The Journal of Behavioral Economics
Journal of Comparative Economics
Journal of Developmental Economics
Journal of Economic Behavior and Organization
Journal of Economic Education
Journal of Economic Issues
Journal of Health Economics
Journal of Labor Research
Journal of Marketing
Journal of Political Economy
Journal of Retailing
Journal of Urban Economics
Labor History
Money
Monthly Labor Review
New England Economic Review
Problems of Communism
Public Choice
Quarterly Review of Economics and Business
Review of Social Economy
Southern Economic Journal

319. Consumer Interest Groups

Alliance Against Fraud in Telemarketing and Electronic Commerce (AAFTEC)
National Consumers League
1701 K Street, NW, Suite 1200
Washington, DC 20006
E-mail: info@nclnet.org
www.nclnet.org

American Council on Consumer Interests (ACCI)
University of Missouri
Columbia, MO 65211
E-mail: acci@showme.misso-suri.edu
www.consumerinterests.org

Coalition Against Insurance Fraud
1012 14th Street NW, Suite 200
Washington, DC 20005
www.InsuranceFraud.org

Consumer Action
717 Market Street, Suite 310
San Francisco, CA 94103
E-mail: info@consumer-action.org
www.consumer-action.org

Consumer Alert
1001 Connecticut Avenue, NW
Suite 1128
Washington, DC 20036
E-mail: info@consumeralert.org
www.consumeralert.org

Consumer Federation of America (CFA)
1424 16th Street, NW, Suite 604
Washington, DC 20036
www.consumerfed.org

Jump$tart Coalition for Personal Financial Literacy
919 18th Street, NW
Washington, DC 20006
E-mail: info@jumpstartcoali-tion.org
www.jumpstart.org

National Coalition for Consumer Education
1701 K Street NW, Suite 1200
Washington, DC 20006
E-mail: ncce@nclnet.org
www.lifesmarts.org

National Consumer Law Center (NCLC)
18 Tremont Street
Boston, MA 02108
E-mail: consumerlaw@nclc.org
www.consumerlaw.org

National Consumers League (NCL)
1701 K Street NW, Suite 1200
Washington, DC 20006
E-mail: info@nclnet.org
www.nclnet.org

National Institute for Consumer Education (NICE)
559 Gary Owen Building
Eastern Michigan University
Ypsilanti, MI 48197
E-mail: gwen.reichbach@emich.edu
www.nice.emich.edu

Public Citizen, Inc.
1600 20th Street, NW
Washington, DC 20009
Fax: 202-588-7799
www.citizen.org

Society of Consumer Affairs Professionals in Business (SOCAP)
801 North Fairfax Street, Suite 404
Alexandria, VA 22314
E-mail: socap@socap.org
www.socap.org

U.S. Public Interest Research Group (U.S. PIRG)
218 D Street, SE
Washington, DC 20003-1900
E-mail: uspirg@pirg.org
www.pirg.org

SECTION V

Lists for
Sociology

320. Careers in Sociology

census analyst
charities administrator
child welfare advocate
clinical social worker
community organizer
consultant
cottage supervisor
criminal justice planner
customer relations
demographer
geriatric social worker
group worker
houseparent
industrial sociologist
interviewer
labor relations
law enforement officer

market researcher
mediator
ministry
population analyst
public opinion pollster
psychiatric social worker
recreation worker
researcher
rural sociologist
school social worker
social services volunteer coordinator
social worker
sociology professor
substance abuse counselor
training and development
urban planner
youth care worker

321. Pioneers in the Field of Sociology

Ruth Benedict
Jeremy Bentham
Charles H. Cooley
John Dewey
W. E. B. DuBois
Erich Fromm
Erving Goffman
William James

Lawrence Kohlberg
Elisabeth Kübler-Ross
Kurt Lewin
Konrad Lorenz
Margaret Mead
David Riesman
Max Weber

Dewey

322. U.S. Social Reformers

Edith Abbott (1876–1957)
Grace Abbott (1878–1939)
Jane Addams (1860–1935)
Susan B. Anthony (1820–1906)
Gamaliel Bailey (1807–1859)
Clara Barton (1821–1912)
Henry Ward Beecher (1813–1887)
Amelia Bloomer (1818–1894)

William Booth (1829–1894)
Elihu Burritt (1811–1879)
Carrie Chapman Catt (1859–1947)
John Jay Chapman (1862–1933)
Dorothy Day (1897–1980)
Eugene Debs (1855–1926)
Dorothea Dix (1802–1887)
Fredrick Douglas (1817–1895)

(continued)

322. *(continued)*

W. E. B. DuBois (1868–1963)
William Lloyd Garrison (1805–1879)
Samuel G. Howe (1801–1876)
Helen Keller (1880–1968)
Martin Luther King, Jr. (1929–1968)
Robert La Follette (1855–1925)
Joshua Leavitt (1794–1873)
Horace Mann (1796–1859)
Lucretia Mott (1793–1880)
Wendell Phillips (1811–1884)
Jacob Riis (1849–1914)
Margaret Sanger (1883–1966)
Elizabeth Cady Stanton (1815–1902)
Lucy Stone (1818–1893)
Harriet Tubman (1820–1913)

Booker T. Washington (1856–1915)
Walter F. White (1893–1955)
Emma Hart Willard (1787–1870)
Frances E. Willard (1839–1898)
Whitney M. Young, Jr. (1921–1971)

Mott

323. Problems Facing Teenagers

Alcohol abuse
Drug abuse
Peer pressures
Teenage pregnancy
AIDS, venereal disease
Career uncertainties
Financing college
Getting along with parents
Getting into college
Grades

Sibling relationships
Physical safety, gangs
Family economics
Unemployment
Fear of war
Parents' divorce
School problems
Teenage suicide
Problems in growing up
Sexual identity

324. Fields of Study in Sociology

criminology
demography
human ecology
marriage and family studies
political sociology
popular culture social psychology

sociolinguistics
sociology of education
sociology of law
sociometry
suicidology
urban sociology

325. Folk Medicines

Ailment	Treatment
asthma	wear a muskrat skin over the lungs
bed-wetting	honey; eat fried mouse pie
bleeding	chimney soot
body odor	baking soda
boils	poultice of ginger and flour
bug bites	apply baking soda or meat
burns	apple honey
chest cold	a mustard-lard plaster placed on chest
chiggers	salty pig skin
colds	onion and honey soup
colds	rub skunk grease on the chest
consumption	tar and egg yolks
cough	mixture of honey, lemon & whiskey
croupe	turpentine in a spoonful of sugar
dandruff	vinegar water
earache prevention	wear wool from a black sheep in the ear
earache	warm vinegar water in the ear
hangover	scrambled owl's eggs
impaired vision	piercing an ear
laziness	balm tea
mosquito bites	baking soda
nose bleeds	tea leaves
onion breath	drink coffee
pimples	apply thin white skin from inside egg shell
pimples	salve made of wheat germ and milk
poison ivy	apply paste made of baking soda and water
rheumatism	wear the eye tooth of a pig
sore throat	gargle with apple cider vinegar
stuffed-up nose	chew honeycomb
sunburn	wash with sage tea
toothache	chew cotton; oil of cloves
upset stomach	boil elm broth; vinegar water; castor oil
varicose veins	apply apple cider vinegar
warts	rub with radish or raw meat
warts	tie a toad around your neck

326. Old Names for Illnesses

apoplexy	stroke
blood poisoning	bacterial infection; septicemia
camp fever	typhoid fever
congestive fever	malaria
consumption	pulmonary tuberculosis
croup	laryngitis, diphtheria, or strep throat
dropsy	congestive heart failure
dropsy of the brain	encephalitis
grippe	influenza, flu
infantile paralysis	polio
lock jaw	tetanus
lung fever	pneumonia
palsy	paralysis or loss of muscle control
pleurisy	inflammation of the thorax
putrid fever	typhus or diphtheria
scrivener's palsy	writer's cramp
shakes	delirium tremens
summer complaint	diarrhea

Source: "Heritage of the High Country: A History of Del Bonita and Surrounding Districts."

327. Esperanto Vocabulary

Esperanto is an international language first proposed by Dr. L. L. Zamenhof in 1887. It is currently spoken by several million people in over 80 countries.

Esperanto	English	Esperanto	English
arbo	tree	donas	give
bel	beautiful	esperaas	hope
besto	animal	far	do, make
bibro	book	fort	strong
blua	blue	gust	taste
bona	good	havas	has, have
ced	yield	instruisto	teacher
cit	quote	ir	go
dankas	thank	jes	yes
diferenc	difference	kredas	believe
diskut	discuss	ne	no, not

327. *(continued)*

Esperanto	English	Esperanto	English
nigra	black	nulo	0
nova	new	unu	1
patro	father	du	2
pren	take	tri	3
ricevas	receive	kvar	4
skribas	writes	kvin	5
tablo	table	ses	6
tago	day	sep	7
tre	very	ok	8
tro	too	nau	9
tute no	not at all	dek	10
venas	come	cent	100
vi	you	mil	1000

For more information, contact:
  Esperanto League
  PO Box 1129
  El Cerrito CA 94530
  Web site: http://www.esperanto-usa.org/
  E-mail: info@esperanto-usa.org

328. Dialects of the United States

Appalachian
Black English
Bostonian
Bronx
Brooklyn
Chesapeake Bay (Maryland &
  Virginia coast)
Conch (Florida Keys)
Creole (Louisiana)
General American
Gullah (South Carolina & Georgia
  coast)
Gumbo
Louisiana Cajun
Midwestern
New York City
Outer Banks (North Carolina coast)

Ozark
Pennsylvania Dutch
Southern
Upper New York State
Western drawl
Yankee (New England)
Yiddish American

329. Languages Spoken in the U.S.

Language	Persons over 5 Years of Age That Speak the language
Speak only English	198,601,000
Spanish	17,339,000
French	1,702,000
German	1,547,000
Italian	1,309,000
Chinese	1,249,000
Tagalog	843,000
Polish	723,000
Korean	626,000
Vietnamese	507,000
Portuguese	430,000
Japanese	428,000
Greek	388,000
Arabic	355,000
Hindi (Urdu)	331,000
Russian	242,000
Yiddish	213,000
Thai (Laotian)	206,000
Persian	202,000
French Creole	188,000
Armenian	150,000
Navajo	149,000
Hungarian	148,000
Hebrew	144,000
Dutch	143,000

Source: U.S. Census Bureau, 1990 Census. (Data for 2000 census were not released at publication time.)

330. Greeting Customs

handshake
high five
hug
bow
curtsy
nod
tip of the hat
military salute

331. Rites of Passage

baby blessing and naming
baptism
bar and bat mitzvahs
birthday party
caps and gowns
circumcision
debutante ball
first communion
graduation ceremony
passing out cigars
quince
retirement party
sorority/fraternity pledging
sweet-16 party
vision quest

332. American Courtship Rituals and Customs

banns of marriage
bridal shower
bundling
chaperones
dating
diamonds
Dutch treat
engagement rings
flirting
kissing
parking
proposing on bended knee

333. American Wedding Rituals and Customs

best man
bridal veil
bridesmaids
bride's parents pay
carrying bride over threshold
cutting the cake
decorating car
eloping
flower girl
garter
giving the bride away
groom
honeymoon
hope chest
June weddings
kissing the bride
ring bearer
throwing rice

trousseaus
ushers
wedding rings
white wedding dress

334. Funeral Rituals and Customs

coffin
embalming
flag at half mast
flowers
gun salute

lighting candles
pall bearers
visitation at funeral home
wakes

335. Traditional Castes of India

Highest to lowest:
Brahmans
Kshatriyas
Vaisyas
Sudras

Below the castes:
Untouchables

336. Anglo-American English Vocabulary

"England and America are two people separated by a common language."
—GEORGE BERNARD SHAW

Anglo	American	Anglo	American
aerodrome	airfield	lido	swimming pool
bags	trousers	lift	elevator
barrister	attorney	litter bin	wastebasket
beaker	cup	Ltd.	Inc.
biscuit	cookie	lorry	truck
bobby	police officer	mackintosh	rain coat
bonnet	hood of a car	mince	ground beef
boot	car's trunk	motorway	highway/freeway
braces	suspenders	nappy	diaper
car park	auto parking lot	net ball	basketball
caravan	trailer	nought	zero
chemist	pharmacist	paper blind	window shade
chips	French fries	petrol	gasoline
clatter	to gossip	pillar box	mail box
conk	nose	private hire	taxi
dust bin	garbage can	public school	private school
elastoplast	bandaid	rambler	hiker
estate car	station wagon	ring up	to telephone
face flannel	wash cloth	round	sandwich
first floor	second floor	scurf	dandruff
flat	apartment	serviette	napkin
jumper	sweater	singlet	T-shirt
gaffer	shop foreman	smalls	underclothing
Girl Guide	Girl Scout	squib	firecracker
gruel	oatmeal	state school	public school
gum	paste, glue	telephonist	telephone operator
holiday	vacation	telly	TV
ironmonger	hardware store	tin	can
knock up	to awaken	torch	flashlight
larder	pantry	w.c.	toilet
let	to rent	wind cheater	windbreaker

337. Emoticons

Emoticons can help avoid misunderstanding a writer's intentions. Usually, emoticons are to be read by tilting your head left so the right side of the emoticon is at the bottom.

:)	Happy	%-6	Brain dead
>:(	Very angry	&-(	Tearful
B)	Cool sunglasses	|-0	Yawning
:O	Indifferent smiley	'-)	Wink; Winking
;)	Winking smiley	(:-$	Ill
:(	Frowney	:-~)	Has a cold
(-D	Laughing	/	Too cool
%-}	Amused	L:-)	Graduate
:-Q	Confused	0:)	Angel; Saint
8)	Near sighted smile	:	Hmmm
:D	Laughing smile	:)~	Drooling
:>	Sarcastic smile	:-)x	Bow tie
:))	Very happy	:-.	"No comment"
(:-(	Very sad; frowning	:-{#}	Braces
:-/	Wry face	:/i	No smoking
!-(	Black eye	:X	Sworn to secrecy
#:-0	Ahhhhhh!	:o	Shocked
:')	Crying	<:-l	Dunce
%)	Cross-eyed	@;-)	Flirt
:-#|	Bushy mustache	:-I	Indifference

338. The Golden Rule in Many Religions

Hurt not others with that which pains thyself.
  —BUDDHISM

Whatsoever ye would that men should do to you, do ye even so to them.
  —CHRISTIANITY

What you don't want done to yourself, don't do to others.
  —CONFUCIANISM

Do naught to others which if done to thee would cause pain.
  —HINDUISM

What is hateful to yourself, don't do to your fellow man.
  —JUDAISM

338. *(continued)*

May I do to others as I would that they should do unto me.
  —Paganism (Plato)

Treat others as thou wouldst be treated thyself.
  —Sikhism

Do not do unto others all that which is not well for oneself.
  —Zoroastrianism

339. Religious Symbols

agnus dei
botonée
Celtic cross
chalice
dove
Greek cross
Jerusalem cross
Latin cross
lotus
Maltese cross
mandala

menorah
om
papal cross
patriarchal cross
Russian cross
shiva
star and crescent
Star of David
tau cross
torii
yin-yang

TAOISM

340. Holy Books

Holy Book	Religion
Bhagavad-Gita	Hinduism
Five Classics	Confucianism
Koran	Islam
New Testament	Christianity
Old Testament	Judaism & Christianity
Talmud	Judaism
Tao-te-ching	Taoism
Torah	Judaism
Upanishads	Hinduism
Veda	Hinduism

341. Major Causes of Death in the United States

Heart disease	725,192
Cancer	549,838
Stroke	167,366
Chronic lower respiratory diseases	132,181
Accidents	97,860
Diabetes mellitus	68,399
Influenza and pneumonia	63,730
Alzheimer's disease	44,536
Nephritis, nephrotic syndrome, and nephrosis	35,525
Septicemia chronic liver disease and cirrhosis	30,680

Source: National Vital Statistics Report, Vol. 49, No. 11, 1999.

342. Words Borrowed from African Languages

banana	dig	hippie	phony
banjo	fuzz	jam	tote
bogus	goober	jamboree	voodoo
boogie	gumbo	mumbo jumbo	
bug	guy	okra	

343. Common Words Borrowed from Spanish Languages

adobe	calaboose	guerrilla	portal
aficionado	canary	hammock	pueblo
alfalfa	canyon	incommunicado	ranch
alligator	cargo	junta	rodeo
armada	chaparral	lariat	savvy
arroyo	chili	lasso	siesta
banana	chocolate	macho	tabasco
barbecue	cigar	maize	tapioca
breeze	cocaine	marijuana	tobacco
bronco	cockroach	mesa	tornado
buffalo	corral	mesquite	tortilla
burro	coyote	patio	vanilla
cabana	desperado	peon	vigilante
cafeteria	filibuster	plaza	

344. Australian Slang

Slang	Meaning
aeroplanes	bow tie
air and exercise	short jail term
Arry gators	thanks
Aussie	an Australian
bad dog	overdue debt
barbie	barbeque
barney over	quarrel
battler	a persistent loser
beano	a fun party
bloke	man
bludger	someone who doesn't do their fair share
blue	a fight
bush	a rural area
chalkie	teacher
crook	defective; sick
dill	a fool
dingo	Australian wild dog
dole bludger	welfare cheat
drongo	a super dill; big fool
drover	cowboy
the dry	annual nine-month drought
fair dinkum	true blue; loyal
flat out	full speed; very fast
flying doe	female kangaroo
galah	silly and dull
garbo	garbage man
gin	aborigine woman
good on you	good for you (sometimes sarcastic)
have kangaroos	to be crazy
jackeroo	cowboy
jillaroo	cowgirl
jumper	sweater
kangarooster	odd person

Slang	Meaning
mozzies	mosquitoes
outback	Australian back country
paddock	field or pasture
postie	postal worker
ringer	cowboy
ripper	great! excellent!
sheila	woman
shot through	went home
skite	to brag; boast
smoko	rest period; a break
squatter	landed gentry
station	cattle ranch
stone the crows	exclamation of surprise or disgust
strewth	It's the truth
swag	bedroll for traveling light
take a sickie	stay home for any reason other than illness
to do your block	to lose your temper
too end	extreme north of Australia
too right	You're so right!
tucker	meal, food
the wet	three-month rainy season
value for money	a good man
you bewdy	you're okay; exclamation of approval

345. Words Borrowed from Native Americans

caucus	papoose	squaw
Chautaugua	pecan	succotash
chipmunk	pemmican	tepee
hickory	persimmon	totem
hogan	podunk	toboggan
hominy	powwow	tomahawk
igloo	quahog	wahoo
moccasin	raccoon	wampum
moose	Sequoia	wigwam
muskrat	skunk	woodchuck
opossum	squash	

346. Contemporary Social Problems

AIDS
Aging population with inadequate health care
Continued racism
Cost of medical care
The cycle of poverty
Date rape
Drug and alcohol abuse
Environmental pollution
Excessive school drop-out rate
Growth in the crime rate
High numbers of homeless persons
High rates of teenage pregancies
High unemployment among black youth
Illiteracy
Increased trends in suicide
Increasing child abuse
Plight of the farmers
Poor educational achievement
Proliferation of firearms and violence
Sexual harassment and sex discrimination
Teenage run-aways
Threat of international terrorism
Violence in the streets

347. Southern Foods

awendaw
beignets
bell peppers
biscuits
black-eyed peas
cabbage
calas
collards
cornbread
corncakes
cowpeas
cracklins
crawfish
cymlings
dumplings
eggplant
figs
fried chicken
grits
gumbo
ham
hoecakes
hush puppies

iced tea
jambalaya
key lime pie
mint julip
molasses
muddle
mutton burgoo
okra
oyster pie
peanut soup
pecan pie
persimmons
pokeweed
pork rinds
pralines
rice
seafood
shoofly pie
sorgum molasses pie
spoon bread
sweet potatoes
turnips
Virginia baked ham

348. Things Not Around in 1960

acrylic paint
aerobics
affirmative action programs
AIDS
air bags
airport metal detectors
alkaline batteries
alkyd paint
aluminum softball bats
Amtrak
Apple Computer
artificial hearts
astroturf
athletic scholarships for women
automatic garage door openers
automatic teller machines
bagelinos
bar codes
Beatles, the
Berlin Wall
Bic pens
bug zappers
cable television
call forwarding
cassette audio tapes
catalytic converters
Catholic church services in English
cellular phones
cigarette package warnings
clear braces
compact discs
computerized tomography
  (CAT scan)
cubic zirconium diamonds
Department of Education
Department of Energy
designer jeans
digital audio tapes
disposable diapers
disposable razors
DNA fingerprinting

Dolby noise-reduction system
drug education programs
Earth Day
electric toothbrushes
express mail
extended-wear contact lenses
fanny packs
fathers in the delivery room
female astronauts
female coal miners
female secret service agents
fiber optics
food processors
food stamps
frequent flyer programs
frozen yogurt
garbage disposals
gene cloning
glosnot
graphite tennis racquets
hang gliders
Head Start programs
heart pacemakers
heart transplants
holograms
home computers
home VCR's
hot-air corn poppers
indoor soccer
instamatic cameras
instant replay
jet skis
laser surgery
legal abortions
liquid crystal display (LCD)
Martin Luther King Day
Mastercharge Cards
MTV
Medicare
microwave ovens
Moscow "hot line"

348. *(continued)*

music synthesizer
national voting age of 18
911 emergency number
National Organization for Women
neutron bombs
1-800 telephone numbers
1-900 telephone numbers
"no fault" divorce
non-smoking sections
orthoscopic surgery
Peace Corps
permanent-press slacks
phosphate-free detergents
plastic garbage bags
pocket calculators
political action committees (PAC's)
push-button telephones
quartz digital watches
radial tires
radioactive waste
rechargeable flashlights
remote control
revolving restaurants
robots
scanners
seat belts
self-serve gas stations
skateboards
smart bombs
smoke detectors
soft contact lenses
sun roofs
supertankers
space shuttle
sports dome
Star Trek
stereophonic radio broadcasts
styling mousse
Styrofoam
Super Bowl
supersonic transport planes

surrogate mothers
synthetic skin
talking cars
televised congressional sessions
TV instant replay
test-tube babies
three-point shots in basketball
touch-tone telephones
twist-ties
two-liter plastic soda bottles
USA Today
unit pricing in supermarkets
Valium
video arcades
waterbeds
windsurfing
word processors
ZIP codes

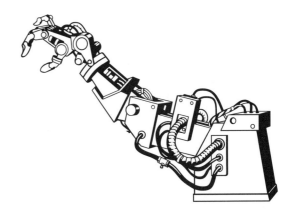

349. Things from 1960 That Are Hard to Find Today

asbestos
auto tire inner tubes
autumn leaf fires
bakelite
black-and-white television programs
Burma Shave signs
car hops
chrome automobile bumpers
cigarette smoking on airplanes
drive-in theaters
Edsels
elm trees
flash bulbs
free air at gas stations
free maps at gas stations
48-star flags
glass milk bottles
Gulf Oil Corporation
home delivery bread men
home delivery milkmen
home movie cameras
Look magazine
manual typewriters
"men wanted" classified ads
military draft
motor scooters

New York Herald Tribune
PCB's
penny gumball machines
percolators
poll taxes
prayers in public schools
prefrontal lobotomies
push lawn mowers
ringer washers
rotary telephones
78-rpm records
shaving brushes
silver in U.S. coins
slide rules
stenographers
Studebakers
Sunday "Blue" laws
29¢ per gallon gasoline
telephone party lines
TV cigarette ads
Thalidomide
toothpaste powder
vacuum tube
"wheat" pennies
"whites only" signs
wood tennis racquets

350. Forms of American Music

acid rock
big band
bluegrass
blues
Cajun
country and western
crooners
folk
folk rock
gospel
grunge

Hawaiian
heavy metal
"hillbilly"
honkey-tonk
jazz
Motown sound
new wave
protest
punk
ragtime
rap

350. *(continued)*

religious rock and roll
rhythm and blues
sacred harp
soul
spirituals
swing
"Tex-Mex"
western swing
zydeco

351. Traditional Wedding Anniversaries

Year	Gift
First	Paper
Second	Cotton
Third	Leather
Fourth	Linen
Fifth	Wooden
Sixth	Iron
Seventh	Copper
Eighth	Bronze
Ninth	Pottery
Tenth	Tin
Fifteenth	Crystal
Twentieth	China
Twenty-fifth	Silver
Thirtieth	Ivory
Fortieth	Woolen
Forty-fifth	Sapphire
Fiftieth	Gold
Sixtieth	Diamond
Seventy-fifth	Diamond

352. Forms of Marriage

Monogamy	marriage of one man and one woman
Polygamy	man having more than one wife
Polyandry	woman having more than one husband
Exogamy	prohibition of marriage to one's relatives
Endogamy	marriage permitted only to a member of one's own family

353. Age at First Marriage: 1890–2000

Median Age at First Marriage

Year	Males	Females
1890	26.1	22.0
1900	25.9	21.9
1910	25.1	21.6
1920	24.6	21.2
1930	24.3	21.3
1940	24.3	21.5
1950	22.8	20.3
1960	22.8	20.3
1970	23.2	20.8
1980	24.7	22.0
1990	26.1	23.9
1993	26.5	24.5
1994	26.7	24.5
1995	26.9	24.5
1996	27.1	24.8
1997	26.8	25.0
1998	26.7	25.0
1999	26.9	25.1
2000	26.8	25.1

Source: U.S. Bureau of the Census. Online at www.census.gov.

354. American Indian Medical Remedies

Ailment	Remedy
acne	wild bergamot
asthma	skunk cabbage, jimson weed
athlete's foot	yellow nut grass tubers
bad breath	geranium roots
bee sting	tobacco
blister	sunflower roots
boil	wild pansies
bronchitis	creosote bush tea
burn	yellow-spined thistle salve, black alder
childbirth pain	wild black cherry
cold	wintergreen colic catnip
cough	aspen bark, sarsaparilla roots
diarrhea	blackberry tea, white oak bark
dysentery	magnolia bark
earache	licorice leaves, ginger
fever	bayberry, white poplar bark
flu	evergreen, fresh hemlock
headache	skunk cabbage
insect bite	wild onion or garlic bulbs, snakeweed
measles	sassafras roots
mumps	sweet everlasting; red cedar tea
poison ivy	gum plant, wormwood
ringworm	red birch, mulberry
stomachache	dandelion tea, snowberry
snake bite	Virginia snakeroot, Beneca snakeroot
sore throat	white pine needles tea, slippery elm tea
stop bleeding	puffballs, wild geranium root
toothache	prickly ash bark
swelling	witch hazel, blue flag (iris) root

355. Advice from Aesop

Wise men say nothing in dangerous times.
Quality comes before quantity.
Slow and steady wins the race.
One man's meat is another man's poison.
Look before you leap.
Figures are not always facts.
It is one thing to propose, another to execute.
Acts speak plainer than words.
Necessity is the mother of invention.
Men are blind to their own faults.
There is no arguing a coward into courage.
Grasp at the shadow and lose the substance.
One good turn deserves another.
Nip evil in the bud.
Spare the rod and spoil the child.
Honesty is the best policy.
Union is strength.
Keep to your place and your place will keep to you.
Example is better than precept.
The lights of heaven are never blown out.
Revenge is too dearly purchased at the price of liberty.
There can be little liking where there is little likeness.
A bird in the hand is worth two in the bush.
He who plays a trick must be prepared to take a joke.

356. Mohandas Gandhi's List of Seven Deadly Sins

Pleasure without conscience
Wealth without work
Knowledge without character
Worship without sacrifice
Politics without principle
Business without morality
Science without humanity

357. Major World Religions

Christianity	1.9 billion
Islam	1.1 billion
Hinduism	324 million
Sikhism	19 million
Judaism	14 million
Baha'ism	6.1 million
Confucianism	5.3 million
Jainism	4.9 million
Shintoism	2.8 million

Source: The Christian Science Monitor, August 4, 1998.

358. Church Attendance Rates of Selected Countries

Percent of population attending church once a week, not counting funerals, christenings, and baptisms:

Country	%	Country	%
Nigeria	89	Austria	30
Ireland	84	Britain	27
N. Ireland	58	Spain	25
Poland	55	France	21
Portugal	47	Switzerland	16
Mexico	46	Australia	16
Italy	45	Denmark	5
U.S.A.	44	East Germany	5
India	42	Japan	3
Canada	38	Russia	2

Source: Institute for Social Research, University of Michigan.

359. Top 10 Organized Religions in the United States, 2001

Religion	Number	Percent
Christianity	159,030,000	76.5%
Judaism	2,831,000	1.3%
Islam	1,104,000	0.5%
Buddhism	1,082,000	0.5%
Hinduism	766,000	0.4%
Unitarian Universalist	629,000	0.3%
Wiccan/Pagan/Druid	307,000	0.1%
Spiritualist	116,000	
Native American Religion	103,000	
Baha'i	84,000	

Note: Does not incude nonreligious, atheist, or agnostic

Source: Barry A. Kosmin, Egon Mayer, & Ariela Keysar. American Religious Identification Survey. The Graduate Center of the City University of New York, at http://www.gc.cuny.edu/studies

360. Major U.S. Disasters

Epidemic, over 30,000 die	1618–1623
East coast hurricane, over 4,000 die	1775
New Madrid, Missouri earthquakes	1811–1812
Cholera epidemic, thousands die	1832
Steamboat *Sultana* explodes, over 1,500 die	1865
Massive forest fires in Michigan, Minnesota, Wisconsin	1871
Chicago fire	1871
Brooklyn Conway Theatre fire	1876
Massive blizzard in eastern U.S., about 400 die	1888
Johnstown, Pennsylvania, flood	1889
Hurricane, over 1,000 die	1893
Galveston hurricane, over 6,000 die	1900
Chicago's second fire	1906
San Francisco earthquake	1906
Monongah, West Virginia, coal mine, 361 die	1907
Titanic sinks	1912
Luisitania sinks	1915
Steamer *Eastland* sinks in Chicago River	1915
Forest fire, Wisconsin & Minnesota	1918
Spanish flu epidemic, 500,000 die	1918
San Paulo, Colorado, dam collapse	1928

360. (continued)

South Florida hurricane	1928
Hurricane in Long Island, New York, and New England, over 600 die	1938
Boston's Cocoanut Grove nightclub fire	1942
Two navy ammo ships explode, Port Chicago, California, 322 die	1944
Freighter *Grandcamp* explodes, 561 die	1947
Hurricane Diane in eastern U.S., 400 die	1955
AIDS epidemic, over 100,000 dead	1980's
Terrorist attacks at World Trade Center, Pentagon, and Pennsylvania, more than 5,000 die	2001

361. Annual American Celebrations

New Year's Day	Memorial Day
Martin Luther King's Birthday	Flag Day
Groundhog Day	Father's Day
Valentine's Day	Independence Day
Presidents' Day	Labor Day
Leap Year Day	Columbus Day
St. Patrick's Day	Halloween
Mardi Gras	Veterans' Day
Ash Wednesday	Thanksgiving
April Fool's Day	Christmas
Easter Sunday	Boxing Day
Passover	New Year's Eve
Mother's Day	birthdays
Arbor Day	wedding anniversaries

362. Celebrity Deaths from Alleged Drug Overdoses

Len Bias	basketball player
John Belushi	comedian
Tommy Bolin	guitarist
John Bonham	member of Led Zeppelin
Lenny Bruce	comedian
Tim Buckley	singer-songwriter
Brian Cole	member of The Association
Sandy Denny	singer
John Entwhistle	member of The Who
Brian Epstein	Beatles manager
Chris Farley	comedian
Judy Garland	actress and singer
Andy Gibb	singer
Tim Hardin	singer-songwriter
Jimi Hendrix	singer-songwriter
Billie Holiday	jazz singer
Brian Jones	member of The Rolling Stones
Little Willie John	singer
Janis Joplin	singer-songwriter
Frankie Lymon	member of The Teenagers
David McComb	member of Australian band The Triffids
Robbie McIntosh	Average White Band drummer
Aimee Semple McPherson	evangelist
Marilyn Monroe	actress
Pam Morrison	wife of Jim Morrison of The Doors
Keith Moon	member of The Who
Nico	member of Velvet Underground
Bradley Nowell	member of Sublime
Gram Parsons	member of The Byrds
Kristen Pfaff	singer
River Phoenix	actor
Dana Plato	"Diff'rent Strokes" actress
Elvis Presley	singer, actor
David Ruffin	singer with The Temptations
Bon Scott	singer with AC/DC
Rory Storme	rock musician
Vinnie Taylor	Sha Na Na guitarist
Gary Thain	Uriah Heep guitarist
Sid Vicious	member of The Sex Pistols
Danny Whitten	Crazy Horse guitarist
Al Wilson	member of Canned Heat
Dennis Wilson	member of The Beach Boys

363. Countries Prohibiting Capital Punishment

At least 108 nations have rejected the use of capital punishment, including the following:

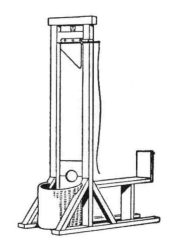

Australia	Italy
Austria	Luxembourg
Bolivia	Netherlands
Canada	New Zealand
Colombia	Nicaragua
Costa Rica	Norway
Denmark	Panama
Dominican Republic	Philippines
Ecuador	Portugal
Finland	Sweden
France	Switzerland
Germany	United Kingdom
Honduras	Uruguay
Iceland	Venezuela
Ireland	

364. States Prohibiting Capital Punishment

Alaska	North Dakota
Hawaii	Rhode Island
Iowa	Vermont
Maine	West Virginia
Massachusetts	Wisconsin
Michigan	District of Columbia
Minnesota	

365. The Physiological Risks of Cocaine Use

damage to the heart muscle
paralysis of breathing muscles
hypertension
chest pain
liver damage
irregularities in the heart beat
cerebral hemorrhage bronchitis
heart attacks
hyperthermia strokes

366. Warning Signs of Alcohol Abuse

drinking as an immediate response to any problem
all celebrations must include alcohol
driving a car while intoxicated
sleep disturbances
blackouts
using alcohol to handle any stress
missing school or work because of drinking
drinking until intoxicated

367. Alcohol and Driving Statistics

- Every 32 minutes, one person dies in an alcohol-related traffic accident. In 2000, 16,653 people were killed in crashes involving alcohol, representing 40 percent of the 41,821 people killed in all traffic crashes.

- In 1999, 63 percent of youth (age 15–20) who died in passenger vehicle crashes were not wearing safety belts. (NHTSA, NCSA, 1999)

- Fatally injured drivers who have been drinking are least likely to have been wearing safety belts. (NHTSA, 1999)

- One out of nine intoxicated drivers in fatal crashes have had a prior DWI conviction within the past three years. (NHTSA, 1999)

- Half of DWI offenders on probation and over half of those in jail reported drinking only beer prior to their arrest. (BJS, 1999)

- Male drivers involved in fatal crashes were nearly twice as likely to have been intoxicated (21.8%) than were females (11.2%). (NHTSA, 1996)

- In 1998, the United States drivers with:
  - BACs (Blood Alcohol Content) of .10 and above were involved in an estimated 999,000 crashes that killed 12,530 and injured 719,000
  - BACs between .08–.09 were involved in an estimated 17,200 crashes that killed 993 and injured 32,000
  - Positive BACs below .08 were involved in an estimated 33,700 crashes that killed 2,412 and injured 70,000

- Alcohol-related crashes accounted for an estimated 16% of the $127 billion in U.S. auto insurance payments. (Public Services Research Institute)

- The number of alcohol fatalities for 1999 of 15,786 (38% of total traffic fatalities for the year), represents a 30 percent reduction from the 22,404 alcohol-related fatalities reported in 1989 (49% of the total). (NHTSA, 1999)

368. Young Drinking Drivers in Fatal Crashes: National Trends

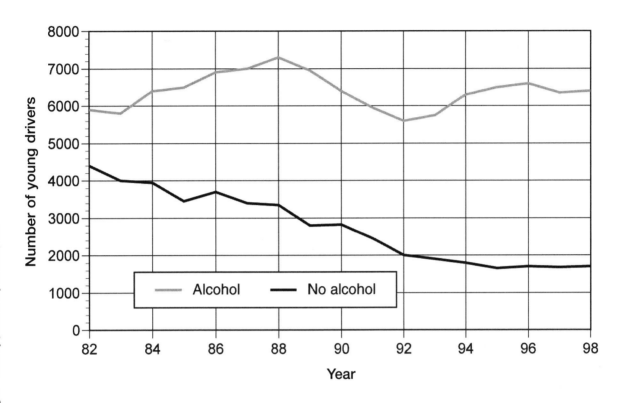

Young Drinking and Non-Drinking Drivers in Fatal Crashes

Source: National Highway Traffic Safety Administration, 2001.

369. Drug Abuse Danger Signals

- sudden change in mood
- possession of drug paraphernalia
- unusual temper outbursts
- abrupt change in friends
- increased absence from school or work
- stealing from others
- increased borrowing of money
- sudden increase in behavioral problems
- poor relationships with parents or friends

370. Largest American Indian Nations

Cherokee	Pueblo
Navajo	Iroquois
Sioux	Apache
Chippewa	Lumbee
Choctaw	Creek

371. Predictors of Successful Marriages

- both partners had a happy childhood
- both sets of parents were successfully married
- both are emotionally well adjusted
- both had good relationships with their parents
- high self-esteem in both partners
- healthy instruction in human sexuality
- of similar religious beliefs
- couple dated at least a year
- bride is at least 19 and groom at least 22
- relatively similar educational backgrounds

372. American Sports Firsts

1839	game of baseball invented by Abner Doubleday
1845	baseball team (Knickerbocker Club)
1845	yacht race
1851	America's Cup yacht race
1859	cricket match (Hoboken, N.J.)
1859	intercollegiate baseball game (Amherst vs. Williams College)
1862	football club (Boston)
1868	women's baseball team
1869	intercollegiate football game (Princeton vs. Rutgers)
1871	professional baseball player (Alfred Reach)
1875	baseball glove
1876	tennis court (Boston)
1880	croquet league (Philadelphia)
1880	bareknuckle world heavyweight championship (Paddy Ryan)
1881	lawn tennis championship
1883	night baseball game
1892	basketball game invented by James Naismith
1892	college basketball team (Mt. Union College)
1892	night football game (Mansfield, Pa.)
1893	18 hole golf course (Wheaton, Ill.)
1895	professional football game
1895	volleyball invented by W. G. Morgan
1896	modern Olympic games started (Athens, Greece)
1903	professional hockey team
1903	world series baseball game (Pittsburgh Pirates beat Boston Americans)
1911	squash tournament
1916	PGA golf championship
1920	curling rink (Brookline, Mass.)
1936	American Badminton Association founded
1967	Super Bowl football game

373. Values

achievement
beauty
bravery
cleanliness
considerateness
cooperation
creativity
diligence
equality
exciting life
family
forgiveness
freedom
friendship
generosity
happiness
hard work
health
intelligence

justice
kindness
lasting contribution
love
loyalty
national security
obedience
openmindedness
order
peace
perseverance
pleasure
power
rationality
recognition
responsibility
salvation
security
self-reliance

self-respect
success
thoughtfulness
tradition
truth
wealth
wisdom

374. Possible Purposes of Schools

To develop skills for work
To learn how to manage money and resources
To learn how to use leisure time
To appreciate beauty
To learn the rules and expectations of the culture
To develop an ethical character
To develop one's abilities to the fullest
To select a career
To develop effective work habits and values
To develop positive self-esteem
To develop good health habits
To become responsible citizens
To learn how to be a worthy family member
To understand and get along with others
To develop basic skills in reading, writing, and mathematics
To learn the skills of effective decision making
To help solve social problems (e.g., poverty, racism, pollution)

375. Research on Effective Schools

In the past two decades substantial attention has been given to studying effective schools. (See the work of Ron Edmunds, Larry Lezotte, John Goodlad.) While no universal blueprint exists, some generalizations can be drawn from the myriad of research studies available. The exact causal nature of these characteristics is difficult to determine. However, the presence of certain specific traits is found in the most outstanding schools. The following characteristics have been identified as exemplifying the most effective schools:

1. The professional staff is committed to the belief that all students can learn.
2. Teachers hold high expectations for their students. Teachers also believe that their efforts do make a difference in the lives of their students.
3. Students believe that their success in school is related to how hard they work.
4. The principal functions as an instructional leader. They are able to set high goals for their buildings and to inspire the staff to move toward those goals.
5. A safe and orderly school environment is provided.
6. Continued professional development is encouraged and facilitated.
7. Firm, consistent and fair enforcement of appropriate student behavior is emphasized. Disruptive and dangerous behaviors are not tolerated. Rules and expectations are clearly communicated to all.
8. A climate of cooperation exists among the staff. The faculty works as a team. Collaboration becomes part of the school culture. Mutually supportive relationships exist between the principal and the staff.
9. Students exhibit a high level of school spirit. They identify with their school and feel good about attending their school.
10. Academic learning time is safeguarded. Frivolous interruptions of class activities are minimized.
11. Parents feel welcome in the school. The community is supportive of their schools.
12. Student progress is systematically monitored.
13. Staff input into instructional decisions is invited.
14. Students' level of on-task behavior is relatively high.
15. An emphasis is placed upon developing basic academic skills in students.
16. Continuity of instruction from one grade level to the next is emphasized.

Source: Ronald Partin, *The Classroom Teacher's Survival Guide.* Paramus, NJ: The Center for Applied Research in Education, 1999.

376. High School Graduation Rate

Percentage who had completed secondary education in selected developed nations:

Canada	83.9%
France	85.5%
Germany	88.9%
Italy	49.1%
United Kingdom	86.1%
United States	87.1%

Source: The Condition of Education 1998. U.S. Department of Education.

377. School Dropout Rate for U.S.

Dropout and Completion Measures	Total*	White Non-Hispanic	Black Non-Hispanic	Hispanic	Asian/Pacific Islander
Percentage of 15- through 24-year-olds who dropped out of grades 10–12, October 1999 to October 2000	4.8	4.1	6.1	7.4	3.5
Percentage of 16- through 24-year-olds who were dropouts in 2000	10.9	6.9	13.1	27.8	3.8
Percentage of 18- through 24-year-olds who were high school completers in 2000**	86.5	91.8	83.7	64.1	94.6

*Due to relatively small sample sizes, American Indians/Alaskan Natives are included in the total but are not shown separately.

**Excludes those still enrolled in high school

Source: U.S. Bureau of the Census, 2000 Population Survey.

378. Length of the School Year

Canada	185 days
Germany	188 days
England	192 days
Japan	220 days*
Korea	222 days
New Zealand	190 days
United States	181 days

Number of year-round schools in the U.S. in 1986–87: 408.
Number of year-round schools in 2001: 3,011.
Number of students who attended year-round schools in 2001–02: 2,184,596.

*All of the nations with more than 220 school days per year meet on Saturday mornings.

Sources: National Association for Year-Round Education at http://www.nayre.org.

379. Highest Level of Education Attained

(U.S. adults over age 25)

	%
Not high school graduate	16.5
High school graduate	33.3
Some college	17.3
Associate	7.5
Bachelor's	17.0
Master's	5.6
Professional	1.4
Doctor's	1.2

Source: U.S. Department of Commerce, Bureau of Census, 1999.

380. Ivy League Colleges

Brown, 1764
Columbia, 1754
Cornell, 1865
Dartmouth, 1769
Harvard, 1636
Pennsylvania, 1740
Princeton, 1746
Yale, 1701

381. Seven Sisters Colleges

Barnard, 1889
Bryn Mawr, 1885
Mount Holyoke, 1837
Radcliffe, 1879
Smith, 1871
Vassar, 1861
Wellesley, 1875

382. Births to Teens

Adolescent Births in Selected Developed Countries

Country	*Number of Children Born to Women 15–19*	*% of Adolescent Births Among Unmarried Women*
France	15,100	78
Germany	24,200	57
Great Britain	41,700	87
Japan	16,000	10
Poland	41,600	31
United States	502,900	62

Source: The Alan Guttmacher Institute, *Into a New World: Young Women's Sexual and Reproductive Lives.* New York: The Alan Guttmacher Institute, 1998.

383. Teen Birth Rate per 1,000 Female Teens

Teen Pregnancies in Selected Developed Countries

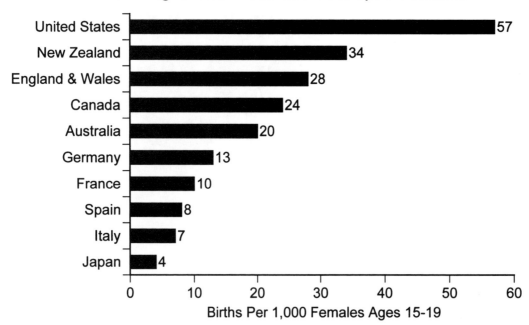

Country	Births Per 1,000 Females Ages 15-19
United States	57
New Zealand	34
England & Wales	28
Canada	24
Australia	20
Germany	13
France	10
Spain	8
Italy	7
Japan	4

Source: The Alan Guttmacher Institute, 1999.

384. Birth Rates by Marital Status

Marital Status and Age	Births per 1,000 Females				
	1960	1970	1980	1990	1999
Marital, 15–19	531	444	350	420	311
Non-marital, ages 15–19	15	22	28	43	40
Non-marital, ages 20–24	40	38	41	65	73
Non-marital, ages 14–44	22	26	29	44	44

Source: National Center for Health Statistics.

385. Teens and Sex: A Few Facts

- About 3 million teenagers (one-fourth of those who are sexually active) will get a sexually transmitted disease this year.

- Annually, about 1 million female teens (10% of all women aged 15-19 and 19% of those who have had sexual intercourse) will become pregnant.

- The teen birth rate reached a record low in 2000, with rates steadily declining throughout the 1990's.

- The proportion of all teen who give birth who are unwed has continued to escalate, from 14 percent in 1940 to 67 percent in 1990 and 79 percent in 2000.

- 56% of teen pregnancies result in births; 14% in miscarriages; 30% abortions.

- Teenage mothers have 13% of the babies born in the U.S.

- 78% of births to teenage mothers are outside of marriage.

- 25% of teenage mothers give birth to a second child within 2 years of their first.

- 64% of the approximately 60 million women aged 15 to 44 practice contraception.

- A screening program of high school students found that almost 12% of girls and 6% of boys were infected with chlamydia.

Sources: Centers for Disease Control and Prevention at http://www.cdc.gov; The Alan Guttmacher Institute at http://www.agi-usa.org/index.html.

386. Most Common Surnames in the U.S.

1. Smith
2. Johnson
3. Williams
4. Jones
5. Brown

6. Davis
7. Miller
8. Wilson
9. Moore
10. Taylor

Source: U.S. Census Bureau, 2000.

387. Most Popular Names for Births in 2001

Rank	Male Name	Female Name
1.	Jacob	Emily
2.	Michael	Hannah
3.	Joshua	Madison
4.	Matthew	Samantha
5.	Joseph	Sarah
6.	Nicholas	Elizabeth
7.	Anthony	Kayla
8.	Tyler	Alexis
9.	Daniel	Abigail

Source: Social Security Administration.

388. Well-Known Adopted Persons

John J. Audubon, naturalist
Halle Berry, actress
Bill Clinton, U.S. President
Faith Daniels, news anchor
Ted Danson, actor
Gerald Ford, U.S. President
Melissa Gilbert, actress
Sara Gilbert, actress
Scott Hamilton, figure skater
Faith Hill, country singer
Herbert Hoover, U.S. President
Jesse Jackson, minister

Steven Jobs, entrepreneur
John Lennon, singer
Greg Louganis, diver
James Michener, author
Marilyn Monroe, actress
Edgar Allan Poe, author
Eleanor Roosevelt, First Lady
Dave Thomas, entrepreneur
Mark Twain, writer
Anthony Williams, politician
Malcolm X, activist

Sources: Adoption Solutions Website at www.adoptionsolutions.com; National Adoption Information Clearinghouse at www.calib.com/naic/index.htm.

389. Healthy Life Expectancy Rankings

Based on the World Health Organization's Disability Adjusted Life Expectancy (DALE)

Country	Overall	Males	Females
Japan	74.5	71.9	77.2
Australia	73.2	70.8	75.5
France	73.1	69.3	76.9
Sweden	73.0	71.2	74.9
Spain	72.8	69.8	75.7
Italy	72.7	70.0	75.4
Greece	72.5	70.5	74.6
Switzerland	72.5	69.5	75.5
Canada	72.0	70.0	74.0
United Kingdom	71.7	69.7	73.7
United States	70.0	67.5	72.6
(Lowest)			
Ethiopia	33.5	33.5	33.5
Mali	33.1	32.6	33.5
Zimbabwe	32.9	33.4	32.4
Rwanda	32.8	32.9	32.7
Uganda	32.7	32.9	32.5
Botswana	32.3	32.3	32.3
Malawi	29.4	29.3	29.4
Niger	29.1	28.1	30.1
Sierra Leone	25.9	25.8	26.0

Disability Adjusted Life Expectancy (DALE) summarizes the expected number of years to be lived in what might be termed the equivalent of "full health." To calculate DALE, the years of ill-health are weighted according to severity and subtracted from the expected overall life expectancy to give the equivalent years of healthy life.

Source: World Health Organization, 2001.

390. Life Expectancy in the U.S., 1900–2000

Year	All races		White		Black*	
	Male	Female	Male	Female	Male	Female
1900	46.3	48.3	46.6	48.7	32.5	33.5
1910	48.4	51.8	48.6	52.0	33.8	37.5
1920	53.6	54.6	54.4	55.6	45.5	45.2
1930	58.1	61.6	59.7	63.5	47.3	49.2
1940	60.8	65.2	62.1	66.6	51.5	54.9
1950	65.6	71.1	66.5	72.2	59.1	62.9
1960	66.6	73.1	67.4	74.1	61.1	66.3
1970	67.1	74.7	68.0	75.6	60.0	68.3
1980	70.0	77.4	70.7	78.1	63.8	72.5
1990	71.8	78.8	72.7	79.4	64.5	73.6
2000	74.1	79.5	74.8	80.0	67.8	74.7

*Prior to 1970, data for the black population are not available. Data shown for 1900–1960 are for the nonwhite population.

Source: National Center for Health Statistics. Online at http://www.cdc.gov/nchs.

391. U.S. Surgeon General's "Leading Health Indicators"

1. Physical activity
2. Overweight and obesity
3. Tobacco use
4. Substance abuse
5. Responsible sexual behavior
6. Mental health
7. Injury and violence
8. Environmental quality
9. Immunization
10. Access to health care

Source: Healthy People 2010 report. Online at www.health.gov.

392. Major Causes of Disability

Males

1. HIV/AIDS
2. Road traffic accidents
3. Unipolar depressive disorders
4. Alcohol use disorders
5. Tuberculosis
6. Violence
7. Self-inflicted injuries
8. Schizophrenia
9. Bipolar affective disorder
10. Iron-deficiency anemia

Females

1. HIV/AIDS
2. Unipolar depressive disorders
3. Tuberculosis
4. Iron-deficiency anemia
5. Schizophrenia
6. Obstructed labor
7. Bipolar affective disorder
8. Abortion
9. Self-inflicted injuries
10. Maternal sepsis

Source: World Health Report, 2001. World Health Organization.

393. Daily Housework Trends

(As percent of Middletown housewives responding)

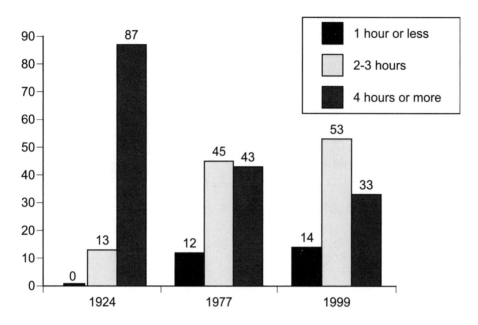

Source: Middletown Community Surveys, I, III, and IV. Cited in *Bowling Alone,* by R. D. Putnam. Simon & Schuster, 2000.

394. Dining In

How often do you and your family eat dinner together?

	%
Almost every night	50
Several times a week	18
Once a week	6
A few times a month	7
A few times a year	5

Source: September 2000 telephone poll by trained interviewers of a representative national sample of 1,010 randomly selected American adults. The Shell Poll, vol. 2, issue 3. Online at http://www.shellus.com.

395. Team Sports Participation

Youth (ages 12–17) participation in team sports during the past year:

Total	61.0%
Males	66.7%
Females	56.2%

Age

12 or 13	67.4%
14 or 15	63.6%
16 or 17	53.5%

Source: National Household Report on Drug Abuse, Department of Health and Human Services, February 2002.

396. Recipe for Avoiding Poverty

1. Finish high school.
2. Marry before having a child.
3. Marry after the age of 20.

Only 8 percent of the individuals following these three practices are poor; 79 percent of those who do, do not live in poverty. "Fifty-one percent of the increase in child poverty observed during the 1980's is attributable to changes in family structure during that period."

Source: William Galston, Professor and Director, Institute for Philosophy and Public Policy, University of Maryland; former domestic policy adviser to President Clinton.

397. Poverty Status of Families

	Percent of Families Living Below the Poverty Level*	
	All Families	Married-Couple Families
2000	8.6	4.7
1990	10.7	5.7
1980	10.3	6.2
1970	10.1	(NA)
1960	18.1	(NA)

*With and without children under 18 years

Source: U.S. Bureau of the Census.

398. Women in the Labor Force

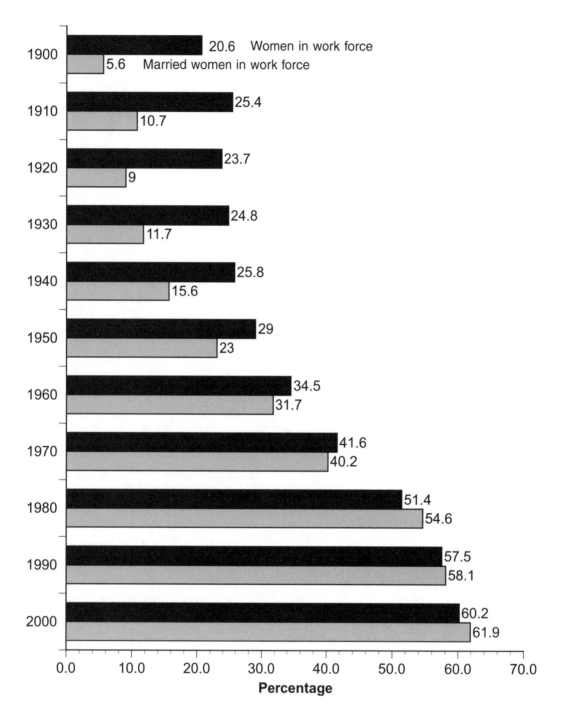

Source: U.S. Bureau of Census and Bureau of Labor Statistics.

398. *(continued)*

Women in the Labor Force: Graph Interpretation Activity

The accompanying graph depicts the percentage of all women in the work force and the percent of married women in the work force. For example in 1900, 20.6 percent of women over the age of 15 were in the paid labor force in 1900. Only 5.6 percent of married women were counted in the labor force.

1. In which year did the percent of married women in the work force first exceed the percent of all women in the work force? What would account for that phenomenon?

2. What percent of married women were working outside the home in 1960?

3. In 1920, what percent of all women were employed outside the home?

4. What factors most likely accounted for the dramatic increase in women employed outside the home in the past century?

Answers: 1. 1980. The percent of unmarried women employed was lower than the percent of married women working outside the home. 2. 31.7%. 3. 23.7%. 4. Smaller families, women's rights movement, transition from a rural economy, rising cost of living, desire to buy more things, more single mothers, higher divorce rate, more educated women, increased social acceptance of women working (especially after WWII).

399. Per Capita Income by Ethnicity

African Americans	$14,397
Hispanic Americans	$11,621
Asian Americans & Pacific Islanders	$21,134
American Indians/Alaska Natives	Not Available
White Americans	$24,109

Source: U.S. Census Bureau, Current Population Reports, Money Income in the U.S., 1999.

400. Population by Race and Hispanic Origin for the U.S., 2000

Race and Hispanic or Latino	Number	Percent of Total Population
RACE		
Total population	281,421,906	100.0
One race	274,595,678	97.6
White	211,460,626	75.1
Black or African American	34,658,190	12.3
American Indian and Alaska Native	2,475,956	0.9
Asian	10,242,998	3.6
Native Hawaiian, Other Pacific Islander	398,835	0.1
Some other race	359,073	5.5
Two or more races	6,826,228	2.4
HISPANIC OR LATINO		
Total population	281,421,906	100.0
Hispanic or Latino	35,305,818	12.5
Not Hispanic or Latino	246,116,088	87.5

Source: U.S. Census Bureau, Census 2000.

401. U.S. Population Center

Each decade, the Census Bureau calculates the center of population. The center is determined as "the place where an imaginary, flat, weightless and rigid map of the United States would balance perfectly if all residents were of identical weight."

Year	Nearest Town	Year	Nearest Town
2000	Edgar Springs, MO	1890	Greensburg, IN
1990	Steelville, MO	1880	Covington, KY
1980	DeSoto, MO	1870	Portsmouth, OH
1970	Mascoutah, IL	1860	Hillsboro, OH
1960	Centralia, IL	1850	Petersburg, WV
1950	Olney, IL	1840	Clarksburg, WV
1940	Carlisle, IN	1830	Parkersburg, WV
1930	Linton, IN	1820	Moorefield, VA
1920	Spencer, IN	1810	Leesburg, VA
1910	Bloomington, IN	1800	Baltimore, MD
1900	Columbus, IN	1790	Chestertown, MD

Source: U.S. Census Bureau, http://www.census.gov.

402. Homicide Victimization, 1950–1999

Year	Homicide Rate per 100,000 Population	Estimated Number of Homicides
1950	4.6	7,020
1960	5.1	9,110
1970	7.9	16,000
1980	10.2	23,040
1990	9.4	23,440
1999	5.7	15,533

Source: FBI, Uniform Crime Reports, 1950–1999.

403. Incarceration Rate, 1980–2000

Number of sentenced inmates incarcerated under State and Federal jurisdiction per 100,000, 1980–2000

1980	139	1987	231	1994	389
1981	154	1988	247	1995	411
1982	171	1989	276	1996	427
1983	179	1990	297	1997	444
1984	188	1991	313	1998	461
1985	202	1992	332	1999	476
1986	217	1993	359	2000	478

Source: Bureau of Justice Statistics, 2001. Online at http://www.ojp.usdoj.gov/bjs/glance/tables/incrttab.htm.

404. Number of Persons Under Sentence of Death, 1955–2000

Year	Number of Prisoners Under Sentence of Death
1955	125
1960	212
1965	331
1970	631
1975	488
1980	692
1985	1,575
1990	2,346
2000	3,593

Source: Capital Punishment 2000, Department of Justice at www.ojp.usdoj.gov/bjs.

405. Fizzled Fashion Fads

Afro haircuts	hot pants	patent leather shoes
blue suede shoes	ironing hair	penny loafers with
butch wax	leisure suits	pennies
button fly jeans	poodle skirts	pillbox hats
coonskin caps	miniskits	pocket protectors with
earth shoes	mood rings	pens
glassless glasses	muttonchop sideburns	saddle shoes
go-go boots	Nehru jackets	taps on street shoes
headbands	paper dresses	zoot suits

406. Greatest Rock and Roll Hits of All Time

"Stairway to Heaven"
"(I Can't Get No) Satisfaction"
"Layla"
"Light My Fire"
"Purple Haze"
"Yesterday"
"Imagine"
"Johnny B. Goode"
"My Generation"
"Like a Rolling Stone"

Source: Selected in a popular poll conducted by the Rock and Roll Hall of Fame and Museum, Cleveland, Ohio

407. Top 10 Movies of All Time

1. *Citizen Kane* (1941)
2. *Casablanca* (1942)
3. *The Godfather* (1972)
4. *Gone with the Wind* (1939)
5. *Lawrence of Arabia* (1962)
6. *The Wizard of Oz* (1939)
7. *The Graduate* (1967)
8. *On the Waterfront* (1954)
9. *Schindler's List* (1993)
10. *Singin' in the Rain* (1952)

Source: Selected by 1,500 leaders from across the American film community. American Film Institute at http://www.afi.com. Used with permission.

408. Sociology Related Journals

Administration in Social Work

The American Journal of Drug and Alcohol Abuse

Behavior Therapy

Child and Adolescent Social Work Journal

Child and Youth Services

Child Welfare

Clinical Social Work Journal

Community Mental Health Journal

Crisis Intervention

Gerontologist

Health and Social Work

Hospice Journal

Indian Journal of Social Work

International Social Work

Intervention

Journal of Divorce

Journal of Independent Social Work

Journal of Marriage and Family

Journal of Social Work and Human Sexuality

Journal of Sociology and Social Welfare

Parenting Studies

Prevention in Human Services

Public Welfare

School Social Work Journal

Small Group Behavior

Social Work

Social Work Research and Abstracts

Social Work Today

Society

Sociology and Social Research

Suicide and Life-Threatening Behavior

Urban and Social Change Review

Youth and Society

409. Online Resources for Teaching Sociology

American Sociological Association
http://www.asanet.org

Ask ERIC: Lesson Plans for Teaching Sociology
http://askeric.org/cgi-bin/lessons.cgi/Social_Studies/Sociology

Centre for Learning and Teaching Sociology, Anthropology and Politics
http://www.c-sap.bham.ac.uk

Crime Statistics
U.S. Department of Justice
www.ojp.usdoj.gov/bjs

Internet Resources for Teaching Sociology of Aging
http://www.crab.rutgers.edu/ ~ deppen/aging.htm

Resources for Teaching of Social Psychology
http://jonathan.mueller.faculty.noctrl.edu//crow

409. *(continued)*

Social Studies Sociology Lessons
http://www.edhelper.com/cat276.htm

Sociology Cases Database Project
www.nd.edu/ ~ dhachen/cases

Sociology Classroom
Internet Resources for High School Students and Teachers
http://home.att.net/ ~ sociologyclassroom/home.html

Sociology: Databases & Centers
http://www.academicinfo.net/socdata.html

Sociology & Psychology Lesson Plans and Activities
http://members.aol.com/Donnpages/Sociology.htm

Sociology of Death and Dying
http://www.trinity.edu/ ~ mkearl/death.html

Social Statistics Briefing Room
http://www.whitehouse.gov/fsbr/ssbr.html

The SocioWeb
http://www.sonic.net/ ~ markbl/socioweb

Teaching Resources: Sociology
University of Nottingham
http://www.nottingham.ac.uk/sociology/index.html

World Civilizations
Washington State University
http://www.wsu.edu:8080/ ~ dee/WORLD.HTM

Lists for
Psychology

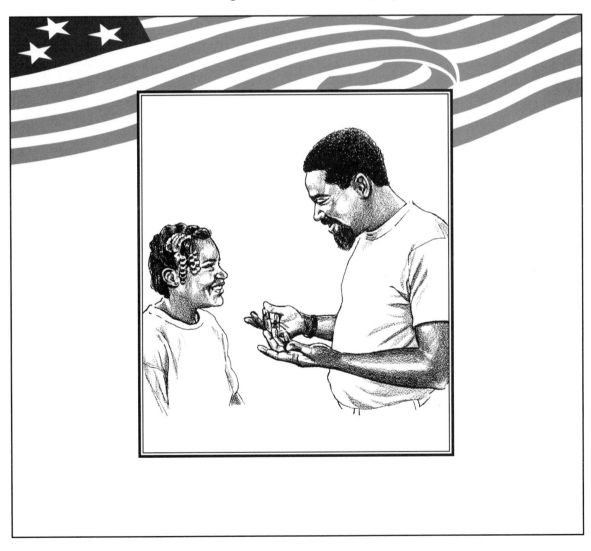

410. Fields of Psychology

adolescent development
animal
behavioral pharmacology
child
clinical
cognitive
community
comparative
consulting
consumer
counseling
developmental
educational
engineering
evaluation and measurement
experimental

forensic
genetic
history of psychology
industrial
learning
military
organizational
personality
philosophical
physiological
psycholinguistics
psychometrics
psychopathology
rehabilitation
school
social

411. Careers in Psychology and Mental Health

career counselor
child psychologist
clinical psychologist
cognitive psychologist
community mental health aide
counseling psychologist
counselor
educational psychologist
group home supervisor
high school psychology teacher
human resource professional
industrial psychologist
intake interviewer
marriage counselor
mental health researcher
organizational consultant
pastoral counselor
probation officer
professor

psychometrician
research technician
school psychologist
social psychologist
substance abuse counselor
test developer
training and development consultant

412. Eminent Pioneer Psychologists

Anne Anastasi	Erik Erikson	Wolfgang Köhler
Albert Bandura	Gustav Fechner	Abraham Maslow
Alfred Binet	Leon Festinger	Maria Montessori
Mary W. Calkins	Arnold Gesell	Ivan Pavlov
Walter Cannon	G. Stanley Hall	Jean Piaget
Raymond Cattell	Hermann Helmholtz	Carl Rogers
Maine de Biran	Mary Henle	B. F. Skinner
John Dewey	Clark Hull	Lewis Terman
Dorothea Dix	William James	Edward Titchener
June Etta Downey	George Kelly	E. L. Thorndike
Hermann Ebbinghaus	Kurt Kofka	Leona Tyler

413. Prominent Figures in the History of Psychiatry

Alfred Adler	Carl Jung
Ruth Benedict	Thomas Kirkbride
Eugen Bleuler	Melanie Klein
Abraham Brill	Emil Kraepelin
Helene Deutsch	Rollo May
Sigmund Freud	Philippe Pinel
Anna Freud	Otto Rank
Erich Fromm	Harry S. Sullivan
Wilhelm Griesinger	E. B. Titchener
Karen Homey	

Freud

414. Phobias

Phobia	Abnormal fear of . . .	Phobia	Abnormal fear of . . .
acrophobia	high places	isophobia	poison
agoraphobia	open spaces	kakorrhaphio-phobia	failure or defeat
aichmophobia	sharp instruments		
ailurophobia	cats	leukophobia	color white
amathophobia	dust	linonophobia	string
anthophobia	flowers	menophobia	being alone
anthropophobia	people	microphobia	germs
aphephobia	touch	murophobia	mice
arachnophobia	spiders	mysophobia	dirt
astraphobia	lightning	nyctophobia	dark
ataxiophobia	disorder	ochlophobia	crows
aulophobia	flutes	ochophobia	riding in cars
blennophobia	slime	ombrophobia	rain
brontophobia	thunder	ophidiophobia	snakes
bymnophobia	nudity	parthenophobia	young girls
cathisophobia	sitting down	phobophobia	fear
claustrophobia	closed places	phonophobia	noise
crystallophobia	glass	photophobia	light
cynophobia	dogs	phrenophobia	going insane
dromophobia	crossing streets	phronemophobia	thinking
entomophobia	insects	pnigophobia	choking
equinophobia	horses	pyrophobia	fire
frigophobia	cold	rhypophobia	filth
galeophobia	sharks	scriptophobia	writing in public
gamophobia	marriage	thanatophobia	death
gephyrophobia	crossing a bridge	theophobia	god
geumophobia	flavors	tonitrophobia	thunder
harpaxophobia	being robbed	trichophobia	hair
hedonophobia	sunlight	triskaidekaphobia	the number 13
heliophobia	pleasure	uranophobia	homosexuality
hydrophobia	water; rabies	vermiphobia	worms
hygrophobia	liquids	xenophobia	strangers
iatrophobia	doctors	zoophobia	animals

415. Counseling Approaches

Theory	*Primary Proponent*
Action Therapy	O'Connell
Actualizing Therapy	Shostrum
Adlerian Individual Psychotherapy	Adler
Art Therapy	Naumburg, Cane, Kramer
Assertion-Structured Therapy	Phillips
Attack Therapy	Synanon
Behavioral Marital Therapy	Jacobson & Margolin
Behavioral Therapy	Wolpe
Bibliotherapy	Gottschalk
Biocentric Therapy	Branden
Bioenergetic Therapy	Reich
Brief Therapy	Smal; Alexander & French
Character Analysis Therapy	Horney
Client-Centered Therapy	Rogers
Cognitive Behavior Modification	Meichenbaum
Cognitive Therapy	Beck
Conjoint Family Therapy	Satir
Conjoint Sex Therapy	Masters & Johnson
Construct Counseling	Kelly
Correspondence Therapy	Parsons
Dance Therapy	Chace
Decision Counseling	Greenwald
Directive Psychotherapy	Thorne
Eclectic Models of Counseling	Egan
Ego Psychotherapy	Federn & Weiss
Existential Therapy	May, Bugenthal
Experimental Therapy	Whitaker & Malone
Family Systems Therapy	Bowen
Freudian Psychoanalysis	Freud
Functional Family Therapy	Barton & Alexander
Gestalt Therapy	Perls
Hypnotherapy	Milton Erickson
Intensive Journal Process	Progroff
Jungian Analytical Psychotherapy	Jung
Learning Theory Psychotherapy	Dollard and Miller
Logotherapy	Franki
Marital Counseling	Mudd, Stone & Stone
Massed-time Therapy	Ries

415. *(continued)*

Theory	*Primary Proponent*
Milan Systemic Family Therapy	Selvini-Palazzoli
Milieu Therapy	Pinel, Rush
Modern Psychoanalysis	Spotnitz
Multimodal Behavioral Therapy	Lazarus
Multiple Family Therapy	Laqueur
Multiple Impact Therapy	McGregor
Music Therapy	Priestly, Nordoff, Robbins
Object Relations Therapy	Kohut
Objective Psychotherapy	Karpman
Occupational Therapy	Dunton, Tracy, Barton
Operant Interpersonal Therapy	Stuart
Orgone Therapy	Reich
Pastoral Counseling	Boisen
Philosophical Psychotherapy	Spinoza
Play Therapy	Axline
Poetry Therapy	Greifer, Leedy, Spector
Primal Therapy	Janov
Provocative Therapy	Farrelly
Psychodrama	Moreno
Psycho-Imagination Therapy	Shorr
Psychosynthesis	Tien
Rational Emotive Therapy	Albert Ellis
Recreational Therapy	Dunton, Davis
Re-evaluation Counseling	Jackens
Relationship Therapy	Patterson
Relaxation Therapy	Kraines, Jacobson
Release Therapy	Levy
Sector Therapy	Deutsch
Sex Therapy	Masters and Johnson
Social Learning Therapy	Bandura
Solution-Focused Brief Therapy	de Shazer
Strategic Family Therapy	Maclanes & Haley
Structural Family Therapy	Minuchin
Supportive Therapy	Watkins
Time-Limited Dynamic Therapy	Strupp and Binder
Total Push Therapy	Myerson
Transactional Analysis	Berne
Transpersonal Psychology	James, Wilber

416. Psychotherapeutic Techniques

bibliotherapy	psychodrama
confrontation	questioning
directives	reflection of feelings
dream analysis	rehearsal
free association	relaxation training
homework	role playing
hypnosis	silence
interpretation	suggestion
paraphrasing	systematic desensitization
persuasion	testing
projective tests	

417. Commonly Used Psychological Tests

Wechsler Adult Intelligence Scale, Revised (WAIS-R)
Minnesota Multiphasic Personality Inventory (MMPI)
Thematic Apperception Test (TAT)
Rorschach Test
Myers-Briggs Type Indicator
Draw-a-Person Test (DAP)
House-Tree-Person Test (HTP)
Wechsler Intelligence Scale for Children, Revised (WISC-R)
Peabody Picture Vocabulary Test (PPVT)
Bender-Gestalt Visual Motor Test
Stanford-Binet Intelligence Test

418. Types of Tests

achievement
aptitude
attitude
intelligence
interest
inventory
personality
projective

419. Famous People Who Did Poorly in School

Winston Churchill was one of the worst students in his class. He was branded as careless and unpunctual by his headmaster. He won the Nobel Prize for literature in 1953.

Thomas Edison was labeled by his teachers as "too stupid to learn." He attended grammar school for only three months because his teachers considered him to be "addled."

Albert Einstein did not talk until he was four, nor read until age nine. He failed a math course. The first time he tried, he failed his entrance examination at Polytechnic Institute in Zurich. He was judged to have "no promise."

William Faulkner was briefly enrolled in Ole Miss. He received a "D" in English.

Isaac Newton flunked mathematics in school.

Carl Sandburg, the poet, flunked out of West Point, supposedly because of "deficiencies in English."

Albert Schweitzer's mother would cry because he received such poor grades.

Woodrow Wilson did not learn his letters until he was nine years old or to read until he was eleven.

Émile Zola once received a zero in French literature and composition.

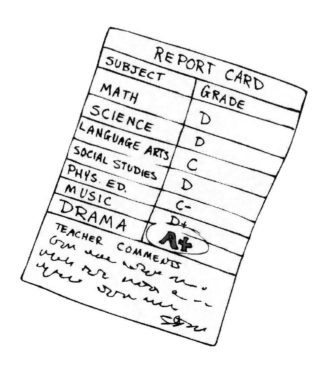

420. Characteristics of Successful Persons

From extensive study of outstanding achievers, a number of researchers have arrived at traits that tend to be possessed by successful persons.

Are committed to their goals

Are able to set priorities

Have learned how to learn

Are results oriented

Continually seek new challenges

Manage stress effectively

Focus on a mission

Learn how to make decisions

Practice mental rehearsal

Take calculated risks

Maintain flexibility

Ask for what they want

Are able to ask the right questions

Keep their promises

Are good listeners

Can tolerate rejection and loss

Practice persistence

Avoid perfectionism

Accept help from successful people

Trust their hunches

Are able to negotiate

Anticipate what can go wrong

Feel good about themselves

Strive to improve

Practice patience

Are assertive when necessary

Are honest

Are able to see the other person's point of view

Avoid self-pity

Use praise more than criticism

Learn to say no

Trust themselves

421. Initial Failures

Burt Reynolds and **Clint Eastwood** were both fired by the same studio on the same day. The opinion was that neither had star potential.

Fred Smith, the founder of Federal Express, lost a million dollars a month for the first two years.

Candice Bergen flunked out of the University of Pennsylvania.

Jerry West was supposedly such a poor basketball player as a boy that other boys would not let him join their games.

Babe Ruth was the New York Yankees' second choice to play right field.

Henry Ford was broke at the age of 40.

Chevy Chase was expelled from Haverford College. He transferred to Bard College.

Vince Lombardi, one of the most outstanding professional football coaches, was a line coach at Fordham University at the age of 43.

Abraham Lincoln was twice defeated in his bid for the U.S. Senate.

Buckminster Fuller was twice expelled from Harvard.

Michael Douglas flunked out of the University of California.

Chester A. Arthur, twenty-first president of the United States, was fired as collector of the port of New York.

William Kennedy's book, *Ironweed*, was rejected by 13 publishers. He later won the Pulitzer Prize for his novel.

Benjamin Harrison was defeated for governor of Indiana and the United States Senate before being elected President of the United States.

Theodore Roosevelt was defeated in his bid for mayor of New York City.

James K. Polk, the eleventh president, was twice defeated for governor of Tennessee.

Joe Namath's SAT scores were too low for admission to the University of Maryland. He ended up as an award-winning quarterback at the University of Alabama before entering the professional ranks.

William Faulkner was turned down for membership by a literary society at Ole Miss.

Michael Jordan was cut from his high school basketball team his junior year.

(continued)

421. *(continued)*

Fred Astaire was evaluated by one casting director as "can't act, slightly bald, can dance a little . . ."

Lucille Ball failed her first drama class. The teacher asserted that Lucille "had no talent."

Lee Iacocca was turned down for a scholarship at Purdue.

Calvin Coolidge was defeated for a school board in Northampton, Massachusetts, prior to his election to the presidency.

Eleanor Roosevelt fainted the first time she tried to speak in public.

Richard Bach's best-selling book *Jonathan Livingston Seagull* was turned down by two dozen publishers

Abraham Lincoln's 1863 Gettysburg Address was judged by *The Chicago Times* as ". . . loose-joined, so puerile, not alone in literary construction, but in its ideas, its sentiments, its grasp. He has outdone himself. He has literally come out of the little end of his own horn. By the side of it, mediocrity is superb."

Robert Pirig's bestselling book, *Zen and the Art of Motorcycle Maintenance*, was rejected by 121 publishers before it was finally accepted.

The Duke of Windsor, the future King Edward VIII of England, failed his entrance exam into the Royal Navy.

Thomas Edison unsuccessfully tried 50,000 different elements for his lightbulb before finding the one that worked.

422. Famous Persons Who Were Learning Disabled

Hans Christian Andersen	Albert Einstein
Cher	Bruce Jenner
Winston Churchill	Greg Louganis
Tom Cruise	George Patton
Leonardo da Vinci	Nelson Rockefeller
Walt Disney	Woodrow Wilson
Thomas Edison	F. W. Woolworth

423. Views of Success

Success is going from failure to failure without loss of enthusiasm.
—WINSTON CHURCHILL

If there is one secret of success it lies in the ability to get the other person's point of view and see things from his angle as well as your own.
—HENRY FORD

Self-trust is the first secret of success. —RALPH WALDO EMERSON

I don't know the key to success; but the key to failure is trying to please everybody. —BILL COSBY

When I was a young man I observed that nine out of ten things I did were failures. I didn't want to be a failure, so I did ten times more work.
—GEORGE BERNARD SHAW

The secret to success in any human endeavor is total concentration.
—KURT VONNEGUT

There is a simple formula for success, and and I'll tell what it is: Always do more than you're paid to do. —SIDNEY SHELDON

There are two ways to climb an oak tree. You can climb it, or you can sit on an acorn. —ZIG ZIGLAR

You become the champion by fighting one more round.
—JAMES J. CORBETT

If you wish to succeed in life, make perseverance your bosom friend, experience your wise counselor, caution your elder brother, and hope your guardian genius. —JOSEPH ADDISON

Try not to become a man (sic) of success but rather try to become a man of value. —ALBERT EINSTEIN

A man is a success if he gets up in the morning and gets to bed at night, and in between he does what he wants to do. —BOB DYLAN

Never continue in a job you don't enjoy. If you're happy in what you're doing, you'll like yourself, you'll have inner peace. And if you have that, along with physical health, you will have had more success than you could possibly have imagined. —JOHNNY CARSON

424. Physiological Needs

appropriate body temperature
elimination of body wastes
food
oxygen
pain avoidance
physical activity
sensory stimulation
sex
sleep and rest
water

425. Psychological Needs

achievement
affiliation
aggression
approval of others
attention
avoidance of embarrassment
avoidance of unpleasant experiences
control; power
creativity; expression
dependence
dominance
fun

knowledge
independence
love
nurturance
orderliness
recognition
revenge
security
self-actualization
self-esteem
sex

426. Being-Values as Postulated by Abraham Maslow

Motivating forces of the most mentally healthy people:

Wholeness: unity; integration; interconnectedness; simplicity
Perfection: necessity, suitability; justice; completeness
Completion: ending; finality; fulfillment, destiny
Justice: fairness, orderliness, lawfulness
Aliveness: spontaneity; self-regulation; full-functioning
Individuality: non-comparability; novelty
Effortlessness: ease, grace
Playfulness: fun; joy; amusement; humor
Truth: honesty; reality; simplicity; richness, completeness
Self-sufficiency: autonomy; independence; self-determining

Source: A. Maslow, *The Psychology of Being,* 2nd ed. p. 83.

427. Mental Health Indicators

Based on research and clinical experiences, Abraham Maslow listed ten describable characteristics of the healthy individual:

Clear, more efficient perception of reality.
More openness to experience.
Increased integration, wholeness, and unity of the person.
Increased spontaneity, expressiveness.
A real self; a firm identity; autonomy, uniqueness.
Increased objectivity, detachment, transcendence of self.
Recovery of creativeness.
Ability to fuse concreteness and abstractions.
Democratic character structure.
Ability to love and be loved.

Source: Maslow, A. H. (1954). *Motivation and Personality.* New York: Harper & Bros.

428. Research-Based Suggestions for a Happier Life

1. **Realize that enduring happiness doesn't come from making it.** People adapt to changing circumstances—even to wealth or a disability. Thus wealth is like health: its utter absence breeds misery, but having it (or any circumstance we long for) doesn't guarantee happiness.

2. **Take control of your time.** Happy people feel in control of their lives, often aided by mastering their use of time-setting goals, breaking them into daily aims. Although we often overestimate how much we will accomplish in any given day (leaving us frustrated), we generally underestimate how much we can accomplish in a year, given just a little progress every day.

3. **Act happy.** We can act ourselves into a frame of mind. Manipulated into a smiling expression, people feel better; when they scowl, the whole world seems to scowl back. So . . . put on a happy face. Talk as if you feel positive self-esteem, optimistic, and outgoing. Going through the motions can trigger the emotions.

4. **Seek work and leisure that engages your skills.** Happy people often are in a zone called "flow"—absorbed in a task that challenges them without overwhelming them. The most expensive forms of leisure (sitting on a yacht) often provide less flow experience than gardening, socializing, or craft work. Off your duffs, couch potatoes.

(continued)

428. *(continued)*

5. **Join the movement movement.** An avalanche of recent studies reveals that aerobic exercise not only promotes health and energy, it also is an antidote for mild depression and anxiety. Sound minds reside in sound bodies.

6. **Get REST.** Happy people live active, vigorous lives, yet reserve time for renewing sleep and solitude. Americans suffer from a growing "national sleep debt," with resulting fatigue, diminished alertness, and gloomy moods. Even a literal day of REST—Restricted Environmental Stimulation Therapy—or smaller, daily doses of solitude in meditation or prayer can spiritually recharge.

7. **Give priority to close relationships.** There are few better remedies for unhappiness than an intimate friendship with someone who cares deeply about you. Confiding is good for soul and body. If married, resolve to nurture your relationship, to not take your partner for granted, to display to your spouse the sort of kindness that you display to others, to affirm your partner, to play together and share together. To rejuvenate your affections, resolve in such ways to act lovingly.

8. **Focus beyond the self.** Reach out to those in need. Happiness increases helpfulness (those who feel good do good). But doing good also makes one feel good. Compassionate acts help one feel better about oneself.

9. **Count your blessings.** People who keep a gratitude journal—who pause each day to reflect on some positive aspect of their lives (their health, friends, family, freedom, education, senses, etc.) experience heightened well-being.

10. **Take care of the soul.** In study after study, actively religious people are happier. They cope better with crises. For many people, faith provides a support community, a sense of life's meaning, feelings of ultimate acceptance, a reason to focus beyond self, and a timeless perspective on life's woes.

Source: David G. Myers, *The Pursuit of Happiness* (Avon Books, 1993). Copyright 2001, David G. Myers, Hope College, Holland, MI 49422. Used with permission.

429. Common Defense Mechanisms

compensation
denial of reality
displacement
fantasy
fixation

intellectualization
introjection
overcompensation
projection
rationalization

reaction formation
regression
repression
sublimation

430. Early Treatments for Mental Illness

administration of hellebore
baths
beating
copious bleeding
dunking head under water
electric shock
execution
exorcism
frontal lobotomy
hot irons applied to the head

insulin shock treatment
lowering afflicted into snake pits
shackling
spinning in a centrifuge
straitjackets
tossing afflicted from high cliffs
trephining (boring a hole in the
  skull)
tying up patient
wrapping in wet sheets

431. Psychology Firsts

c. 800	mental asylums in the world (Baghdad; Damascus)
1409	mental hospital in Europe (Valencia, Spain)
1556	mental hospital in America (Mexico)
1773	mental hospital in the U.S. (Williamsburg, Virginia)
1834	psychophysicist, Ernst Heinrich Weber
1844	Association of Medical Superintendents of American Institutions for the Insane established
c. 1869	systematically study individual differences (Galton)
1879	psychology laboratory founded (by Wilhelm Wundt)
1881	psychology laboratory in the United States (G. Stanley Hall)
1886	psychology book published in America, by John Dewey
1892	American Psychological Association founded
1895	first book on psychoanalysis, *Studies on Hysteria*, by Freud and Breuer, published
1896	American psychiatric institute founded (New York City)
1901	psychiatric ward in an American general hospital established (Albany)
1904	intelligence test (Binet & Simon)
1916	American intelligence test (Stanford-Binet)
1930	mental hygiene international congress held

432. Nonsense Syllables for Learning Experiments

BAZ	MIB	POB
NOC	SOZ	FIW
DIH	HUW	REJ
ZIR	BAX	NIW
PIW	PAZ	WEM
KOG	GIK	ZON
LIR	BUV	LOS
VIT	WUB	LIX
ROX	FUP	ZUF
LIG	PW	JOL
TIY	FOS	KIF
PUH	SEF	RIW
KOL	POF	JIK
SIM	LOZ	SIF
ZEL	KOD	WIR

433. Five-Letter Anagrams

STRTU	HSEOR	LSUKL
ESROC	CELNU	CONEA
PTNLA	VRPEO	ADRAR
OIENS	EESRA	HTMUO
ROBDA	VREDI	UOFLR
EPALP	TROOM	UTTRH
STIRW	ACEDN	PESLE
ELNGA	NCOWL	PRUES
TNIAR	SRIEF	ROTAC
SETNO	ICJEU	ERGEN
YELAR	WTEIH	STAPA
ASTRI	KKNUS	NEPUR
FTIUR	KCRTA	RTAXE
EPNOH	OMBRO	VRBEA
OOCRL	VRSEE	EWRKC
WBNOR	BZRAE	DCUOL
EOCNA	STATO	SASRG
SHUOE		

434. Four-Letter Anagrams

NVEO	LBLI	TWIA	SETR
RNOB	TOVE	ELGU	LBAL
NEHA	TXEI	OBNR	ENIM
SKED	VLEO	ATUN	MBOC
KWLA	PCHA	SNIK	RTNU
SNOE	ORHE	NZEO	VDEO
RHIA	EBUL	ISMW	PEGA
KIEH	UROF	PDNO	ODFO
KCSO	YBBA	XITA	TMBO
GHHI	GFOL	MEDO	SKIC
HCOE	RKOF	NOCR	LPLI
TUOA	ONNO	LDAO	IEMC
TBAH	TDEA	IDLO	ERTE
KOBO	EIAD	SHDI	OABT
TIHC	PNAL	ALGO	RALO

435. Items for Creativity Brainstorming

Brainstorm creative uses for:

baseball bat
cane fishing pole
cardboard tube from paper towels
chalkboard eraser
claw hammer
colander
deck of cards
discarded Christmas trees
fruitcake
horseshoe
ice cube tray
jump rope
Manhattan telephone book
megaphone
newspaper
nylon stockings
old shoes
paper clip
pencil
pie pan
plastic milk jug

railroad spike
school bus
shovel
socks with holes in them
soft-drink can
square yard of carpet
Styrofoam egg carton
thousand ping pong balls
used auto tires
volleyball

436. Self-Help Groups

Abused Women's Aid in Crisis
  (AWAIC)
Adoptee's Liberty Movement
  Association
Al-Anon
Alateen
Alcoholics Anonymous (AA)
American Diabetes Association
Arthritis Foundation
Batterers Anonymous
Brain Tumor Support Group
Breathing Partners
Burns Recovered
Calix Society
Candlelighters
Co-dependents Anonymous
Compassionate Friends, The
Debtors Anonymous
Down's Syndrome Congress
Emotions Anonymous
Epilepsy Foundation
Families Anonymous
Gain-Anon
Gamblers Anonymous
Gray Panthers
Heart to Heart
Hospice
International Parents' Organization
Juvenile Diabetes Foundation
Lupus Foundation of America
Make Today Count
Mended Hearts

Mensa
Mothers of Twins Club
Muscular Dystrophy Association
Narcotics Anonymous
National Anorexic Aid Society
National Association for
  Retarded Citizens
National Ataxia Foundation
National Federation of the Blind
National Hemophilia Foundation
National Multiple Sclerosis Society
National Society for Autistic Children
Neurotics Anonymous
Overeaters Anonymous
Paralyzed Veterans of America
Parents and Friends of
  Lesbians and Gays
Parents Anonymous
Parents Without Partners
Reach to Recovery
Recovery, Inc.
Spina Bifida Association
Stroke Clubs
Take Off Pounds Sensibly (TOPS)
Theos Foundation
Tourette-Syndrome Association
United Cerebral Palsy
United Ostomy Association
Widowed Persons
Women for Sobriety
Women Who Love Too Much

437. Feelings

adequate	despondent	frantic	jubilant
afraid	determined	frightened	jumpy
agitated	disappointed	frustrated	leery
alarmed	disconcerted	fulfilled	left out
ambitious	disconsolate	furious	lonely
amused	disenchanted	gay	lost
angry	disgruntled	gentle	loved
anguished	disgusted	glad	loving
annoyed	dismayed	gleeful	low
anxious	disoriented	gloomy	lucky
apathetic	displeased	glum	mad
appalled	distracted	good	marvelous
appreciated	distraught	great	mean
apprehensive	distressed	grieved	melancholy
assertive	distrustful	happy	merry
bad	disturbed	hateful	miserable
baffled	doubtful	healthy	mixed up
befuddled	down	helpless	moody
bold	downtrodden	hopeless	motherly
bored	ecstatic	horrified	mournful
bothered	elated	hostile	needed
brave	empathetic	hurt	negative
bubbly	enduring	ill	nervous
burdened	energetic	inadequate	out of it
calm	enthralled	incapable	outraged
capable	envious	independent	overjoyed
caring	euphoric	indestructible	panicky
cheerful	excited	indignant	peaceful
compassionate	exasperated	ineffective	perplexed
confident	exhausted	infuriated	persecuted
confused	exuberant	intense	pleasant
content	fearful	intimidated	pleased
courageous	fed up	invisible	positive
critical	fine	irate	powerless
cross	firm	irked	proud
deflated	flabbergasted	irritated	relieved
dejected	flustered	jealous	remorseful
delighted	forceful	jolly	resentful
depressed	fortunate	jovial	resistant
desperate	fragile	joyful	revengeful

437. (continued)

run down	spiteful	tranquil	upset
sad	strong	trapped	useless
satisfied	stunned	troubled	vibrant
secure	surprised	turned off	vulnerable
serene	terrible	uncomfortable	weak
serious	terrified	uneasy	wonderful
somber	thankful	unloved	worn out
sore	thrilled	unsure	worried
sorrowful	tickled	unwanted	
sorry	timid	up	
spirited	tormented	uplifted	

438. Most Common Fears

speaking before a group	dogs	losing friends
not having enough money	dying	looking foolish
insects and bugs	flying	tests
heights	loneliness	bodily injury
sickness	deep water	
	failing	
	making mistakes	

439. Commonly Abused Drugs

Name	Street Name
alcohol	booze
amphetamines	speed, uppers
barbiturates	ludes, yellow jackets, reds
cocaine	coke, toot, snow, crack
hashish	herb
heroin	smack, junk, skag
inhalants; aerosols	cans
LSD	acid, dots
MDMA	ecstasy
marijuana	grass, ganja, acapulco
mescaline	cactus
peyote	buttons
psilocybin	magic mushrooms
phencydidine (PCP)	angel dust

440. Risks of Chronic Alcohol Use

alcohol-induced depression
anxiety
birth defects in offspring
blood-clotting problems
brain damage
cancer, especially esophagus and stomach
chronic gastritis
cirrhosis of the liver
decreased red blood cell formation
delirium tremens (DTs)
fetal alcohol syndrome heart disease
inflammation of the pancreas
inflammation of the stomach lining
lower disease resistance
lowered REM sleep
heart muscle tissue damage
memory loss
premature aging syndrome
shorter lifespan (average: 15 years less)

441. Growth Changes of Puberty

Boys	Girls
acne	acne
beard	breast development
chest hair	enlargement of genitals
enlargement of genitals	menstruation
pubic hair	pubic hair
underarm hair	rounding of body shape
voice change	underarm hair

442. Famous Twins

Nat & Eli Bremer	Members of a quartet named Amen
Aaron Carter	Pop singer
Edward Montgomery Clift	Actor
Jacqueline & Pauline Cuff	Rock & roll singers
Kim & Kelley Deal	Members of rock group The Breeders
John Elway	Professional football player
Horace & Harvey Grant	NBA basketball players
Deidre & Andrea Hall	Actresses
Jill & Jacqueline Hennessy	Actresses
Heather & Jennifer Kinley	Country music performers
Marcus & Adam Krings	Members of a quartet named Amen
Patsy & Peggy Lynn	The Lynns, country music performers
Debbie & Carrie Moore	Moore & Moore, country music singers
Tia & Tamera Mowry	Actresses
Ashley & Mary-Kate Olsen	Actresses, singers
Tommy & Tony Perrone	Musical duo Gemini
Auguste & Jean Picard	Underwater exploration pioneers
Jackson Pollack	Painter
Elvis Presley	Singer, actor (brother Jesse died at birth)
Liz & Jean Sagal	Television actresses
Rick & Ron Saul	Professional football players
Jen & Patti Stirling	Members of pop-rock group Stirling
Ed Sullivan	Television show host
Jim Thorpe	Olympic athlete
Nicholle & David Tom	Actress & actor
Gene & Marv Upshaw	Professional football players
Tom & Dick Van Arsdale	Professional basketball players
Abigail Van Buren & Ann Landers	Advice columnists

Source: National Organization of Mothers of Twins Clubs. Online at http://www.nomotc.org.

443. Substance Abuse: National Hotlines

Organization	Phone
Cocaine Helpline	1-800-COCAINE
National Council on Alcoholism	1-800-662-2255
National Federation of Parents for Drug-Free Youth	1-800-554-KIDS
National Institute on Drug Abuse, Abuse Workplace Helpline	1-800-843-4971
National Institute on Drug Abuse Information and Referral Line	1-800-662-HELP
Parents Resource Institute for Drug Education (PRIDE)	1-800-241-9746

444. Substance Abuse: Educational Resources

Al-Anon/Alateen

http://www.al-anon-alateen.org/index.html

Al-Anon Family Groups, which includes Alateen, provide support to those affected by someone else's drinking. Al-Anon's online monthly magazine, *The Forum*, contains many personal stories of inspiration.

Canadian Centre on Substance Abuse

http://www.ccsa.ca

A non-profit organization working to minimize the harm associated with the use of alcohol, tobacco, and other drugs.

Mothers Against Drunk Driving (MADD)

http://www.madd.org

This grassroots organization seeks effective solutions to the drunk driving and underage drinking problems, while supporting those who have already experienced the pain of these senseless crimes.

National Clearinghouse for Alcohol and Drug Information

http://www.health.org

Find information on publications, calendars, and related Internet sites, as well as "For Kids Only" materials including games, "really cool" links, and an "Are you Curious? Ask US!" page that allows visitors to ask experts questions about drugs.

National Families in Action Online

http://www.emory.edu/NFIA/index.html

Locate the latest scientific information about the effects of drugs on the brain and body. Visitors can ask neuroscience experts questions about drugs.

444. *(continued)*

National Highway Traffic Safety Administration (NHTSA)

http://www.nhtsa.dot.gov

A valuable resource for information on the effects of drunk driving.

National Inhalant Prevention Coalition (NIPC)

http://www.inhalants.org

The NIPC serves as an inhalant referral and information clearinghouse, stimulates media coverage about inhalant issues, develops informational materials, produces *ViewPoint* (a quarterly newsletter), provides training and technical assistance and leads a week-long national grassroots inhalant education and awareness campaign.

National Institute on Drug Abuse

http://www.nida.nih.gov

This site offers information on drugs of abuse, NIDA publications and communications, agency events, and links to other drug-related Internet sites.

Neuroscience for Kids

http://faculty.washington.edu/chudler/neurok.html

This site provides answers to commonly-asked questions about the brain and neuroscience, with information on neurotransmission, brain and spinal cord anatomy and physiology, and the effects of specific drugs on the nervous system.

Partnership for a Drug-Free America

http://www.drugfreeamerica.org/

The Partnership works to decrease demand for drugs and other substances by changing societal attitudes which support, tolerate or condone drug use.

Substance Abuse & Mental Health Services Administration (SAMHSA)

http://www.samhsa.gov/about/about.html

This Federal agency is charged with improving the quality and availability of prevention, treatment, and rehabilitative services in order to reduce illness, death, disability, and cost to society resulting from substance abuse and mental illnesses.

Tobacco Information and Prevention Source (TIPS)

http://www.cdc.gov/tobacco/index.htm

This Office on Smoking and Health (OSH) program maintains a vast database of educational materials, reports, and statistics on the use and effects of tobacco.

Science in the News

http://whyfiles.news.wisc.edu

This site provides articles on science items that have been in the news.

445. Common Superstitions

Bad luck to:

walk under a ladder
let a black cat cross your path
sing carols before Christmas season
hang a calendar before January 1
lose a water bucket at sea
see the wedding dress by candlelight
halt a funeral procession
have bride and groom see each other on their wedding day before the
    wedding starts
go on a trip on a Friday, especially the 13th
give a person a gift of a knife unless you include a coin
hang a horseshoe open-end down on your wall
spill ink
spill salt
burn a peach tree
open an umbrella indoors
light three cigarettes on one match
break a mirror
meet on the stairs
turn a feather bed on Sunday
cross knives at the table
enter a house with the left foot
first plant seeds the last three days of March
kill a sparrow

Good luck to:

put money in a wallet given as a gift
carry a silver dollar
wear one's hat backwards
be followed by a strange dog
throw rice at weddings
rub a rabbit's foot
hang a horseshoe open-end up on your wall
find a four-leaf clover
receive a coin with a hole in it
wear "something borrowed, something blue, something given, and something
    new" as a bride
be the seventh child
eat cabbage on New Year's Day

445. *(continued)*

Predictions

Dropping a knife or fork on the floor foretells a visitor.
A howling dog predicts a death.
A falling window sash or a dog howling at night foretells a death.
Two spoons in one saucer predict a wedding.
Bubbles on tea foretell a kiss is coming.
Cutting hair or nails in a calm sea will bring rough weather.
Children who play with mirrors become vain.
If your right ear tingles, someone is saying good things about you.
If your left ear tingles, someone is speaking ill of you.
Washing your hands in water in which eggs were boiled will bring you warts.
Eating both ends of a loaf of bread before eating the middle will predict
   difficulty managing finances.
Smelling flowers growing on a grave may destroy one's sense of smell.

446. Barriers to Effective Communication

Overuse of close-ended questions
Criticizing and labeling
Becoming distracted
Daydreaming
Sugar-coated reassurance
Preaching or moralizing
Interrupting
Advice giving
Fixing other people's problems
Listening only to content; not hearing feelings
Not attending to nonverbal cues
Finishing another person's sentences
Prejudging the speaker
Jumping to conclusions
Talking, not listening
Leading questions
Interpreting, diagnosing
Incongruent body language

Source: Ronald Partin (1999). *The Classroom Teacher's Survival Guide.* Paramus, NJ: Center for Applied Research in Education.

447. Leadership Qualities

Qualities teens say are most essential to be a good leader in society:

	%
honesty	89
not afraid to speak up	85
maturity	75
strong moral character	72

Source: PRIMEDIA/Roper National Youth Opinion Survey/Roper's 1998 Year in Review.

448. Common Nonverbal Gestures

ankles crossed
applause
clasped hands
crossed arms
crossing fingers
crying
eye contact
eyes fluttering
folded arms
frown
genuflection
hands on hips
head in hands
head nods
leaning forward
legs crossed
"OK" sign
raised eyebrows
"raspberries"
rubbing back of neck

rubbing bridge of nose
rubbing forehead
rubbing hands together
scratching head
shoulder shrug
sigh
skipping
smile
steepling hands
sticking tongue out
thumbs up/down
"V" sign
waving
wink
yawn

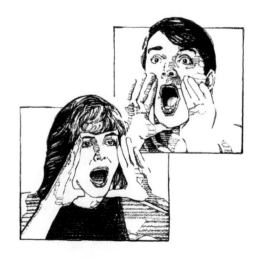

449. The Endocrine System

adrenal glands

pancreas

parathyroid

pineal gland

pituitary gland

reproductive glands

thyroid gland

450. Parts of the Brain

forebrain:

telencephalon

—cerebrum

—basal

—corpus callosurn

diencephalon

—thalamus

—hypothalamus

midbrain:

interior colliculi

superior colliculi

hindbrain:

cerebellum

pons

medulla

451. Right Brain–Left Brain Thinking Modes

Right	*Left*
nonverbal	verbal
nonrational	rational
concrete	symbolic
holistic	linear
intuitive	logical
better at remembering faces	better at remembering names
expresses feelings	tends to hold on to feelings
short attention span	good ability to concentrate
risk taker	less likely to take risks
likes to draw	likes to read
not concerned with details	likes structure
impulsive	organized
difficulty meeting deadlines	punctual, time conscious
may be messy	neat and tidy

452. Multiple Intelligences: 8 Ways of Being Smart

Logical-Mathematical Intelligence—the ability to detect patterns, reason deductively and think logically; scientific and mathematical thinking.

Verbal-Linguistic Intelligence—well developed verbal skills, excels in the use of language.

Visual-Spatial Intelligence—gives one the ability to manipulate and create mental images in order to solve problems.

Musical Intelligence—encompasses the capability to recognize and compose musical pitches, tones, and rhythms.

Bodily-Kinesthetic Intelligence—the ability to coordinate one's own bodily movements; skilled with one's body such as the surgeon, dancer, athlete.

Interpersonal Intelligence—ability to perceive and understand other people.

Intrapersonal Intelligence—self-awareness and insight into one's own motives, emotions, intentions, and thoughts and the ability to transform oneself.

Naturalist Intelligence—ability to recognize and categorize plants, animals, and other objects in nature.

Source: Howard Gardner (1999). *Intelligence Reframed: Multiple Intelligences for the 21st Century.* Basic Books.

453. Indicators of Emotional Intelligence

Emotional self-awareness

- Improvement in recognizing and naming own emotions
- Better able to understand the causes of feelings
- Recognizing the difference between feelings and actions

Managing emotions

- Better frustration tolerance and anger management
- Fewer verbal put-downs, fights, and classroom disruptions
- Better able to express anger appropriately, without fighting
- Less aggressive or self-destructive behavior
- More positive feelings about self, school, and family
- Better at handling stress
- Less loneliness and social anxiety

Motivation: Harnessing emotions productively

- More responsible
- Better able to focus on the task at hand and pay attention
- Less impulsive; more self-control

Empathy: Reading emotions

- Better able to take another person's perspective
- Improved empathy and sensitivity to others' feelings
- Better at listening to others

Handling relationships

- Increased ability to analyze and understand relationships
- Better at resolving conflicts and negotiating disagreements
- Better at solving problems in relationships
- More assertive and skilled at communicating
- More popular and outgoing; friendly and involved with peers
- More concerned and considerate
- More "prosocial" and harmonious in groups
- More sharing, cooperation, and helpfulness
- More democratic in dealing with others

Source: Goleman, D. (1995). *Emotional Intelligence.* New York: Bantam.

454. Sample Decibel Levels

200	Saturn rocket at close range
150	jet airplane taking off
140	threshold of pain
130	pneumatic hammer, stock car races
120	rock music amplifiers (5 feet), thunder
110	power mower, riveter
100	circular saw, snowmobile
90	Niagara Falls, vacuum cleaner, subway train
80	truck engine, telephone ringing
70	automobile, hairdryer
60	normal conversation
50	average office noise, rainfall
40	quiet residential area, library
30	bedroom at night
20	whisper, rustling leaves
10	breathing, quiet recording studio

455. Forms of Propaganda

Bandwagon—Urges us to "get on the bandwagon" because everyone else is "on board." It appeals to our need not to be left out or seen as nonconforming.

Testimonial—Because a celebrity endorses a product, candidate, or movement, we should as well.

Repetition—Hearing the same message numerous times softens resistance.

Emotional Words—Employs words like *love, beautiful, exquisite,* or *save* to elicit positive feelings in the listener.

Name-calling—Negative words are used to form negative attitudes toward the targeted person or their ideas.

Mistaking Correlation for Causation—Implies that because one thing occurs with another, one caused the other.

Plain Folks—Tying a candidate or ideology to "regular folks."

Fear—Employing scare tactics to persuade people.

455. *(continued)*

Transfer—Using symbols, images, or quotations of famous people to enhance the positive feelings toward a possibly unrelated idea of person.

Glittering Generalities—Using broad, stirring words (like rights, American, freedom) to arouse positive feelings and win over the listener without examining the evidence.

Ad Hominem—Attacking the person instead of the argument.

Source: Irving M. Copi, Carl Cohen (1968). *Introduction to Logic.*

456. Sentence Stems for Debriefing Experiential Activities

I confirmed . . .   I realized . . .
I discovered . . .   I recognized . . .
I felt . . .   I was surprised . . .
I reinforced . . .   I wonder . . .
I was puzzled . . .   I was disppointed . . .
I learned . . .   I relearned . . .
I reaffirmed . . .   I was pleased . . .

457. Symptoms of Major Depression

sleep disturbance (insomnia), sleeping too much
crying
"empty" feeling
loss of interest in usually enjoyable activities
difficulty in thinking clearly
feelings of guilt or worthlessness
loss of concentration
lowered self-esteem
not as talkative as usual

excessive fatigue
prolonged sadness
loss of appetite
socially withdrawn
persistent permission
significant weight loss
irritability
persistent thoughts of death or suicide
attempted suicide

458. Major Stressors for Adolescents

Moving or changing schools
Conflicts with peers
Injuries or severe illness
Grades, tests, homework
Pressure to use drugs and alcohol
Bullying or teasing by peers
Illness of family member
Changes in their bodies
Loss of anything valuable
Separation or divorce of parents
Insufficient physical resources—food, clothing, shelter, etc.
Death of a loved one
High expectations of others
Family financial problems
Insufficient sleep
Fear of physical harm traveling to or from school
Insecurity about one's looks, clothing, athletic ability, etc.
Rejection by friends, girlfriend, or boyfriend
Death or suicide of another child
Taking on too many activities

Source: Understanding Childhood Stress from the Family Forum Series, info@at-risk.com.

459. Physical Symptoms of Stress

acne
accelerated heart rate
asthma attack
backache
blushing
cold hands
colds
constipation
diarrhea
dilated pupils
dry mouth
exhaustion
fainting
fatigue
erratic heart beat
hands shaking

headache
higher blood pressure
hunger
muscle pain
nausea
neck ache
nervousness
perspiration
sexual dysfunction
shortness of breath
skin rash
sleep disturbance
sweaty palms
trembling
upset stomach

460. Mental Symptoms of Stress

critical of others
decreased creativity
denial
diminished fantasy life
forgetfulness
helplessness
impaired concentration
impatience
indecisiveness
inflexibility
loss of confidence
loss of objectivity
loss of sense of humor

lowered self-esteem
overplanning
pessimism
poor decision making
preoccupation
problem avoidance
sarcasm
self-defeating thoughts
selfishness
self-pity
sense of urgency
stubbornness
short temper

461. Emotional Symptoms of Stress

alarm
anger
anxiety
apprehension
burdened
depression
dread

fear
frustration
grief
guilt
hopelessness
inadequacy
irritability

moodiness
panic
resentment
restlessness
tension
terror
worry

462. Behavioral Responses to Stress

absenteeism
acting out
aggression
alcohol abuse
arguing
behavioral tics
change in sleep patterns
change of work habits
clenching one's jaw
compulsive behaviors
crying
drug abuse
excessive chatter

excessive eating
excessive risk taking
fidgeting
fighting
grinding teeth in sleep
hitting
nail biting
nervous laughter
pacing
ritualistic behaviors
screaming
self-indulgence

shifty eyes
shopping
sighing
smoking
staring into space
stuttering
tantrums
throwing things
using obscenities
voice tone change
withdrawing
working

463. Early Warning Signs of Job Stress

headaches
sleep disturbances
difficulty in concentrating
low morale
upset stomach
job dissatisfaction

Source: Stress at Work, National Institute for Occupational Safety and Health. Online at http://www.cdc.gov/niosh/homepage.html.

464. Stress Prevention Techniques

avoid catastrophizing
avoid getting too wrapped up in
    yourself
avoid overcommitment
avoid perfectionism
avoid putting yourself down
avoid unnecessary arguments
be an actor, not a reactor
be prepared
be thankful
choose to be happy
clarify the expectations of others
clarify your expectations
cultivate new relationships
decorate your environment
develop a support network
develop self-affirming habits
distinguish between needs and wants
do one thing at a time
eat a healthy diet
eliminate self-defeating behavior
eliminate needless worry
exercise regularly
find some time to be alone
forgive
get adequate rest and sleep
get organized

get up 10 minutes earlier
have a good belly laugh
have a pet
help others
keep a balance in your activities
keep a journal
know and accept yourself
learn responsible assertiveness
learn to say "no"
list your strengths and successes
maintain a sense of humor
maintain supportive relationships
make effective planning a habit
monitor your stress level
reexamine your "shoulds" and
    "musts"
remember to play
set long-range goals
set priorities
smile
stop to smell the roses
strive for an open mind
take time to relax
treat others with kindness
try to remain flexible
unclutter your life
volunteer for a worthy cause

465. Stress Reduction Techniques

apologize
ask someone for help
challenge your assumptions
challenge your irrational self-talk
cry
dance
do aerobic exercise
engage in a hobby
get a massage
go for counseling
hug someone
join a self-help group
just listen
keep things in perspective
listen to favorite music
make a list
meditate
never make important decisions after
   midnight
play a musical instrument

problem solve
read
recall a pleasant experience
relax your jaw
remember that tomorrow is a
   new day
seek a different perspective
sing
stretch
take a break
take a nap
take a walk
take a warm bath
take three slow, deep breaths
talk with someone you trust
use biofeedback
use progressive relaxation
use self-affirmation
visualize a calming scene
write a letter

466. Leisure Time of Adults

Of these activities, how much time do you spend on them? Responses of working-age adults.

	Favorite Activity (%)	Spend a Lot of Time Doing (%)
Talking or visiting with family or friends	57	38
Spending time outdoors such as going to a park	54	21
Reading for pleasure	48	18
Attending religious services	34	21
Attending children's activities	38	19
Attending an amateur or professional sporting event	34	6
Participating in a sports activity	33	11
Exercising or working out	27	14
Watching television	19	24
Doing chores around the house or in the yard	18	47
Using the Internet	15	12
Running errands such as grocery shopping	9	29

Source: September 2000 telephone poll by trained interviewers of a representative national sample of 1,010 randomly selected American adults. *The Shell Poll*, volume 2, issue 2, Spring 2000. Online at http://www.shellus.com.

467. Hours of Sleep on a Weekday

Fewer than 6	13%
6 hours	18%
7 hours	31%
8 hours	28%
9 hours	7%
10 or more	3%

Source: Results from a telephone survey of adults 18 or over conducted by the National Sleep Foundation, 2001. Online at www.sleepfoundation.org.

468. Sedentary Adults

Percent of U.S. adults who were sedentary in terms of their leisure time physical activities (that is, never engaged in ANY vigorous, moderate, or light physical activities for at least 20 minutes).

Men	%
18–24 years	25.8
25–44 years	31.8
65 years and over	50.5

Women	%
18–24 years	37.1
25–44 years	36.5
45–64 years	44.4
65 years and over	61.4

Source: National Center for Health Statistics,1997. Online at http://www.cdc.gov/nchs.

469. Smoking Behavior

Percent of adults over 18 who smoke:

United States (1965)	41.9
United States (1998)	24.0

Percent of U.S. teens who smoke:

8th graders (1991)	14.3
8th graders (1997)	19.4
10th graders (1991)	20.8
10th graders (1997)	29.8
12th graders (1991)	28.3
12th graders (1997)	36.5

Source: Centers for Disease Control and Prevention. Online at www.cdc.gov.

470. Time Management Strategies

Know your goals. What do you want to accomplish?

Set priorities.

Handle each piece of paper once.

Think through a job before starting.

Make a list of points to discuss before telephoning.

Have an organized filing system.

Finish one task before beginning another.

Group routine and trivial tasks.

Practice increasing reading speed.

Listen carefully.

Do the most important things first.

Throw away all the paper you can.

Keep an orderly desk and room.

Maintain a "TO DO" list.

Consolidate shopping and errands.

Terminate non-productive activities as soon as possible.

Don't dwell on the past.

Guard your physical health with sufficient sleep and exercise.

Allow flexibility in your schedule for unexpected events.

Set deadlines for yourself.

Break major goals into subgoals.

Anticipate disruptions; have a backup plan.

Keep a calendar of important events.

Don't abuse the time of others.

Allow enough time for planning.

Fix a starting and finishing time for each project.

Develop an idea notebook.

Be selective in television viewing.

Reward yourself for completion of projects.

Work smarter, not harder.

Keep a time log to see how you are using your time.

Minimize interruptions when studying.

Recognize when you are procrastinating.

Eliminate tasks which do not contribute to your goals.

Set aside quiet think time.

Take occasional short breaks.

Put waiting time to good use; read or work on small tasks.

Do least enjoyable chores first.

Use your wastebasket freely.

Learn to say "no."

Plan as far ahead as possible.

Break big jobs into smaller tasks.

Have a place for everything.

Examine old habits for time wasters.

Eat a light lunch to avoid afternoon drowsiness.

Don't mistake activity for productivity.

Maintain a balance between work, school, and leisure activities.

Discover your most creative time of day.

Keep a notepad by your bed.

Combine tasks whenever possible.

Develop checklists in planning.

Designate a specific place where you place all items to be taken to school with you the next day.

Take sufficient time to carefully weigh important decisions.

Know thyself. Be aware of your strengths and limitations.

Periodically evaluate the progress toward your goals.

Do one thing at a time.

Don't rely upon your memory for important events, ideas, or dates. Write them down on your calendar or notebook.

Don't dwell on unimportant decisions.

471. Children's Weekly Time Use, 1981 and 1997*

(In hours and minutes)

Activity	1981	1997	Difference
School	21:22	29:22	+8:00
Playing	15:54	12:58	−2:56
TV viewing	15:12	13:09	−2:03
Eating	9:08	8:18	−0:50
Sports	2:20	5:17	+2:57
Studying	1:25	2:07	+0:42
Reading	0:57	1.16	+0:19
Household work	2:27	5:39	+3:12

*Children ages 3-11; selected activities

Source: 1997 Panel Study of Income Dynamics, Child Development Supplement. University of Michigan.

The average youth living in the U.S. watches television 25 hours a week and plays computer games an additional seven hours.

Source: National Institute on Media and the Family, 1998 study.

472. Degree of Effort and Challenge

Percentage responding "yes" in a representative sample of American teenagers:

It is important to me that I do my best in all my classes	72%
The amount of work I do in school now is important to my success later in life	66%
I try to take the most difficult and challenging courses I can	51%
Doing homework is a priority for me. I complete it before participating in other activities	43%

Source: The State of Our Nation's Youth 2001. Horatio Alger Association.

473. Time Use Scavenger Hunt

Collect the autographs of people in this room who qualify for the following:

- Two people who do not wear wristwatches.
- Two people who exercise at least three times a week.
- Two people who have ever written a list of goals they want to achieve in their lifetimes.
- One person who keeps a journal.
- Two people who sleep more than eight hours each night.
- One person who makes a to-do list at least once a week.
- One person who has a tidy locker.
- An individual who was late getting started today.
- One person who did not watch television yesterday.
- A person who keeps a note pad by their bed.

474. Time Management: Introductory Activity

Introduce the idea of time usage by asking the class to brainstorm proverbs and quotations related to the use of time. Then have the class discuss the meanings of each and whether they believe it to be true. Are there exceptions when a saying might not be true?

Here are some you might suggest if the students do not mention them:

"Time heals all wounds."
"Haste makes waste."
"Anything worth doing is worth doing well."
"How time flies when you're having fun!"
"A stitch in time saves nine."
"Lost time is never found."
"To spend your time is to spend your life."
"Time is money."
"Time is on our side."
"Misspending time is a kind of homicide."
"There is no time like the present"
"A man before his time."
"Time reveals all."
"So little time to do so much."
"We don't have time."
"Work expands to fill the time available."

475. Causes of Procrastination

"Procrastination is the art of keeping up with yesterday."
—DON MARQUIS (1878–1937)

- Poor time management, overestimating how much time is available
- Not seeing value or relevance in the task
- Inability to prioritize
- Getting bogged down in details
- Inability to say "no"; overcommitment
- Fear of being evaluated
- Excessive anxiety about the task at hand, worrying rather than doing
- Fear of failure
- Perfectionism, unrealistic high expectations
- Avoidance of difficult or unpleasant activities

476. Procrastination Checklist

Are you eligible for membership in the Procrastinator's Club of America, but haven't gotten around to sending your application? Their motto, "We're behind you all the way," has been accepted by many students. Are you one? Test your eligibility right now! Don't put it off another minute.

Answer each of the following now:

	Yes	No
Do you frequently finish tasks at the last minute?	_____	_____
Are you regularly late handing in assignments?	_____	_____
Do you find it difficult to get started on the big projects?	_____	_____
Do you frequently tell people that you work better under pressure?	_____	_____
Do you frequently feel guilty because you have not completed a task?	_____	_____
Do you have difficulty getting jobs completed because they may not be perfect?	_____	_____
Do you tend to avoid unpleasant tasks?	_____	_____
Do you have difficulty staying on-task?	_____	_____
Do you frequently say, "I'll do it tomorrow"?	_____	_____
Do you regularly have to stay up late to finish papers or projects?	_____	_____

Count the number of "yes" responses. Compare your score with the following scale:

0–3 **Early starter.** By doing things today you are free to do them again tomorrow if you choose.

4–7 **Amateur procrastinator.** Some potential problem areas may create stress for you and annoyance in those around you.

8–10 **Professional procrastinator.** Putting things off until the last minute is a way of life.

477. Just Do It! Confronting Procrastination

The easiest thing to procrastinate is doing something about procrastination. You may be tempted to allow short-term avoidance to overpower the longer-term advantages. If you have become a slave to deadlines, immobilized by the big and small projects you face, it may be time to combat procrastination.

- It is best to pick one area in which you find procrastination most annoying (e.g., grading exams, answering letters, filing papers).

- Begin small and progress as you experience success. Be patient.

- Establish your own deadlines, and announce them to others involved. Be realistic in setting a timetable.

- Break the project into smaller parts. Chip away at it in small bites. Don't wait for that "big chunk" of time.

- Set a definite beginning point. You must break the inertia of inactivity. If getting started is especially troublesome, set a timer for 10 or 15 minutes. Commit yourself to doing something on the project until the timer rings. Then you can decide whether to stop or continue. Chances are you will gain momentum and continue after the timer stops. If not, try another 10 minutes later in the day.

- Do the most important things first. Avoid the distractions of the trivial and routine tasks when a higher priority job needs to be done. Examining each task in light of your goals will help you set priorities.

- Reward yourself for completing parts of a major task. It may be something as simple as a 10-minute walk, a soft drink, or a social phone call. Contract with yourself for a big reward for completion of important tasks. A night on the town, sleeping late on a weekend, or a purchase you have been wanting to make may help motivate you to complete the job. Be nice to yourself.

- Avoid perfectionism. Excellence is a sufficient level of performance for most things in life, and for many tasks (doing the dishes, a new sport or hobby, dusting the lampshades) adequacy is all that is necessary. Give yourself permission to be less than perfect. You might double the amount of time spent typing a test, attempting to get the spacing and typing perfect. Could that extra time be better spent in another activity which will better benefit our students or yourself? Probably so.

- Procrastination is a learned habit, and can be supplanted with a more constructive habit, giving you greater control over your life. If procrastination has limited your achievements, do something about it now!

478. Perfection—Quotations

Perfection consists not in doing extraordinary things, but in doing ordinary things extraordinarily well. Neglect nothing; the most trivial action may be performed to God. —ANGELIQUE ARNAULD

This is the very perfection of a man, to find out his own imperfection. —SAINT AUGUSTINE

We are what we are; we cannot be truly other than ourselves. We reach perfection not by copying, much less by aiming at originality, by constantly and steadily working out the life which is common to all, according to the character which God has given us. —RICHARD BAXTER

The perfection of any matter, the highest or the lowest, touches on the divine. —MARTIN BUBER

Bachelor's wives and old maid's children are always perfect. —SEBASTIEN ROCH NICOLAS DE CHAMFORT

Aim at perfection in everything, though in most things it is unattainable. However, they who aim at it, and persevere, will come much nearer to it than those whose laziness and despondency make them give it up as unattainable. —PHILIP DORMER CHESTERFIELD

The perfection preached in the Gospels never yet built up an empire. Every man of action has a strong dose of egotism, pride, hardness, and cunning. But all those things will be forgiven him; indeed, they will be regarded as high qualities, if he can make of them the means to achieve great ends. —CHARLES DE GAULLE

A good garden may have some weeds. —THOMAS FULLER

Among the older excellencies of man, this is one, that he can form the image of perfection much beyond what he has experience of in himself, and is not limited in his conception of wisdom and virtue. —DAVID HUME

Everything in the world is perfect except our judgment of what perfection is. —SIDNEY MADWED

Trifles go to make perfection, And perfection is no trifle. —MICHELANGELO

The acorn does not become an oak in a day; the ripened scholar is not made by a single lesson; the well-trained soldier was not the raw recruit of yesterday; there are always months between the seed time and harvest. So the path of the just is like the shining light, which shines more and more unto the perfect day. —B. NICHOL

479. I AM: A Time Management Activity

Instructions: Tell students you are going to read several activites. If their answer to the statement is true, they should stand up. (If that is apt to be too noisy, you can have them just raise their hands.)

Stand up and then sit down if any of the following applies to you:

- You have a calendar with you.
- You've made out a to-do list in the past week.
- Got started late this morning.
- Think of yourself as a perfectionist.
- Wear a watch every day.
- Love to go to meetings.
- Tend to lose things frequently.
- Hate to wait for people.
- Are prone to procrastinate starting tasks.
- Never seem to have enough time.
- Have a job.

480. Effective Study Strategies

Read the text assignments before going to class.
Sit in the front of the classroom.
Write down clear directions for all assignments.
Focus on *what* the teacher is saying, not how.
Scan reading materials before reading.
Type papers when possible.
Develop mnemonics when possible.
Keep a calendar of major events including tests, deadlines, etc.
Set up a study area for that purpose only.
Work on one assignment at a time.
Keep all the supplies and materials you need readily available.
Take periodic breaks (5–10 minutes each hour).
Underline major points in your notes.
Get together study groups to review before tests.
Pay special attention to the first and last five minutes of the class.
Ask questions if you don't understand.
Several shorter study periods are better than one long one.
Break large assignments into a number of smaller tasks.
Get a good night's rest before an exam.
Read through the entire exam before beginning.
Answer the easiest questions first.
Pace yourself to allow adequate time for each question.
Use five-minute blocks of free time to review notes.

481. Self-Discovery Sentence Stems

One thing I do well is . . .

My greatest peeve is . . .

One thing I would like to do better
  is . . .

I enjoy . . .

Success in life is . . .

If I were rich I would . . .

I value . . .

I am deeply concerned about . . .

I would most like to improve . . .

I want to . . .

Probably my strongest asset is . . .

I work best when . . .

People are . . .

When I don't get my way I . . .

I am happiest when . . .

I wish my parents would . . .

I am sad when . . .

If I were 21 I would . . .

I resent . . .

I wish I had . . .

I feel important when . . .

I believe . . .

My favorite teacher . . .

I worry about . . .

People would be happier if they . . .

Most people treat me . . .

Someday I expect to . . .

If I had one wish it would be . . .

I suffer most from . . .

If I were president, I would . . .

I am . . .

My greatest ambition is . . .

My favorite place is . . .

I become angry when . . .

I am scared when . . .

I feel uncomfortable when . . .

I hope to . . .

I think I am . . .

I know I can . . .

I am not afraid to . . .

A true leader is . . .

I admire people who . . .

I sometimes wonder . . .

I would like to learn . . .

One risk I took was . . .

I am probably too . . .

My body is . . .

For me, school has usually been . . .

The high point of my week was . . .

A good friend will . . .

Next year I hope to . . .

The best teachers are the ones
  who . . .

I want to be remembered as . . .

I like people who . . .

Religion is . . .

I wish I knew how to . . .

I'd like to change . . .

I enjoy being with . . .

Happiness is . . .

It is unfair that . . .

I get down in the dumps when . . .

I plan to . . .

I appreciate my parents for . . .

I find it easy to . . .

It is difficult for me to . . .

Most people think I am . . .

Most people would be surprised to
  know that I . . .

The most frustrating thing for me
  is . . .

Teachers usually treat me . . .

If people only knew . . .

Our school needs . . .

482. Self-Discovery Questions

What do you enjoy most?

Who are you?

What do you hope to be doing in five years?

What makes you happy?

What do you do well?

What is the best thing that could happen to you?

How would you like to be remembered?

What would you like to change in your life?

How do you deal with anger?

Do you have any dreams?

Whom do you admire most?

What is your biggest peeve?

What three words would you most want others to use in describing you?

When do you like yourself best?

How do you have fun?

How would you define success?

What would you like to tell your teacher?

What would you like to learn that they haven't taught you in school?

483. Dialogue Starters

Reflect on the following topics and, to the degree you feel comfortable, share your answers with your partner.

What would an ideal friend be like?

How do you define success?

If you could meet any one person in the world, who would it be?

Name two people you greatly admire. Why?

Describe your ideal job.

How do you respond to failure?

Describe one goal you hope to achieve within five years.

Describe one of the most joyful moments of your life.

Describe the most mentally healthy person you know.

Which do you value most: wealth, happiness, or health? Explain.

What qualities does an outstanding teacher possess?

What qualities does an outstanding student possess?

484. Life Goals

Aid my favorite charity.
Be a community leader.
Be a public speaker.
Be in a play.
Be more assertive.
Become a good conversationalist.
Become a millionaire.
Become more positive.
Build my dream house.
Climb a mountain.
Cultivate a flower garden.
Earn a college degree.
Gain public distinction.
Get married.
Help those less fortunate.
Improve family relationships.
Learn to fly an airplane.
Learn to play a musical instrument.
Learn to relax.
Live a long life.

Lose weight.
Make new friends.
Manage time better.
Move to somewhere with a different climate.
Own a special car.
Own my own business.
Participate in professional sports.
Play in a rock band.
Quit smoking.
Raise a large family.
Retire financially secure.
Run a marathon.
Star in a movie.
Start my own business.
Travel.
Win a beauty contest.
Work to spread my religion.
Write a book.

485. Traits of Peak Performers

Researchers have been able to identify traits shared by high achievers. The following list represents a composite of the characteristics possessed by peak performers.

Peak performers . . .

Know what they want. They are passionately committed to a mission and are driven by goals and activities that support their mission. The goals tell them what they want, the mission tells them why.

Manage their time well. They are able to say "no" to distractions and set priorities. They are able to focus their efforts on their goals and mission.

Are actors, not reactors. They are active decision makers, making choices to shape their destiny. They design their own futures.

Treat other people decently. They invest in developing relationships with others. They listen well, express empathy for others, and convey positive expectations.

(continued)

485. *(continued)*

Believe in themselves. They are convinced they have the talents and disposition to succeed. They can accept failures as part of the learning process.

Practice visualization. They use mental rehearsal to rehearse and meticulously plan their performance before executing.

Master their fears (and other debilitating emotions). Optimism tends to characterize their personality.

Discover and nurture potential talents. They are driven toward continuous improvement and become absorbed by interesting and challenging activities.

Handle stress well. They possess a degree of resiliency and self-esteem that enable them to thrive in stressful situations. They have a high need to be challenged, but also build in time for reflection and relaxation.

Sources: Peak Performance and Peak Performers by Charles Garfield; *Seven Habits of Highly Effective People* by Stephen Covey.

The following questions and activities can be used singly or in clusters to stimulate self-reflection on topics related to becoming a peak performer. They might be written in a personal journal, or sometimes shared in pairs or small groups. You might have each student assemble his or her responses into a "Success Portfolio."

How do you invest your time each week? What percent of your time is devoted to your top ten life goals? What does your time allocation tell you about your priorities?

What activities give you the greatest joy and provide meaning to your life?

Discover your purpose. Express it as a personal mission statement.

Which activities would you like to spend more time doing in the future? How can you increase the time for these now, even if only one hour a week?

Which activities drain your energy and enthusiasm?

What skills, experiences and attitudes make you good at what you do?

Make a list of all the things you know how to do.

In great detail, describe what your perfect day would be like.

What words would the three people who know you the best use to describe you?

What three words would you most like others to use in describing you?

If you knew you would not fail, what dream would you pursue?

485. *(continued)*

What five people whom you have personally met do you most admire? What traits did they possess that you would like to emulate?

List five persons you have not met, but admire. What adversities did they have to overcome in their lives? Develop a dossier of articles about such persons. Review your file periodically for inspiration.

Define success . . .

Keep a "stinkin' thinkin' " log of negative and irrational self-talk. How do you verbally defeat yourself? Seek to substitute more constructive self-talk. What would have been a more reasonable self-conversation?

List the guiding principles or values by which you hope to live your life. What evidence is there that you are following these ideals?

Describe one thing you would really like to learn more about. Where could you begin? Commit yourself to continuous learning. Set up your own independent study to learn everything you can about that topic in the next six months.

Whom do you blame for your shortcomings and failures?

Which three persons have been most influential in your life? Have you ever told them how important they were? Send an appreciative note to those who are living.

Describe three successes you have achieved in the past six months. What did you learn from them?

What three things would most help you reach your full potential?

486. Hearing Impaired Persons of Note

Jack Ashley	1922–	member of British Parliament
Ludwig van Beethoven	1770–1827	composer
Linda Bove	1945–	"Sesame Street" actress
John Brewster, Jr.	1766–1854	American artist
Ray Charles	1930	singer
John Louis Clark	1881–1970	wood sculptor
John W. Cornforth	1917–	Nobel chemist
Rolando Lopez Dirube	1928–	Cuban artist
Buddy Ebsen	1936	actor
Thomas Alva Edison	1847–1931	inventor
Nanette Fabray	1920–	actress
Phyllis Frelich	1944–	actress
Evelyn Glennie	1966–	classical percussionist
Antonio Feu Gómez	1907–1984	Spanish artist
John Goodricke	1764–1786	astronomer
Francisco Goya	1746–1828	Spanish artist
John R. Gregg	1867–1948	shorthand inventor
Olof Hanson	1862–1933	architect
Florence Henderson	1934–	actress, singer
William Hoy	1862–1961	major league baseball player
George Hyde	1882–1968	historian
Jack Jones	1923–1983	cultural historian
Helen Keller	1880–1968	author, lecturer
Rush Limbaugh	1951–	radio talk-show host
Judith G. Low	1860–1927	founded Girl Scouts of America
Richard Petty	1937–	auto racer
René Princeteau	1843–1914	French painter
Ronald Reagan	1911–	U.S. President
Laura Searing	1840–1923	journalist
Erastus Smith	1787–1837	scout for Sam Houston
Barbra Streisand	1942–	singer, actress
Alfred Thomson	1894–1979	artist
Douglas Tilden	1860–1935	sculptor
Cadwallader Washburn	1866–1965	artist
Peter Wolf	1945–	TV, film director
Frances Woods	1907–	dancer
David Wright	1920–	poet

487. Famous People Who Stuttered

Clara Barton	founder of American Red Cross
Peter Bonerz	televison actor, director
Lewis Carroll	author
Ty Cobb	baseball player
Charles Darwin	naturalist, author
Demosthenes	Greek orator
George VI	King of England
Ron Harper	NBA basketball player
James Earl Jones	actor
Peggy Lipton	actress
Bob Love	NBA basketball player
Robert Merrill	opera singer
Marilyn Monroe	actress
Sam Neill	actor
Carly Simon	singer-songwriter
John Stossel	television reporter
Mel Tillis	country music singer
John Updike	author
Bill Walton	NBA basketball player
Bruce Willis	actor

488. Famous People with Epilepsy

Alexander the Great	Hannibal
Napoleon Bonaparte	Margaux Hemingway
Lord Byron	Michelangelo
Julius Caesar	Isaac Newton
Truman Capote	Alfred Nobel
Lewis Carroll	Blaise Pascal
Winston Churchill	William Pitt
Leonardo da Vinci	Edgar Allen Poe
Charles Dickens	Pythagoras
Fyodor Dostoevsky	Socrates
Gustave Flaubert	Peter Tchaikovsky
Peter the Great	Harriet Tubman
Georg Friedrich Handel	Vincent van Gogh

489. Migraine Headache Sufferers

Alexander Graham Bell
Lewis Carroll
Frederic Chopin
Charles Darwin
George Eliot
Sigmund Freud
Ulysses S. Grant
Thomas Jefferson
Immanuel Kant
Friedrich Nietzsche
Edgar Allan Poe

Grant

490. Famous Persons Who Experienced Depression

Marlon Brando
Truman Capote
Winston Churchill
Ty Cobb
Calvin Coolidge
John Denver
Patty Duke
Judy Garland
Ernest Hemingway
Billy Joel
Abraham Lincoln

Jack London
Marilyn Monroe
Richard M. Nixon
Rosie O'Donnell
Gen. George S. Patton
Theodore Roosevelt
Diana Spencer (Princess Diana)
Mark Twain
Vincent van Gogh
Mike Wallace
Tammy Wynette

Sources: Joy IkelMan, Bipolar Disorder, at http://www.frii.com; assorted individual biographies.

491. Left-Handed Presidents

James Garfield
Herbert Hoover
Gerald Ford
Harry S Truman
Ronald Reagan
George Bush
Bill Clinton

Source: Famous Left-Handers at http://www.indiana.edu/ ~ primate/left.html#U.S. % 20Presidents.

492. Behavioral and Mental Disorders in Fiction

Bartleby the Scrivener, Herman Melville

The Black Wedding, Isaac Singer

The Crack-Up, F. Scott Fitzgerald

Diary of a Madman, Nicolai Gogol

The End of the Party, Graham Greene

The Eternal Husband, Fyodor Dostoevsky

Flotsam and Jetsam, W. Somerset Maugham

Hamlet, William Shakespeare

He? Guy de Maupassant

Home of the Brave, Arthur Laurents

Jordi, Theodore Isaac Rubin

The Judgment, Franz Kafka

Louis Lambert, Honoré de Balzac

The Lost Phoebe, Theodore Dreiser

Macbeth, William Shakespeare

Madam Bovary, Gustave Flaubert

One Flew Over the Cuckoo's Nest, Ken Kesey

Pigeon Feathers, John Updike

The Room, Jean-Paul Sartre

Tender Is the Night, F. Scott Fitzgerald

The Vagabond, Collette

Waiting for Godot, Samuel Beckett

Ward No. 6, Anton Chekhov

The Yellow Wallpaper, Charlotte Perkins Gilman

493. Common Personality Characteristics

absent-minded
affectionate
aggressive
aloof
altruistic
ambitious
anxious
assertive
bossy
calm
candid
cautious
charming
cheerful
clever
cocky
compassionate
competitive
compulsive
confident
conforming
cooperative
critical
defensive
dependable
dependent
determined
dishonest
disorderly
dominant
dull
energetic
excitable
exuberant
feminine
fickle
flexible
friendly
frivolous
funny
generous
good-natured

gregarious
happy
helpless
honest
hostile
humane
humble
humorous
imaginative
impulsive
indecisive
independent
indifferent
intolerant
irritable
jealous
jovial
kind
lazy
liberal
miserly
moralistic
optimistic
outgoing
overbearing
passionate
persistent
pessimistic
placid
pleasant
poised
polite
popular
practical
proper
pushy
reasonable
rebellious
reliable
reserved
restless
rude

sadistic
sarcastic
self-centered
selfish
sensitive
sentimental
serious
shrewd
shy
sincere
sly
sociable
sophisticated
strong
stubborn
studious
suspicious
sympathetic
tactless
temperamental
tense
timid
tolerant
understanding
uninhibited
unreliable
unstable
versatile
vibrant
warm
weak
wise

494. Psychology Related Journals

Adolescence
American Journal of Drug and Alcohol Abuse
American Journal of Orthopsychiatry
American Journal of Psychology
American Psychologist
Child Development
Contemporary Psychology
Counseling and Development Journal
Developmental Psychology
Family Therapy
Gerontologist
Journal of Abnormal Psychology
Journal of Applied Behavioral Analysis
Journal of Applied Psychology
Journal of Community Psychology
Journal of Comparative and Physiological Psychology
Journal of Contemporary Psychotherapy
Journal of Counseling Psychology
Journal of Creative Behavior
Journal of Cross-Cultural Psychology
Journal of Educational Psychology
Journal of Emotional Education
Journal of the Experimental Analysis of Behavior

Journal of Experimental Child Psychology
Journal of Experimental Psychology
Journal of General Psychology
Journal of History of the Behavioral Sciences
Journal of Humanistic Psychology
Journal of Individual Psychology
Journal of Offender Counseling, Services and Rehabilitation
Journal of Personality
Journal of Personality and Social Psychology
Journal of Psychology
Journal of Social Issues
Journal of Social Psychology
Journal of Transpersonal Psychology
Journal of Vocational Behavior
Journal of Youth and Adolescence
Perceptual and Motor Skills
Psychological Record
Psychological Reports
Psychological Research
Psychological Review
Psychology in the Schools
Psychology Today
Rehabilitation Psychology
Scientific American
Small Group Behavior
Youth and Society

495. Online Resources for Teaching Psychology

American Psychological Association
http://www.psychwww.com

Approaches to Teaching & Learning Psychology
http://www.ryerson.ca/ ~ glassman/Frame.html

AskEric: Lesson Plans for Teaching Psychology
http://askeric.org/cgi-bin/lessons.cgi/Social_Studies/Psychology

Atlases of the Brain and Body
http://www9.biostr.washington.edu/da.html

Internet Psychology Lab
http://kahuna.psych.uiuc.edu/ipl/index.html

National Institute of Mental Health (NIMH)
http://www.nimh.nih.gov

National Mental Health Association
http://www.nmha.org

Positive Psych Teaching Resources
http://www.teachpositivepsych.org

Positive Psychology: A Seven-Day Unit Plan for High School Psychology
http://psych.upenn.edu/seligman/teachinghighschool.htm

Psych Resources on the Web
http://www.psychwww.com

Psych Web
http://www.psychwww.com

Resources for the Teaching of Social Psychology
http://jonathan.mueller.faculty.noctrl.edu//crow

Snapshots of Medicine and Health
National Institutes of Health
http://science-education.nih.gov/newsnapshots/index.html

Society for Neuroscience Brain Backgrounders
http://www.sfn.org/backgrounders

Teaching Clinical Psychology
http://www.rider.edu/users/suler/tcp.html

Teachers of Psychology in Secondary Schools (TOPSS)
http://www.apa.org/ed/topsshomepage.html

SECTION VII

Lists for
Geography

496. Current Names of Old Places

Current Name	Old Name	Current Name	Old Name
Bangladesh	East Pakistan	Namibia	South West Africa
Beijing	Peking; Peiping	Naples, Italy	Neapolis
Belize	British Honduras	New York City	New Amsterdam
Benin	Dahomey	Oslo	Christiania
Botswana	Bechuanaland	Paris	Lutetia Parisiorium
Cambodia	Kampuchea	Pittsburgh	Fort Dusquene
Central African Republic	Ubangi-Shari	Pyongyan, North Korea	Heijo
Cologne	Colonia Agrippa	Salvador	Bahia
Detroit	Fort Lernoult	Seoul, South Korea	Keijo
Donesk, USSR	Stalino		
Ethiopia	Abyssiia	Shanghai, China	Hu-tsen
France	Gaul	Shenyang, China	Mukden
Gdansk	Danzig	Singapore	Singhapura
Ghana	Gold Coast	Sofia, Bulgaria	Sardica
Gorky, USSR	Nizhni Novgorod	Sri Lanka	Ceylon
Ho Chi Minh City	Saigon	St. Petersburg	Leningrad
Hyderabad, India	Golconda	Sudan	Nubia
Indonesia	Netherlands (East) Indies	Sverdlovsk, Russia	Ekaterinburg
		Thailand	Siam
Iran	Persia	Tanzania	German East Africa
Iraq	Mesopotamia	Tokyo	Edo
Istanbul	Constantinople; Byzantium	Toronto	Fort Rouille; York
		Tripoli, Libya	Oea
Kinshasa, Zaire	Leopoldville	Turin, Italy	Augusta Taurinorum
Malagasy Republic	Madagascar	Turkey	Ottoman Empire
Malawi	Nyasaland	Vancouver	Granville
Marseilles, France	Massilia	Vietnam	Indochina
Mexico City	Tenochtitlan	Volgograd	Stalingrad; Tsaritsyn
Myanmar	Burma	Zimbabwe	Rhodesia

497. Types of Maps

aeronautical chart
atlas
celestial globe
globe
physical map
political map
relief map

road map
survey map
terrain map
terrestrial globe
transportation map
weather map

498. Map Features

equator	Mercator projection
graphic scale	meridian
grid line	parallels
index	projection
latitude	scale
longitude	symbols

499. Topographical Features

bays	forests	ravines
beaches	glaciers	rivers
canals	gorges	roads
canyons	grasslands	savannas
caves	hills	shoals
cities	islands	streams
dams	jungles	swamps
deltas	lakes	tundra
deserts	mountains	tunnels
dunes	oceans	valleys
fiords	plains	waterfalls
floodplains		

500. The Continents

Continent	Square Miles
Asia	17,226,000
Africa	11,667,000
Antarctica	5,500,000
Australia	3,000,000
Europe	4,056,000
North America	9,355,000
South America	6,878,000

501. The Seas and Oceans

Andaman Sea
Arctic Ocean
Atlantic Ocean
Baltic Sea
Bering Sea
Black Sea
Caribbean Sea

East China Sea
Gulf of Mexico
Hudson Bay
Indian Ocean
Mediterranean Sea
North Sea
Pacific Ocean

Persian Gulf
Red Sea
Sea of Japan
Sea of Okhotsk
South China Sea
Yellow Sea

502. States and Their Capitals

State	Capital	State	Capital
Alabama	Montgomery	Montana	Helena
Alaska	Juneau	Nebraska	Lincoln
Arizona	Phoenix	Nevada	Carson City
Arkansas	Little Rock	New Hampshire	Concord
California	Sacramento	New Jersey	Trenton
Colorado	Denver	New Mexico	Santa Fe
Connecticut	Hartford	New York	Albany
Delaware	Dover	North Carolina	Raleigh
Florida	Tallahassee	North Dakota	Bismarck
Georgia	Atlanta	Ohio	Columbus
Hawaii	Honolulu	Oklahoma	Oklahoma City
Idaho	Boise	Oregon	Salem
Illinois	Springfield	Pennsylvania	Harrisburg
Indiana	Indianapolis	Rhode Island	Providence
Iowa	Des Moines	South Carolina	Columbia
Kansas	Topeka	South Dakota	Pierre
Kentucky	Frankfort	Tennessee	Nashville
Louisiana	Baton Rouge	Texas	Austin
Maine	Augusta	Utah	Salt Lake City
Maryland	Annapolis	Vermont	Montpelier
Massachusetts	Boston	Virginia	Richmond
Michigan	Lansing	Washington	Olympia
Minnesota	St. Paul	West Virginia	Charleston
Mississippi	Jackson	Wisconsin	Madison
Missouri	Jefferson City	Wyoming	Cheyenne

503. Abbreviations of the States

Alabama	AL	Montana	MT
Alaska	AK	Nebraska	NE
Arizona	AZ	Nevada	NV
Arkansas	AR	New Hampshire	NH
California	CA	New Jersey	NJ
Colorado	CO	New Mexico	NM
Connecticut	CT	New York	NY
Delaware	DE	North Carolina	NC
Florida	FL	North Dakota	ND
Georgia	GA	Ohio	OH
Hawaii	HI	Oklahoma	OK
Idaho	ID	Oregon	OR
Illinois	IL	Pennsylvania	PA
Indiana	IN	Rhode Island	RI
Iowa	IA	South Carolina	SC
Kansas	KS	South Dakota	SD
Kentucky	KY	Tennessee	TN
Louisiana	LA	Texas	TX
Maine	ME	Utah	UT
Maryland	MD	Vermont	VT
Massachusetts	MA	Virginia	VA
Michigan	MI	Washington	WA
Minnesota	MN	West Virginia	WV
Mississippi	MS	Wisconsin	WI
Missouri	MO	Wyoming	WY

504. Nicknames of the States

Alabama	Heart of Dixie; Yellowhammer State; Camellia State
Alaska	Land of the Midnight Sun; The Last Frontier
Arizona	Grand Canyon State; Copper State
Arkansas	Hot Water State; The Land of Opportunity
California	Golden State
Colorado	Centennial State; Highest State
Connecticut	Constitution State; Nutmeg State
Delaware	First State; Diamond State
Florida	Sunshine State; Orange State
Georgia	Peach State; Goober State
Hawaii	Aloha State; Pineapple State

504. *(continued)*

Idaho	Gem State
Illinois	Prairie State; Land of Lincoln
Indiana	Hoosier State
Iowa	Hawkeye State
Kansas	Sunflower State; Jayhawk State
Kentucky	Bluegrass State; Tobacco State
Louisiana	Bayou State; Fisherman's Paradise; Pelican State
Maine	Border State; Pine Tree State
Maryland	Old Line State; The Free State
Massachusetts	Pilgrim State; Bay State
Michigan	Wolverine State; Auto State; Great Lake State
Minnesota	North Star State; Gopher State
Mississippi	Magnolia State; Eagle State
Missouri	Show Me State; Ozark State
Montana	Big Sky Country; Bonanza State; Treasure State
Nebraska	Tree Planter State; Cornhusker State
Nevada	Sage State; Silver State
New Hampshire	Granite State; Mother of Rivers
New Jersey	Garden State; Clam State
New Mexico	Cactus State; Land of Enchantment
New York	Empire State; Knickerbocker State
North Carolina	Old North State; Tarheel State; Terpentine State
North Dakota	Sioux State; Flickertail State; Peace Garden State
Ohio	Buckeye State
Oklahoma	Sooner State
Oregon	Beaver State
Pennsylvania	Keystone State; Quaker State
Rhode Island	Plantation State; Ocean State
South Carolina	Rice State; Swamp State; Iodine State
South Dakota	Sunshine State; Coyote State
Tennessee	Volunteer State
Texas	Lone Star State
Utah	Beehive State
Vermont	Green Mountain State
Virginia	Old Dominion; Cavalier State
Washington	Evergreen State; Chinook State
West Virginia	Mountain State
Wisconsin	Badger State; Copper State
Wyoming	Equality State; Cowboy State

505. Origins of State Names

Alabama	Creek Indian for "place of rest"
Alaska	from Eskimo word *alakshak* which means "peninsula, or "great lands"
Arizona	derived from Indian word for "little place of springs" or from Aztec *arizuma* which means "silver bearing"
Arkansas	from French name for the Oglala Sioux
California	from Spanish *caliento forno* or "hot furance," the name of a fictitious Spanish paradise
Colorado	derived from Spanish word for red
Connecticut	probably from Indian word "Quonoktacut" given the river which ran through that area
Delaware	after Lord De La Warr, the Virginia governor
Florida	from Spanish *Pascua floride* or flowery Easter, named by Ponce de Leon in his 1513 visit
Georgia	named in honor of King George II of England
Hawaii	probably from native word *hawaiki* or "homeland"
Idaho	supposedly from an Indiana word for "light on the hills"
Illinois	from French version of *Illini*, Indian word for men
Indiana	"land of the Indians"
Iowa	possibly from Sioux word meaning "sleepy waters" or "drowsy ones"
Kansas	after the Kansas Indian tribe; meaning "south wind people"
Kentucky	perhaps from the Indian name *Kentake* for "plains" or "meadow lands"
Louisiana	in honor of French King Louis XIV
Maine	from old French word meaning "province"
Maryland	named after Queen Henrietta Maria of England
Massachusetts	from Algonquin word *Massadchu-es-et* meaning great hills
Michigan	from Indian word for "great water"
Minnesota	from Sioux word for "cloudy water" or "muddy water" describing the Minnesota River
Mississippi	from Indian word for great river
Missouri	from an Indian tribe whose name meant "muddy stream"
Montana	from Spanish or Latin word for "mountain"
Nebraska	from Omaha Indian word for "broad river" or "shallow river"
Nevada	from Spanish for "snow covered"
New Hampshire	named after Hampshire County, England
New Jersey	named for Isle of Jersey in the English Channel
New Mexico	after the Aztec god, *Mexiti*
New York	in honor of the Duke of York

505. *(continued)*

North Carolina	from Latin word for Charles; in honor of King Charles I
North Dakota	from a Sioux name meaning "ally"
Ohio	from Iroquois word meaning "good river" or "beautiful river"
Oklahoma	from Choctaw Indian word for "red man"
Oregon	uncertain; perhaps from an Indian word meaning "beautiful water"
Pennsylvania	in honor of William Penn, the state's founder
Rhode Island	perhaps from Dutch word for "red clay"
South Carolina	from Latin word for Charles; in honor of King Charles I
South Dakota	from a Sioux name meaning "ally"
Tennessee	from a Cherokee village called *tanasse*
Texas	after the Texas Indian tribe
Utah	named for the Ute Indians
Vermont	probably from French, *vert mont*, or green mountain
Virginia	named for the Virgin Queen of England, Elizabeth I
Washington	in honor of George Washington
West Virginia	carved from Virginia during the Civil War
Wisconsin	from Chippewa word *Miskonsin* meaning "grassy place"
Wyoming	from Indian word for "large prairies"

506. Population of the 50 States and the District of Columbia

	*2000 Census**	*1990 Census**	*2000 State Rank**	*1990 State Rank**
Alabama	4,447,100	4,040,587	23	22
Alaska	626,932	550,043	48	49
Arizona	5,130,632	3,665,228	20	24
Arkansas	2,673,400	2,350,725	33	33
California	33,871,648	29,760,021	1	1
Colorado	4,301,261	3,294,394	24	26
Connecticut	3,405,565	3,287,116	29	27
Delaware	783,600	666,168	45	46
District of Columbia	572,059	606,900	(NA)	(NA)
Florida	15,982,378	12,937,926	4	4
Georgia	8,186,453	6,478,216	10	11
Hawaii	1,211,537	1,108,229	42	41
Idaho	1,293,953	1,006,749	39	42
Illinois	12,419,293	11,430,602	5	6
Indiana	6,080,485	5,544,159	14	14
Iowa	2,926,324	2,776,755	30	30

(continued)

506. *(continued)*

	2000 Census*	1990 Census*	2000 State Rank*	1990 State Rank*
Kansas	2,688,418	2,477,574	32	32
Kentucky	4,041,769	3,685,296	25	23
Louisiana	4,468,976	4,219,973	22	21
Maine	1,274,923	1,227,928	40	38
Maryland	5,296,486	4,781,468	19	19
Massachusetts	6,349,097	6,016,425	13	13
Michigan	9,938,444	9,295,297	8	8
Minnesota	4,919,479	4,375,099	21	20
Mississippi	2,844,658	2,573,216	31	31
Missouri	5,595,211	5,117,073	17	15
Montana	902,195	799,065	44	44
Nebraska	1,711,263	1,578,385	38	36
Nevada	1,998,257	1,201,833	35	39
New Hampshire	1,235,786	1,109,252	41	40
New Jersey	8,414,350	7,730,188	9	9
New Mexico	1,819,046	1,515,069	36	37
New York	18,976,457	17,990,455	3	2
North Carolina	8,049,313	6,628,637	11	10
North Dakota	642,200	638,800	47	47
Ohio	11,353,140	10,847,115	7	7
Oklahoma	3,450,654	3,145,585	27	28
Oregon	3,421,399	2,842,321	28	29
Pennsylvania	12,281,054	11,881,643	6	5
Rhode Island	1,048,319	1,003,464	43	43
South Carolina	4,012,012	3,486,703	26	25
South Dakota	754,844	696,004	46	45
Tennessee	5,689,283	4,877,185	16	17
Texas	20,851,820	16,986,510	2	3
Utah	2,233,169	1,722,850	34	35
Vermont	608,827	562,758	49	48
Virginia	7,078,515	6,187,358	12	12
Washington	5,894,121	4,866,692	15	18
West Virginia	1,808,344	1,793,477	37	34
Wisconsin	5,363,675	4,891,769	18	16
Wyoming	493,782	453,588	50	50
Total Resident Population	**281,421,906**	**248,709,873**	**(NA)**	**(NA)**

*All data are as of April 1.

Source: U.S. Census Bureau.

507. 2000 U.S. Census: Population Data

	Number	Percent
Total population	281,421,906	100.0
Male	138,053,563	49.1
Female	143,368,343	50.9
Under 5 years	19,175,798	6.8
5 to 9 years	20,549,505	7.3
10 to 14 years	20,528,072	7.3
15 to 19 years	20,219,890	7.2
20 to 24 years	18,964,001	6.7
25 to 34 years	39,891,724	14.2
35 to 44 years	45,148,527	16.0
45 to 54 years	37,677,952	13.4
55 to 59 years	13,469,237	4.8
60 to 64 years	10,805,447	3.8
65 to 74 years	18,390,986	6.5
75 to 84 years	12,361,180	4.4
85 years and over	4,239,587	1.5

Source: U.S. Census Bureau.

508. 20 Largest Cities in the United States

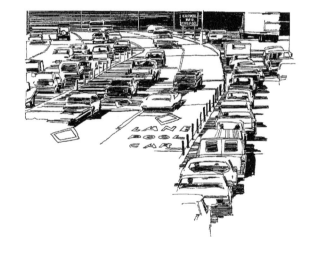

1.	New York City	8,008,278
2.	Los Angeles	3,694,820
3.	Chicago	2,896,016
4.	Houston	1,953,631
5.	Philadelphia	1,517,550
6.	Phoenix	1,321,045
7.	San Diego	1,223,400
8.	Dallas	1,188,580
9.	San Antonio	1,144,646
10.	Detroit	951,270
11.	San Jose	894,943
12.	Indianapolis	791,926
13.	San Francisco	776,733
14.	Jacksonville	735,617
15.	Columbus	711,470
16.	Austin	656,562
17.	Baltimore	651,154
18.	Memphis	650,100
19.	Milwaukee	596,974
20.	Boston	589,141

Source: 2000 U.S. Census.

509. Provinces and Territories of Canada

Province	Capital
Alberta	Edmonton
British Columbia	Victoria
Manitoba	Winnipeg
New Brunswick	Fredericton
Newfoundland	St. John's
Nova Scotia	Halifax
Ontario	Toronto
Prince Edward Island	Charlottetown
Quebec	Quebec
Saskatchewan	Regina

Territory	Capital
Northwest Territory	Yellowknife
Yukon Territory	Whitehorse

510. The 20 Most Populous Countries (in millions)

1.	China	1,273
2.	India	1,029
3.	United States	278
4.	Indonesia	228
5.	Brazil	174
6.	Russia	145
7.	Pakistan	145
8.	Bangladesh	131
9.	Japan	127
10.	Nigeria	127
11.	Mexico	102
12.	Germany	83
13.	Philippines	82
14.	Vietnam	80
15.	Egypt	70
16.	Turkey	66
17.	Iran	66
18.	Ethiopia	66
19.	Thailand	62
20.	United Kingdom	60

511. Longest Rivers

Name	Location
Nile	Africa
Amazon	South America
Yangtze	Asia
Huang Ho	Asia
Congo	Africa
Amur	Asia
Lena	Asia
Irtysh	Asia
Mackenzie	North America
Mekong	Asia
Niger	Africa
Yenisey	Asia
Paraná	South America
Mississippi	North America
Missouri	North America

512. Active Volcanoes in the United States

Volcano	State
Gareloi	Alaska
Cleveland	Alaska
Okmok	Alaska
Akutan	Alaska
Pavlof	Alaska
Veniaminof	Alaska
Redoubt	Alaska
Kilauea	Hawaii
Mount St. Helens	Washington

513. Weather Signs from American Folklore

If crows fly low, winds going to blow.

Crows fly high, winds going to die.

Red sky in the morning, sailors take warning.

Red sky at night, sailor's delight.

Onion skins thin, mild winter coming in.

Onion skins tough, winter will be rough.

When the grass is dry at morning light, look for rain before the night. When the dew is on the grass, rain will never come to pass.

When leaves show their undersides, be very sure rain betides.

Thicker corn husks predict a cold winter.

Flies bite more right before a rain.

If the groundhog sees his shadow on February 2, there will be six more weeks of winter.

The wider the middle band on the wooly bear, the milder the winter ahead.

When the wind is in the east 'tis neither good for man nor beast.

If the first snowflakes of the storm are large, it will not last long.

If autumn is foggy expect more snow this winter.

High clouds foretell good weather.

Clear moon, frost soon.

If your hair becomes limp rain is near.

A sunshiny shower won't last an hour.

When the smoke descends, good weather ends.

Crickets chirp slower as it gets colder.

Leaves turning inside out precede the onset of rain.

If it is wet on Friday, Saturday, and Sunday, expect it to be wet all week.

Cows or mules or woolyworms growing thick hair foretells a cold winter.

A large crop of walnuts or acorns predicts cold winter.

Dust devils predict bad weather.

Tough apple skins foretell a hard winter.

Bees stay close to their hives when rain is coming.

Swallows fly close to the ground before a rain.

If the first of April is foggy, there will be floods in June.

A Saturday rainbow will be followed by a week of rain.

Trees grow dark before a storm.

Northeast winds in winter bring heavy snow.

A hog carrying a stick of wood forebodes bad weather.

A morning rainbow in the western sky suggests rain will be coming.

A year of snow, a year of plenty.

514. Weather Extremes

Lowest temperature	−129.0° F	Antarctica	1989
Highest temperature	136.4° F	Libya	1922
Lowest precipitation	.03″	Arica, Chile	average
Heaviest rainfall	73.6"/24 hrs.	Reunion Island	1952
Wettest year	1042″	Cherrapunji, India	1861

515. Types of Clouds

altocumulus
altostratus
cirrocumulus
cirrostratus
cirrus
cumulonimbus
cumulus
nimbostratus
stratocumulus
stratus

516. Weather Terms

air mass	gale	sleet
barometric pressure	hail	snow
blizzard	high-pressure area	squall
breeze	humidity	storm
cloud	hurricane	sunshine
cloudburst	ice	temperature
cyclone	jet stream	thunder
dew point	lightning	thunderstorm
drought	low-pressure area	tide
fog	monsoon	tornado
flood	precipitation	typhoon
front	rain	waterspout
frost	rainbow	wind

517. Major Crops of the United States

alfalfa	potatoes
barley	rye
bean	sorghum
corn	soybeans
cotton	tobacco
fruit	tomatoes
oats	wheat
peanuts	

518. Farm Animals

cattle	goats	rabbits
chicken	horses	sheep
ducks	pigs	turkeys

519. Fields of Geology and Geography

Field	*Study of . . .*
climatology	patterns of weather
cultural geography	location and spread of cultures
economic geology	geologic materials of use to industry
economic geography	location and distribution of economic activities
environmental geology	solving environmental problems using geological knowledge
geomorphology	the earth's surface and its changes
geophysics	development and composition of the earth
glacial geology	glaciers and their effect on the earth's surface
historical geography	changes and patterns of human activities
human geography	patterns of human activity and interaction with environment
hydrology	distribution and movement of water on the earth
mineralogy	minerals

519. *(continued)*

Field	Study of . . .
oceanography	oceans and ocean life forms
paleontology	fossils
petrology	origin, characteristics and structure of rocks
planetology	physical and chemical make-up of the planets
population geography	changes in patterns of population
sedimentology	sediment and how it is deposited
seismology	earthquakes
soil geography	distribution of soils
structural geology	the shapes and positions and movements of rocks deep beneath the earth's surface
urban geography	cities and urban areas
zoogeographers	animal habitats

520. Careers in Geography

cartographer	land-use specialist
census planner	park ranger
cultural geographer	political geographer
demographer	population analyst
ecologist	teacher
geographer	weather forecaster

521. The Great Lakes

Lake	Maximum Depth (feet)
Erie	210
Huron	750
Michigan	923
Ontario	802
Superior	1,333

522. Largest Lakes

Caspian Sea	Lake Michigan
Lake Superior	Lake Tanganyika
Lake Victoria	Great Bear Lake
Aral Sea	Lake Baikal
Lake Huron	Lake Nyasa

523. Major Deserts

Desert	Location
Atacama	Chile
Gobi	Mongolia
Great Arabian	Middle East
Great Australian	Australia
Kalahari	South Africa
Kara Kum	Kazakhstan and Turkmenistan
Kyzyl Kum	Kazakhstan and Uzbekistan
Libyan	Libya
Mojave	U.S.
Painted Desert	U.S.
Sahara	North Africa
Takia Makan	China
Thar	India-Pakistan

524. Largest Islands

Greenland	Sumatra
New Guinea	Great Britain
Borneo	Honshu
Madagascar	Victoria
Baffin	Ellesmere

525. Tallest Buildings in North America

Building	City	Height (feet)
Sears Tower	Chicago	1,450
Empire State Building	New York City	1,250
Aon Center	Chicago	1,136
John Hancock	Chicago	1,127
Chrysler Building	New York City	1,046
Bank of America Plaza	Atlanta	1,023

The CN Tower in Toronto, Ontario is 1,821 feet tall, making it North America's tallest self-supporting structure.

526. Lowest Spots on Each Continent

Continent	Location	Feet below sea level
Asia	Dead Sea (Israel & Jordan)	1,290
Africa	Quattara Depression (Egypt)	440
Australia	Lake Eyre	39
Europe	Caspian Sea (U.S.S.R.)	96
North America	Death Valley (United States)	282
South America	Salinas Grande (Argentina)	131

527. Types of Volcanoes

Cinder cones
Composite volcanoes
Lava domes
Shield volcanoes
Submarine volcanoes

528. Geographic Nicknames

Name	Nickname
Alexandria, Egypt	Mother of Books
Atlantic Ocean	The Herring Pond
Australia	New Holland
Balkans	Powder Keg of Europe
Boston	Bean Town
Chicago	Windy City
Dallas	Big "D"
Denver	Mile High City
Detroit	Motor City
Europe	Old World
Hispania	Spain
Hollywood	Film Capital of the World
Iceland	Land of Frost and Fire
Ireland	Emerald Isle
Italy	Garden of Europe
Kiev	Russian Mother of Cities
Los Angeles	LA; City of the Angels
Mexico	New Spain
Nashville	Music City, U.S.A.
New York City	The Big Apple
Panama	Crossroads of the World
Paris	City of Light
Philadelphia	Philly; City of Brotherly Love
Pittsburgh	The Steel City
St. Louis	Gateway of the West
San Francisco	Frisco; The Golden Gate City

529. World Currencies

Country	Unit	Equivalent
Afghanistan	afghani	100 puls
Argentina	peso	100 centavos
Australia	dollar	100 cents
Botswana	pula	100 thebe
Brazil	real	100 centavos
Bulgaria	lev	100 stotinki
Canada	dollar	100 cents
China	yuan	100 fen

529. *(continued)*

Country	Unit	Equivalent
Egypt	pound	100 piasters
European Union	euro	100 euro-cents
Great Britain	pound	100 pence
Haiti	gourde	100 centimes
India	rupee	100 paisa
Iran	rial	100 dinars
Israel	new shekel	100 new agorot
Italy	lira	100 centesimi
Japan	yen	100 sen (not used)
Korea	won	100 chon
Mexico	peso	100 centavos
Peru	sol	100 centavos
Poland	zloty	100 groszy
Russia	ruble	100 kopecks
South Africa	rand	100 cents
Switzerland	franc	100 centimes
Turkey	lira	100 kurus
United States	dollar	100 cents
Yugoslavia	dinar	100 paras
Zimbabwe	dollar	100 cents

530. Soybean Products

adhesive tape
baby food
candles
candy
carbon paper
cattle feed
cooking oil
cosmetics
disinfectants
explosives
fertilizer
fire extinguisher fluid
ice cream

insect sprays
leather softeners
linoleum
mayonnaise
medicines
paint
processed meat
salad dressings
soaps
soy sauce
textiles
varnishes

531. Major Wine Producing Countries

(in order of production)

France
Italy
Spain
United States
Argentina
South Africa
Portugal
Germany
Romania

532. Major Wheat Producing Countries (in order of production)

China
India
United States
Canada
Australia
Pakistan
Turkey

Source: US Department of Agriculture, 2001.

533. Major Crude Oil Producing Countries

Saudia Arabia
Russia
North Sea
United States
Iran
China
Norway
Mexico
Canada
Iraq
United Arab Emirates
Nigeria
Kuwait

534. U.S. Peanut Crop Summary, 1990–2000

Year	Area Planted (1,000 acres)	Area Harvested (1,000 acres)	Yield per Acre (pounds)	Production (1,000 pounds)
1990	1,846.0	1,815.5	1,985	3,603,650
1991	2,039.2	2,015.7	2,444	4,926,570
1992	1,686.6	1,669.1	2,567	4,284,416
1993	1,733.5	1,689.8	2,008	3,392,415
1994	1,641.0	1,618.5	2,624	4,247,455
1995	1,537.5	1,517.0	2,282	3,461,475
1996	1,401.5	1,380.0	2,653	3,661,205
1997	1,434.0	1,413.8	2,503	3,539,380
1998	1,521.0	1,467.0	2,702	3,963,440
1999	1,534.5	1,436.0	2,667	3,829,490
2000	1,536.8	1,329.0	2,448	3,252,775

Source: National Agricultural Statistics Service, USDA.

U.S. Peanut Crop: Data Interpretation

Directions: Answer the questions below using data from the accompanying table, *United States Peanut Crop Summary, 1990–2000.*

1. What year did peanut farmers have the greatest yield per acre?

2. Which year had the lowest total number of pounds of peanuts harvested?

3. How many acres of planted peanuts did not get harvested in 2000?

4. How many pounds of peanuts were harvested in 1995?

5. The total number of pounds of peanuts produced increased almost 36% from 1990 to 1991. What data from the table accounts for this sharp increase?

6. What external factors likely caused the increase of almost 200 pounds per acres between 1997 and 1998?

Answers:

1. 1998
2. 2000
3. 207,800 pounds
4. 3,461,475,000 pounds
5. The yield per acre was higher in 1991. More acres were planted in 1991 than the previous year. More acres were harvested than the year before.
6. Weather conditions may have been more favorable in 1998. Insects may have cuased less damage. More fertilizer might have been used. More herbicides might have been used to contain weeds.

535. Countries and Capitals of South America

Country	Capital
Argentina	Buenos Aires
Bolivia	La Paz (administrative); Sucre (judicial)
Brazil	Brasilia
Chile	Santiago
Colombia	Bogotá
Ecuador	Quito
Guyana	Georgetown
Paraguay	Asunción
Peru	Lima
Surinam	Paramaribo
Uruguay	Montevideo
Venezuela	Caracas

536. Countries and Capitals of North and Central America

Country	Capital
Antigua and Barbuda	St. John's
Bahamas	Nassau
Barbados	Bridgetown
Belize	Belmopan
Canada	Ottawa
Costa Rica	San Jose
Cuba	Havana
Dominica	Roseau
Dominican Republic	Santo Domingo
El Salvador	San Salvador
Grenada	St. George's
Guatemala	Guatemala City
Haiti	Port-au-Prince
Honduras	Tegucigalpa
Jamaica	Kingston
Mexico	Mexico City
Nicaragua	Managua
Panama	Panama City
St. Christopher and Nevis	Basseterre
St. Lucia	Castries
St. Vincent and the Grenadines	Kingstown
Trinidad and Tobago	Port-of-Spain
United States	Washington, D.C.

537. Countries and Capitals of Asia

Country	Capital	Country	Capital
Afghanistan	Kabul	Malaysia	Kuala
Armenia	Yerevan	Maldives	Male
Azerbaijan	Baku	Mongolia	Ulan Bator
Bahrain	Manama	Myanmar	Rangoon
Bangladesh	Dhaka	Nepal	Kathmandu
Bhutan	Thimphu	Oman	Muscat
Cambodia	Phnom Penh	Pakistan	Islamabad
China	Beijing	Philippines	Manila
Cyprus	Nicosia	Qatar	Doha
India	New Delhi	Saudi Arabia	Riyadh
Indonesia	Jakarta	Singapore	Singapore
Iran	Teheran	Sri Lanka (official)	Colombo
Iraq	Baghdad	Syria	Damascus
Israel	Jerusalem	Taiwan	Taipei
Japan	Tokyo	Tajikistan	Dushanbe
Jordan	Amman	Thailand	Bangkok
Kazakhstan	Astana	Turkey	Ankara
North Korea	Pyongyang	Turkmenistan	Ashgabat
South Korea	Seoul	United Arab Emirates	Abu Dhabi
Kuwait	Kuwait City	Uzbekistan	Tashkent
Kyrgyzstan	Bishkek	Vietnam	Hanoi
Laos	Vientiane	Yemen	Sana
Lebanon	Beirut		

538. 15 New Commonwealth of Independent States

(formerly the U.S.S.R.)

Country	Capital	Country	Capital
Armenia	Yenevan	Lithuania	Vilnius
Azerbaijan	Baku	Moldavia	Kishinev
Byelorussia	Minsk	Russia	Moscow
Estonia	Tallinn	Tajikistan	Dushanbe
Georgia	Tbiisi	Turkmenistan	Ashkhabad
Kazakhstan	Alma Ata	Ukraine	Kiev
Kirghizia	Frunze	Uzbekistan	Tashkent
Latvia	Riga		

539. Nations of Africa

Algeria	Libya
Angola	Malawi
Benin	Mali
Botswana	Mauritania
Burkina Faso	Morocco
Burundi	Mozambique
Cameroon	Namibia
Central African Republic	Niger
Chad	Nigeria
Congo (formerly Zaire)	Republic of the Congo
Djibouti	Rwanda
Egypt	South Africa
Equatorial Guinea	Sierra Leone
Eritrea	Senegal
Ethiopia	Somalia
Gabon	Sudan
Gambia	Swaziland
Ghana	Tanzania
Guinea-Bissau	Togo
Ivory Coast	Tunisia
Kenya	Uganda
Lesotho	Zambia
Liberia	Zimbabwe

Source: U.S. State Department, January 2001.

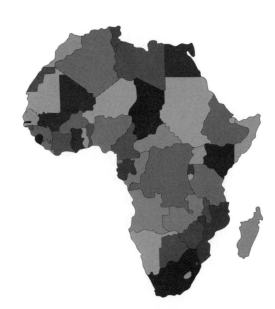

540. Countries and Capitals of Europe

Country	Capital	Country	Capital
Albania	Tirane	Ireland	Dublin
Andorra	Andorra la Vella	Italy	Rome
		Latvia	Riga
Austria	Vienna	Liechtenstein	Vaduz
Belarus	Minsk	Lithuania	Vilnius
Belgium	Brussels	Luxembourg	Luxembourg
Bosnia-Herzegovina	Sarajevo	Macedonia	Skopje
Bulgaria	Sofia	Malta	Valletta
Croatia	Zagreb	Moldova	Chisinau
Czech Republic	Prague	Monaco	Monaco
Denmark	Copenhagen	Netherlands (official)	Amsterdam
Estonia	Tallinn	Netherlands (admin.)	The Hague
Finland	Helsinki	Norway	Oslo
France	Paris	Poland	Warsaw
Georgia	Tbilisi	Portugal	Lisbon
Germany	Berlin	Romania	Bucharest
Greece	Athens	Russian Federation	Moscow
Hungary	Budapest	San Marino	San Marino
Iceland	Reykjavik	United Kingdom	London

Source: U.S. State Department, January 2001.

541. World's Most Populous Metropolises (in millions)

		2002	2015 (projected)
1.	Tokyo	26.4	26.4
2.	Mexico City	18.1	19.2
3.	Bombay	18.1	26.1
4.	São Paulo	17.8	20.4
5.	New York	16.6	17.4
6.	Lagos	13.4	23.2
7.	Los Angeles	13.1	14.1
8.	Shanghai	12.9	14.6
9.	Calcutta	12.9	17.3
10.	Buenos Aires	12.6	14.1
11.	Dhaka	12.3	21.1
12.	Karachi	11.8	19.2
13.	Delhi	11.7	16.8
14.	Osaka	11.0	11.0
15.	Jakarta	11.0	17.3
16.	Metro Manila	10.9	14.8
17.	Beijing	10.8	12.3
18.	Rio de Janeiro	10.6	11.9
19.	Cairo	10.6	13.8

Source: Population Division, United Nations, January 2002.

542. Conventional Names: Quiz Time!

The names we use for places are not necessarily the names used there. Sometimes the first name we use for a country sticks with us, even though that country is known as something completely different at home.

See if you can match the English-form name of the following countries with their Native-form names.

English-form Name	Native-form Name
A. Albania	1. Oesterreich
B. Japan	2. Espana
C. Austria	3. Bharat
D. Cambodia	4. Sverige
E. Morocco	5. Deutschland
F. China	6. Shqiperia
G. Sweden	7. Hellas
H. Croatia	8. Kampuchea
I. Hungary	9. Nippon
J. Greece	10. Suomi
K. India	11. Hrvatska
L. Spain	12. Al Maghrib
M. Finland	13. Zhong Guo
N. Germany	14. Magyarorszag

Source: U.S. Department of State, World Geographic News. Online at http://geography.state.gov.

Quiz Answers: Conventional Names

English-form name		Native-form name	
A.	Albania	6.	Shqiperia
B.	Japan	9.	Nippon
C.	Austria	1.	Oesterreich
D.	Cambodia	8.	Kampuchea
E.	Morocco	12.	Al Maghrib
F.	China	13.	Zhong Guo
G.	Sweden	1.	Hrvatska
H.	Croatia	14.	Magyarorszag
I.	Hungary	7.	Hellas
J.	Greece	3.	Bharat
K.	India	2.	Espana
L.	Spain	10.	Suomi
M.	Finland	5.	Deutschland
N.	Germany		

543. Most Destructive Known Earthquakes

Date	Location	Number of Deaths	Magnitude
January 23, 1556	China, Shansi	830,000	N/A
July 27, 1976	China, Tangshan	255,000* (official)	8.0
August 9, 1138	Syria, Aleppo	230,000	
May 22, 1927	China, near Xining	200,000	8.3
December 22, 856	Iran, Damghan	200,000	
December 16, 1920	China, Gansu	200,000	8.6
March 23, 893	Iran, Ardabil	150,000	
September 1, 1923	Japan, Kwanto	143,000	8.3
October 5, 1948	USSR (Turkmenistan, Ashgabat)	110,000	7.3

*Estimated death toll as high as 655,000

Note: Some dates are prior to 1000 A.D.

Source: USGS National Earthquake Information Center.

544. Common Contaminants

Common Sources	Contaminants	Potential Health Effects
Household Items, such as	mercury	Toxic to kidneys.
Batteries, Thermometers, and Paints		Can cause eye and skin irritation; chest pain; tremor; fatigue; weakness.
Car Radiators and De-Icing Agents	ethylene glycol	Can cause abdominal pain; vomiting; weakness; dizziness; central nervous system depression.
Photocopy Machines Chrome Plating	chromium	Toxic to kidneys; potential human carcinogen.
Chemical Manufacturing	benzene; ethyl benzene; toluene; xylene	Benzene suppresses bone marrow function, causing blood changes; chronic exposure can cause leukemia.
		Central nervous system depression: decreased alertness, headaches, sleepiness, loss of consciousness.
Dry Cleaning Agents and Degreasers	trichloroethane and trichloroethylene	Central nervous system depression: decreased alertness, headaches, sleepiness, loss of consciousness.
		Kidney changes: decreased urine flow, swelling (especially around eyes), anemia.
		Liver changes: fatigue, malaise, dark urine, liver enlargement.
Herbicides for Vegetation Control	chlorophenoxy compounds; 2;4-dichlorophenoxyacetic acid	Chloracne, weakness or numbness of arms and legs, long-term nerve damage.
	dioxin	Dioxin causes chloracne and may aggravate pre-existing liver and kidney disease.

(continued)

544. *(continued)*

Common Sources	Contaminants	Potential Health Effects
Pesticides	chlorinated ethanes; DDT; lindane	Acute symptoms of apprehension, irritability, dizziness, disturbed equilibrium, tremor, and convulsions.
	cyclodienes (aldrin; chlordane; dieldrin; endrin); chlorocyclohexanes	All cause a chain of internal reactions leading to neuromuscular blockage. Acute symptoms include headaches, fatigue, dizziness, increased salivation and crying, profuse sweating, nausea, vomiting, cramps, diarrhea, tightness in the chest, and muscle twitching.
	organophosphates: diazanon; dichlorovos; dimethoate; trichlorfon; malathion; methyl parathion; parathion carbamate: aldicarb; baygon; zectran	All cause a chain of internal reactions leading to neuromuscular blockage. Acute symptoms include headaches, fatigue, dizziness, increased salivation and crying, profuse sweating, nausea, vomiting, cramps, diarrhea, tightness in the chest, and muscle twitching.
Electrical Transformers and Other Industrial Uses	polychlorinated biphenyls (PCBs)	Various skin ailments, including chloracne. May cause liver toxicity. Carcinogenic to animals.
Various Commercial and Industrial Manufacturing Processes	arsenic; beryllium; cadmium; chromium; lead; mercury	All are toxic to kidneys. Decreased mental ability, weakness, headache, abdominal cramps, diarrhea, and anemia. Also affects blood-forming mechanisms and the peripheral nervous system. Long-term exposure to lead can cause permanent kidney and brain damage.

Source: U.S. Environmental Protection Agency. Online at http://www.epa.gov.

545. Forms of Hazardous Waste

Most hazardous waste is identified by one or more of its dangerous properties or characteristics: corrosive, ignitable, reactive, or toxic.

- **Corrosive**—A corrosive material can wear away (corrode) or destroy a substance. For example, most acids are corrosives that can eat through metal, burn skin on contact, and give off vapors that burn the eyes.
- **Ignitable**—An ignitable material can burst into flames easily. It poses a fire hazard; can irritate the skin, eyes, and lungs; and may give off harmful vapors. Gasoline, paint, and furniture polish are ignitable.
- **Reactive**—A reactive material can explode or create poisonous gas when combined with other chemicals. For example, chlorine bleach and ammonia are reactive and create a poisonous gas when they come into contact with each other.
- **Toxic**—Toxic materials or substances can poison people and other life. Toxic substances can cause illness and even death if swallowed or absorbed through the skin. Pesticides, weed killers, and many household cleaners are toxic.

Source: Superfund for Students and Teachers, Environmental Protection Agency. Online at http://www.epa.gov/super fund/students/clas_act/haz-ed/ff_01.htm. Used with permission.

546. Potential Effects of Pollution

- Gaps in vital food chains or nutrient cycles
- Reproductive problems (such as eggshell thinning or loss of nesting materials)
- Developmental effects (such as malformed chick beaks)
- Tumors (such as fish tumors)
- Critical organ damage (such as liver, kidney, or skin lesions)
- Immune system dysfunction (leading to, for example, viral infections in dolphins)
- Altered individual or population growth rates
- Changes in population and community organization
- Loss of total biomass (flora and fauna)
- Relative loss of taxa or species abundance in defined areas (such as fish kills, amphibian mortality, macroinvertebrate depletion)
- Loss of species diversity

Source: Superfund for Students and Teachers, Environmental Protection Agency. Online at http://www.epa.gov/super fund/students.

547. U.S. Waste Generation

Waste Generation Rates—1960 to 2000

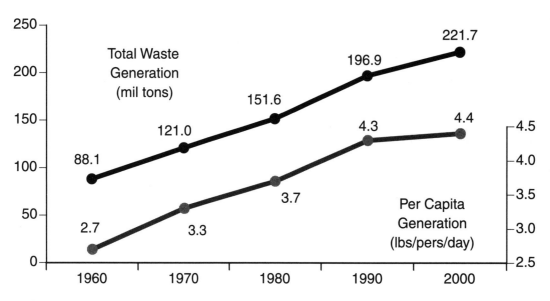

Source: Characterization of MSW in the U.S.: 1996 Update, U.S. EPA.

Questions for consideration:

1. How many million tons of waste did the U.S. generate in 1960?
2. On average, how many pounds of waste per person did the U.S. produce in 1970?
3. How many tons of waste did the U.S. generate each day in 1990?
4. What do you suspect accounted for the leveling off in the per capita waste production over the past decade?

Answers: 1. 88.1 tons 2. 3.3 lbs. 3. 537,978 tons each day. 1990 was a leap year, hence 366 days. 4. increased recycling efforts

548. Water Consumption Rates

Flushing toilets	3–5 gallons of water per flush
Brushing teeth	3–5 gallons of water per minute for running tap
Washing dishes	3–5 gallons of water per minute for running tap
Showering	5–7 gallons of water per minute
Bathing	35–50 gallons of water per bath

Source: The World Bank at http://www.worldbank.org.

549. U.S. Consumption of World Resources

(as percentage of total world consumption)

Population	4.5%
Cotton	19.1%
Energy, all sources	25.3%
Internet users	46.0%
Oil	26.1%
Paper	33.0%
Plastic	33.0%
Pharmaceuticals	40.0%
Rice	.9%
Tobacco	7.2%
Wine	9.1%

Source: 2001 Statistical Abstract of the United States; U.S. Department of Energy; U.S. Department of Agriculture.

550. U.S. Energy Sources

Source	*% of Total Consumption*
Oil	38.8
Natural Gas	23.2
Coal	22.9
Nuclear	7.6
Hydroelectric	3.8
Geothermal	0.3
Biomass	3.2
Solar	0.07
Wind	0.04
TOTAL	100.00

Source: EIA Annual Energy Review 1998.

551. White Christmas Becoming a Memory

Statistics provided by researchers at Oak Ridge National Laboratory indicate a decreasing number of white Christmases over the past four decades. Snowfall data from 16 U.S. cities show that the number of white Christmases per decade declined from 78 during the 1960s to 39 in the 1990s.

Following are the metropolitan areas used in the study, followed in parentheses by the number of white Christmases for the 1960s, 1970s, 1980s and 1990s:

Atlanta	(0, 0, 0, 0)
Boston	(8, 5, 5, 2)
Chicago	(7, 5, 4, 2)
Cincinnati	(3, 0, 2, 2)
Denver	(4, 4, 7, 2)
Detroit	(9, 7, 5, 3)
Kansas City, Mo.	(4, 0, 6, 2)
Knoxville/Oak Ridge	(4, 1, 0, 0)
Memphis	(3, 0, 0, 0)
Minneapolis/St. Paul	(8, 7, 7, 8)
Nashville	(2, 0, 0, 0)
New York City	(5, 1, 1, 1)
Salt Lake City	(7, 7, 8, 8)
Seattle	(2, 0, 0, 0)
Tahoe City, Calif.	(8, 7, 8, 9)
Washington, D.C.	(4, 0, 0, 0)

Source: Dale Kaiser, a meteorologist with the Carbon Dioxide Information Analysis Center at the U.S. Department of Energy's Oak Ridge National Laboratory, and Kevin Birdwell, a meteorologist in the lab's Computational Science and Engineering Division.

552. Paper Facts

- It takes 17 trees to make a ton of paper.
- The U.S. consumes over 100 million tons of paper each year—nearly 800 pounds per person.
- Over 5.2 million tons of catalogs and other direct mailings entered the municipal solid waste stream in 1998.
- The U.S. Postal Service delivers more than 200 billion pieces of mail a year.
- In 1998, only 18.9% of bulk mail was recycled.
- Each of the U.S. Postal Service's 293,000 letter carriers delivers almost 18 tons of bulk mail every year.
- Nearly 470,000 tons of phone directories are published in the U.S. each year.

552. *(continued)*

- The average American spends 8 months in his or her lifetime opening bulk mail.
- Approximately 44% of all junk mail is thrown away unopened.
- U.S. companies spent $39.3 billion on direct mail in 1998.
- U.S. nonprofit organizations annually send 12 billion pieces of bulk mail.
- The typical U.S. office worker uses about 10,000 sheets of copy paper each year.
- 84 million tons of paper ended up in U.S. municipal solid waste in 1998.
- 49.4 million tons of paper and paperboard get recycled each year.
- Recycling 1 ton of paper saves 17 trees and 7,000 gallons of water.
- It takes more than 500,000 trees to make the newspapers Americans consume in one Sunday.
- 4.5 million tons of junk mail are produced each year, requiring 100 million trees for the paper.
- 90% of the 12 billion magazines published each year are discarded; 75% of these are incinerated or landfilled.

Sources: American Paper & Forest Association; National Waste Prevention Coalition; Environmental Protection Agency (EPA); U.S. Postal Service; Center for a New American Dream.

553. Online Resources for Teaching Geography

American Geographical Society
http://www.amergeog.org

Ask ERIC Geography Lesson Archive
http://askeric.org/cgi-bin/lessons.cgi/Social_Studies/Geography

EPA Office of Environmental Education
http://www.epa.gov/enviroed

Geographic Learning Site, U.S. Department of State
http://geography.state.gov/text/tstatehome.html

Geography Education Program
National Geographic Magazine
http://www.nationalgeographic.com/resources/ngo/education/ideas.html

Internet Resources for Geography and Geology
http://www.uwsp.edu/geo/internet/geog_geol_resources.html

National Council for Geographic Education
http://www.ncge.org

National Geographic Society
http://www.nationalgeographic.com/index.html

Project WET (Water Education for Teachers)
http://www.montana.edu/wwwwet

Searching for China WebQuest
Pacific Bell
http://www.kn.pacbell.com/wired/China/ChinaQuest.html

Society for Ecological Restoration
http://www.ser.org

The Teacher's Guide
http://www.theteachersguide.com/socialstudies.html

Understanding Developing Nations
http://www.davison.k12.mi.us/academic/pugh3.htm

U.S. Geological Survey
http://mapping.usgs.gov/www/html

World Fact Book
Central Intelligence Agency
http://www.odci.gov/cia/publications/pubs.html

554. Environmental Education Resources

Alliance to Save Energy
http://www.ase.org

Center for Environmental Education (CEE)—Antioch
http://www.cee-ane.org

Citizens' Environmental Coalition
http:// www.cectoxic.org

Cornell Center for the Environment
Cornell University
http://www.cfe.cornell.edu

Earth 911
http://www.earth911.org

EnviroLink Network
The Online Environmental Community®
http://envirolink.netforchange.com

The Environmental Education and Training Partnership
http://eetap.org

EPA Environmental Education Center
http://www.epa.gov/teachers

Keep America Beautiful
http:// www.kab.org

Master Composter
http:// www.mastercomposter.com

NAAEE Affiliates Network
http://eelink.net/naaeeaffiliatesnetwork.html

NEEAP - National Environmental Education Advancement Project
http://www.uwsp.edu/cnr/neeap

National Environmental Education and Training Foundation (NEETF)
http://www.neetf.org

National Project for Excellence in Environmental Education
http://www.naaee.org/npeee

Natural Resources Conservation Service
U.S. Department of Agriculture
http://www.nrcs.usda.gov

North American Association for Environmental Education (NAAEE)
http://www.naaee.org

Student Conservation Association
http://www.sca-inc.org